GONE BUT NOT
FORGOTTEN

# GONE
## BUT NOT
# FORGOTTEN

## ATLANTANS
## COMMEMORATE
## THE CIVIL WAR

### WENDY HAMAND VENET

*Published in association
with Georgia Humanities*

THE UNIVERSITY OF
GEORGIA PRESS
ATHENS

This publication is made possible in part through a grant
from the Bradley Hale Fund for Southern Studies.

© 2020 by the University of Georgia Press
Athens, Georgia 30602
www.ugapress.org
All rights reserved
Designed by Kaelin Chappell Broaddus
Set in 9.5/13.5 Miller Text by Kaelin Chappell Broaddus

Most University of Georgia Press titles are
available from popular e-book vendors.

Printed digitally

Library of Congress Cataloging-in-Publication Data

Names: Venet, Wendy Hamand, author.
Title: Gone but not forgotten : Atlantans commemorate the Civil War / Wendy Hamand Venet.
Description: Athens : The University of Georgia Press, [2020] | Includes bibliographical references
    and index.
Identifiers: LCCN 2020016294 | ISBN 9780820358123 (hardback) | ISBN 9780820358314 (paperback)
    | ISBN 9780820358130 (ebook)
Subjects: LCSH: Collective memory—Georgia—Atlanta. | Memorialization—Georgia—Atlanta. |
    United States—History—Civil War, 1861–1865—Influence. | Atlanta (Ga—History. | Atlanta
    (Ga.)--Race relations.
Classification: LCC E468.9 .V56 2020 | DDC 973.7/36—dc23
LC record available at https://lccn.loc.gov/2020016294

For my students

# CONTENTS

# ABBREVIATIONS

| | |
|---|---|
| ACWRT | Atlanta Civil War Round Table |
| ALMA | Atlanta Ladies Memorial Association |
| CWCC | Civil War Centennial Commission |
| KKK | Ku Klux Klan |
| NAACP | National Association for the Advancement of Colored People |
| SCV | Sons of Confederate Veterans |
| SMCMA | Stone Mountain Confederate Monumental Association |
| SMMA | Stone Mountain Memorial Association |
| UCV | United Confederate Veterans |
| UDC | United Daughters of the Confederacy |

# Solomon Luckie and the Lamppost

O N DECEMBER 14, 1939, as part of the festivities related to the premiere of the film *Gone with the Wind*, members of a ceremonial militia unit, the Old Guard Battalion of Atlanta's Gate City Guard, dedicated a gaslight at the intersection of Whitehall and Alabama Streets. They were joined by members of the United Daughters of the Confederacy. Hollywood stars, some of whom had already arrived in the city for the movie premiere, did not attend the morning ceremony. This event was intended for local people. The gaslight, one of the few remaining among fifty lit for the first time on Christmas Day 1855, had been struck by an artillery shell during the 1864 Siege of Atlanta, leaving a large hole at its base. In 1918, the Old Guard added a bronze tablet dedicating the lamppost to the memory of Colonel Andrew J. West, commander of one of the battalions that unsuccessfully defended the city from General William T. Sherman's army. Twenty-one years later, the Daughters lit the gaslight and dedicated it as the "Eternal Flame of the Confederacy."

But this lamp has a history beyond the Confederacy. The shell that struck the post ricocheted and hit Solomon Luckie, an African American barber. Although doctors amputated his leg, he died of shock a few hours later. One of the city's few free black residents, Luckie was successful and well liked, but the Old Guard and the Daughters ignored his life and death, and his story lapsed into obscurity. For many years, Atlantans were largely unaware of the lamppost's history, but in 2017, the city quietly authorized the lamppost's removal and its relocation to the campus of the Atlanta History Center. In a museum exhibit about "Memory, Myth, and a Lamppost," the History Center now focuses on Solomon Luckie's story as a free man in a slave city who despite his name was unlucky to be aboveground during a period of Union shelling.[1]

Historian Fitzhugh Brundage has written that historical memory involves the act of transmitting "selective knowledge about the past"; in a nutshell, the story of Solomon Luckie and the lamppost captures Atlanta's dominant narrative of its Civil War history.[2] The lamppost tells the story of a city targeted by General Sherman because of its immense importance to the Confederate war effort, of besieged civilians, and of the city's surrender and partial destruction in 1864. The lamppost also reveals a narrative about the efforts of the Old Guard and the United Daughters of the Confederacy to interpret the war in a way that highlights Atlanta's status as the casualty of an aggressive military commander but excludes African Americans from the story. In 1939, these efforts played out against a backdrop of *Gone with the Wind*'s spectacular movie premiere, a seminal event that drew national attention to Atlanta as the setting of the novel and film.

Scholarly literature on Civil War memory is compelling and varied, but most books and articles focus on individual groups such as veterans, topics such as monuments that commemorate the war, or themes such as sectional reconciliation.[3] This book takes a different approach, examining Civil War commemoration in the city of Atlanta over the span of 150 years. Atlanta's importance to the war and postwar periods cannot be overstated. By 1864, Atlanta had become the second-most-important city in the Confederacy after the capital, Richmond—a transportation and supply center, an industrial center, and a hospital center. The target of Sherman's army in 1864, the city fell into Union hands after a military campaign that included the destruction of vital railroads, the bombardment of the city center, and the deaths of some of its citizens. Atlanta's surrender on September 2, 1864, led to the de facto end of slavery in the city, helped President Abraham Lincoln's reelection effort, and hastened the Confederacy's defeat. With the city's rapid rebuilding and its success in lobbying to become the new state capital in 1868, Atlanta emerged from the war as the center of political and economic power in Georgia and the leader of an emerging New South.

For much of the past 150 years, white and black Atlantans remembered the war separately and very differently. White people focused on the city's subjugation by an invading army and its phoenix-like rebirth after the war. Annual commemorations of Confederate Memorial Day (April 26) became quasi-official holidays in the city. With annual commemorations of Emancipation Day (January 1), black people in Atlanta focused on the war's liberation of slaves and on the empowering theme of freedom. The separate commemorations collided during the centennial of the Civil War, 1961–65. Since that time, a greater level of consensus about the war has emerged, but Civil War memory remains a contested subject in the twenty-first century.

In some ways, Atlanta is representative of the South. After the Civil War, a variety of dynamics led most white Atlantans to ignore the role that slavery played in causing the war and the importance of emancipation as an outcome. Confederate heritage groups, including the Atlanta Ladies Memorial Association and the United Daughters of the Confederacy, held important roles in constructing and maintaining the "Lost Cause" myth well into the twentieth century. However, Atlanta is not representative of the South in every regard. Because of the city's bombardment and sur-render, the expulsion of its civilian population, and its partial destruc-tion, Atlanta's dominant narrative of the war includes the civilian story to a greater degree than is the case in many areas of the South. The home front—and women in particular—played a major role in the development of the Lost Cause ideology.

Atlanta's leaders have always focused on the future more than the past. Unlike many other important southern cities, Atlanta's history does not predate the American Revolution. The city originated with railroads, busi-nessmen, and entrepreneurs in the 1830s, and early leaders adopted a commercial ethos emphasizing growth, infrastructure improvement, and ties with the North. At roughly 20 percent of the total, Atlanta's enslaved population was lower than that in other southern cities, and its bonds-people were employed in foundries and factories, not in agriculture. At-lanta's relative youth, the commercial vision of its leaders, its more mod-est investment in slavery, and its relatively progressive outlook gave the city less of a stake in enshrining the Old South and a greater stake in rec-onciling with the North after the Civil War, a process that began earlier than it did in many other southern cities. Moreover, modern Atlanta lacks physical reminders of the Civil War because the city center was destroyed by Sherman's soldiers. Unlike Charleston, where the building that housed the city's slave market still stands; Richmond, where the structure that once contained the Tredegar Iron Works is partially extant; and Savannah, where the antebellum Marshall House welcomed hotel guests in the 1860s and welcomes them today, Atlanta has no buildings where slaves were sold, no structure that once housed the Confederate Arsenal, no hotel or theater or jail that serves as a reminder of the Civil War city. Over the years, Atlanta has had its share of inept mayors and city council members; however, in the twentieth century, an emphasis on consensus building regarding Civil War commemoration benefited the city at several critical moments, and mayors often took the lead. Sometimes called the "Atlanta Way," this process involves political and business leaders engaging in dialogue with stakeholders to achieve compromise on contentious issues, including Civil War monuments. Of course, Atlanta has not always taken a progressive path, as the race riot of 1906 and the rise of the Ku Klux Klan in the 1920s demonstrate.

This volume offers a reappraisal of several topics. Henry W. Grady's economic blueprint for a New South boosted Atlanta's profile in the 1880s. Although many historians have studied Grady's ideology, his less well-known role in Civil War commemoration is considered here. Although the film *The Birth of a Nation*, based on the writings of Thomas Dixon, has long been understood for its cultural and racial significance, less well known is the role played by Dixon's *The Clansman*, a novel and stage play that helped to ignite the Atlanta Race Riot of 1906. This volume reconsiders the origin, development, and completion of the Confederate carving at Stone Mountain (1914–70) and views it through the lens of the United Daughters of the Confederacy during the peak of the group's influence in the early twentieth century. Changing perceptions of Robert E. Lee are reflected in the unveiling ceremonies of the mountain carving in 1924, 1928, and 1970. Margaret Mitchell's novel, *Gone with the Wind*, and the film based on it came to dominate Civil War memory in Atlanta and the nation. *Gone with the Wind* is considered in the context of artists, writers, and historians of the 1920s and 1930s who attempted to provide a more factual retelling of the war than the one provided by the Lost Cause generation. Their efforts, successful on some levels, did not reflect the reality of slavery or postslavery race relations.

With the Civil War centennial, the white and black narratives of Civil War Atlanta collided. While African Americans, individually and sometimes collectively, challenged the dominant white narrative of the war before 1961, the civil rights movement provided a large-scale, direct, and effective challenge to traditional thinking about the war's meaning. The book closes by examining the period after 1970, when Atlanta became a majority–African American city. Seeking to forge consensus, black mayors navigated a variety of contentious issues, including preservation efforts involving the Atlanta Cyclorama painting and the Margaret Mitchell House, changes to the state flag, and how to present the city's Civil War past to the world during the Olympic Games in 1996.

This book considers Civil War commemoration in Atlanta, including Fulton County (home to the City of Atlanta) and DeKalb County (home to the neighboring city of Decatur and the Confederate carving on Stone Mountain). It does not include Cobb County or Kennesaw Mountain. This book also does not include every important individual or event in Atlanta's Civil War remembrance. Leading figures, including John B. Gordon, Henry Grady, Margaret Mitchell, and Martin Luther King Jr., are highlighted, but so are those who are less well known, including Edward R. Carter, whose 1894 book, *The Black Side*, provided African Americans with a history of one of the war's defining outcomes and challenged white Atlantans to reconsider their assumptions about the war. Although most writers about sectional reconciliation were male, Myrta Lockett Avary wrote books at the turn of the twentieth century that reveal a white woman's perspective. Journalist Sam Small composed a series of articles for the *Atlanta Constitution* during the 1920s in which he took direct aim at the Lost Cause. In so doing, he reminds us that some white Atlantans did not subscribe to the prevailing narrative. Professor Bell Irvin Wiley of Emory University helped to shape the Civil War centennial nationally and provoked local and national conversations about the meaning of Robert E. Lee when Stone Mountain's Confederate carving was unveiled in 1970.

Many friends and colleagues helped me with this project. My husband, Allen; our sons; and my sister, Carol, always demonstrate enthusiasm for my scholarship. I thank my colleagues Glenn Eskew, Anne Farrisee, Tim Crimmins, and Diane Willen for their support and encouragement. I am grateful to the College of Arts and Sciences at Georgia State University for a release from classroom instruction during the spring semester of 2018, time that allowed me to conduct research in Washington, D.C., and elsewhere. Several Atlanta-area residents agreed to be interviewed about their family memories of Civil War commemoration. Bill Kurtz of Madison, Georgia, talked with me about his distinguished grandfather, Atlanta artist and historian Wilbur G. Kurtz. Rosemary Cox grew up at Stone Mountain, where her father, Harold, served as horticulturist. She shared memories of the Confederate carving's unveiling.

Many archivists and librarians helped me to research Civil War commemoration in Atlanta. At the Atlanta History Center, they include Staci Catron, Paul Crater, Erica Hague, Helen Matthews, and Sue Verhoef. At Emory University's Stuart A. Rose Manuscript, Archives, and Rare Book library, I received invaluable help from Kathy Shoemaker, and Mary Linnemann helped me at the University of Georgia's Hargrett Library. I received additional assistance from John Wright at the Atlanta Public Library; Tiffany Atwater at the Atlanta University Center's Robert W. Woodruff Library; Derek Mosley at the Auburn Avenue Research Library on African American Culture and History; Steven Engerrand at the Georgia Archives; and Marcy Breffle and Mary Woodlan at Historic Oakland Cemetery. Michelle Asci helped me to search the vast photographic collections at Georgia State University.

The staff of the University of Georgia Press supported my project from the beginning. I thank Mick Gusinde-Duffy for guiding me through the acceptance and editorial process and the anonymous readers who helped develop the book. I am indebted to Ellen Goldlust, whose skillful editing made my manuscript much more readable. It has been a privilege to work with her for the second time as well as with production manager Jon Davies, a legend at the press.

After a career of thirty-five years in the classroom, I am retiring from teaching. I dedicate this book to my students at Eastern Illinois University and Georgia State University. Thanks for many happy memories.

GONE BUT NOT
FORGOTTEN

# CHAPTER 1

# The Lost Cause

**O**N APRIL 26, 1875, Atlantans gathered to celebrate Confederate Memorial Day, an annual commemoration begun in 1866 that included speeches, prayers, and the decoration of soldiers' graves at Oakland Cemetery. A decade after the war's end, Atlantans heard a speech by Captain Henry Jackson at DeGive's Opera House before heading to the cemetery. Thousands of listeners heard Jackson's classic Lost Cause oration, which emphasized the Confederacy's dedication to creating an "independent republic," interpreted Confederate surrender as a "defeat of principle," and venerated the Army of Northern Virginia and its commander, Robert E. Lee (1807–70). "If the infinite wisdom of the Almighty has ever permitted this earth to be trod by the foot of one perfect man, he was that man," Jackson insisted. He did not acknowledge the Confederacy's western army, for no one in attendance wanted to be reminded of its failure to protect Atlantans from General William T. Sherman (1820–91). When the crowd reached the cemetery, they found its grounds festooned with fresh flowers, including roses in the shape of a Confederate flag. The city's leading newspaper, the *Constitution*, praised the members of the Atlanta Ladies Memorial Association (ALMA) who were responsible for the floral tributes, lauding the efforts of "Georgia's daughters / Fairest of the southern land," who "Come to place o'er fallen heroes / Flowers rich and rare and bright, / Heroes who in vain had fought for— / *Southern free-*

1

*dom—Southern Right."* No one said anything about freedom for African Americans.[1]

In the decade after the Civil War, Atlanta's white population adopted an interpretation of the war that emphasized the notion that the Confederacy fought for abstract constitutional principles and not to preserve slavery. Gone was any mention of the possibility of spreading southern interests, including slavery, into the Caribbean and northern Mexico, as Confederate provisional president Jefferson Davis (1808–89) had suggested when he visited Atlanta in February 1861. Instead, white Atlantans, like white southerners throughout the region, wanted to honor the dead and reexamine the war's causes through a lens that left out or minimized important parts of the story, including the role that slavery played in causing the war and the importance of emancipation as an outcome. They wanted to honor men they regarded as heroes, especially Robert E. Lee, and sought to honor themselves so that they could claim a moral victory in spite of the region's military defeat. To a greater extent than other areas of the South, white people in Atlanta included the civilian narrative in their version of the Lost Cause to reflect Atlanta's subjugation by Sherman and his army. Their postwar collective memory included neither the many Atlantans who opposed secession in 1860 nor the wartime divisions over politics, military policies, and economic struggles that left deep scars among civilians from 1861 to 1865. Instead, they emphasized civilian unity and resilience under Sherman's bombardment and focused on the city's rise from the ashes of its destruction to become capital of a New South.[2]

The Lost Cause narrative played out against a backdrop of resentment toward the federal government. During Reconstruction, southern whites resented the military occupation of their region, for the army's purpose— protecting the civil and voting rights now guaranteed to black men under the Constitution—posed a direct challenge to white political dominance. White people in the South resented the U.S. government's decision to rebury in a series of national cemeteries those Union soldiers hastily interred near Civil War battlefields. When burial crews finished this work in 1871, at a cost of four million dollars, seventy-four national cemeteries contained the reinterred bodies of more than three hundred thousand Union dead, but the states of the former Confederacy received no federal help with the reburials of their soldiers. White southerners found another source of resentment in the late nineteenth century when Congress increased its appropriation to support Civil War pensions. Although some

northerners expressed dismay at the lack of assistance for Confederate reburials, Union veterans vehemently opposed granting pensions to former
rebels. Confederate veterans might receive modest annual stipends from
their states but would receive nothing from their national government.[3]

African Americans in Atlanta and elsewhere offered another interpretation that challenged white southerners: the Civil War had brought regret-
table destruction to the South but ended slavery and offered the potential
for blacks to enjoy the rights of citizenship. In Atlanta, black pastors, ora-
tors, and writers expounded on these themes. Nonetheless, over time, the
Lost Cause interpretation merged with a growing national emphasis on
sectional reconciliation. Among white people in both the North and the
South, reconciliation became the dominant historical memory of the war.
As historian David Blight has pointed out, Union and Confederate veterans led this effort, emphasizing the theme of national healing, which was
clearly apparent when former enemies clasped hands in 1913 on the fiftieth anniversary of the Battle of Gettysburg. The war's causes and the fate
of African Americans during and after the war were often ignored.[4]

Before the war, Atlanta was a young city focused on business and transportation. Founded in the 1830s as the terminus to the Western and Atlantic Railroad, Atlanta grew during the following two decades from a tiny
rail center to a prosperous commercial hub for four railroads. With its
commercial economy and strong ties to the North, Atlanta was not a place
where secessionist views prevailed during the years leading up to the Civil
War. Indeed, in the 1860 presidential election, 63 percent of Atlanta voters cast ballots for one of two Unionist candidates for president instead of
the southern rights candidate, John Breckinridge, who carried Georgia.
However, with Abraham Lincoln's election and the onset of war, Atlantans' loyalties shifted, and most residents appeared to embrace Confederate independence, at least during the first half of the war, when prospects
for military victory appeared bright.[5]

As a rail center, Atlanta's importance to the Confederacy was never in
doubt, and by the second half of the war, Atlanta had become the Confederacy's second-most-important city—a rail and supply center, an industrial center, and a place where thousands of wounded and ill soldiers
were treated in government and private hospitals. However, wartime Atlanta was a tough place to live. The Confederate Arsenal's multiple workshops employed white men, women, and children as well as enslaved men.
Privately owned factories also drove the economy. But economic change

also attracted new residents, the population of the city doubled, and both housing and food were in short supply. Over time, Confederate military losses, food shortages, inflation, and waves of infectious disease led to deteriorating conditions for all Atlantans and destitution for the city's neediest civilians. In desperation, a small number of gun-wielding women looted a butcher shop in 1863, one of several "bread riots" in the Confederate states. By 1864, crime had become rampant as hungry people stole vegetables from local gardens and chickens from coops; more brazen thieves broke into stores and made off with sacks of flour, bolts of cloth, and pairs of shoes. Slaves took advantage of Atlanta's upheaval by running away, both singly and in groups.[6]

In the midst of a domestic situation that was spiraling downward, Sherman launched what would become an infamous campaign to capture Atlanta, and his success boosted not only the general's reputation but also northern morale and Lincoln's chances for reelection in November 1864. Before seizing the city on September 2, Sherman shelled it in July and August, leading to dire circumstances for the remaining population. Most residents took shelter in "bombproofs," makeshift shelters constructed by digging holes in the ground, or cellars covered by sheet metal or wood. Those who lived through these fearful times would never forget them. At least twenty people died, and many others were injured. After capturing the city, Sherman ordered the expulsion of civilians, leading to objections not only from Atlanta's mayor but also from some of Sherman's officers. Atlanta's most destitute civilians rode in wagons south to the town of Rough and Ready, where they were handed over to Confederate authorities. Many spent the remainder of the war living a pitiful existence in Macon and the surrounding area. Even Jefferson Davis's attempt to restore morale by visiting Macon in September 1864 had little apparent impact. Never a gifted orator, Davis faced a daunting task in seeking to convince Atlantans to continue the fight for Confederate independence from outside their city.[7]

While Confederate civilians bemoaned Atlanta's surrender, black people and Unionist white people celebrated it. When Sherman's soldiers entered the city, slaves cheered. Told that they were free to leave their masters, some did so immediately, including Patience, who was enslaved by a local merchant and who stole enough food to sustain her in the coming weeks. Other freedpeople waited a few days to make sure that freedom was a reality and not an illusion. Mary, a slave owned by the Berry family, waited five days before departing, prompting eleven-year-old Carrie Berry to write in her diary, "Mary went off this evening and I don't expect that she will come back any more." In the ensuing months, African Americans feared reenslavement and consequently avoided white people whenever possible.[8]

As the Union army vacated Atlanta in November to begin its famous March to the Sea, Sherman ordered the destruction of buildings that had military value; many other buildings had been damaged during the shelling or by departing Confederate soldiers, burned by arsonists, or bore damage from vandalism. In Sherman's wake, the city took on a ghostly appearance, with shell casings, animal carcasses, and garbage littering the streets.[9]

Many Atlantans returned to the city after the war ended, and its rapid recovery from the devastation impressed visitors from the South, the North, and even Europe. The city council sold bonds as a kind of substitute currency to replace worthless Confederate dollars and authorized the rebuilding of the central market so that farmers could bring produce and meat to feed hungry residents and the city could begin collecting tax revenue. By 1867 all four of the city's major rail lines had been reconstructed, further fueling economic growth. City leaders acquiesced to congressional Reconstruction policy, including the occupation of the city by General John Pope and federal soldiers. Members of the business and political elite welcomed Pope with a reception and enlisted his help in making Atlanta the host for Georgia's 1867 constitutional convention. They scored an even bigger prize when Atlanta was chosen to replace Milledgeville as the new state capital, making it the center of Georgia's political as well as economic power. When the Democratic Party defeated Republicans in the 1870s and dominated state politics, white people in Atlanta celebrated the state's "redemption" from Reconstruction. Black men, legally enfranchised, lost political rights as whites used a variety of tactics, including poll taxes, to suppress the black vote.[10]

At the same time that Atlantans rebuilt the city, they also needed to confront the recent past. Residents recalled the war when they read newspaper obituaries, including that of James M. Calhoun (1811–75), the wartime mayor. When he died in 1875, the local bar association held a meeting at the courthouse to celebrate his life and leadership. As reported in the *Atlanta Constitution*, Calhoun won praise for his efforts to support the city's impoverished and besieged wartime citizens and his protest of

Sherman's 1864 expulsion order. Like many testimonials, this one celebrated Atlanta's return to prosperity after the war when "oppression" was
followed by "opulence and refinement" for Mayor Calhoun's city and its
wartime survivors.[11]

Calhoun had opposed secession, a point that his obituary did not emphasize; indeed, many of Atlanta's Unionist leaders had obituaries that
downplayed their previous roles. James L. Dunning, a Unionist and Reconstruction-era postmaster, petitioned the city council in 1867 to erect
a statue of Abraham Lincoln. Instead of voting down the project directly,
the council responded by requiring that Dunning spend $750,000 to
$1,000,000 to improve parkland for the proposed monument, a sum the
councilmen knew he could not raise, and the project was not carried forward. When Dunning died in 1874, the *Atlanta Constitution*'s brief obituary included no details about his life and instead observed only that he
had faults as well as virtues. Another Unionist, Nedom Angier, died in
1882. After noting his opposition to secession, the *Constitution* suggested
that Angier ultimately embraced Confederate independence. In reality,
Angier escaped from Atlanta during the war and met with members of
the Lincoln cabinet in Washington, D.C., but the perception of Angier's
Confederate sympathies helps to explain his election as mayor in 1877, the
last Republican to serve in this capacity. Angier was succeeded by William
Lowndes Calhoun, a Confederate veteran. Emphasizing a theme that the
city's boosters loved to repeat, the *Constitution* proclaimed that Atlanta
"is torn by no internal passions." The city "always comes up bright and
cheerful—all elements united" to support progress.[12]

William Markham (1811–90), Atlanta's wealthiest Unionist and a one-
term mayor during the 1850s, tried and failed to revive his political career after the war, running unsuccessfully for another term as mayor and
for Congress. An industrialist who established the city's first rolling mill
before selling it to the Confederate government rather than support the
war effort, Markham made another postwar fortune in real estate, with
extensive holdings that included the Markham House Hotel. When he
died in 1890, his obituary acknowledged that he had given "speech after
speech" in opposition to secession during 1860–61 and that he identified
with the Republican Party. Former Unionists and Confederates alike attended Markham's funeral and those of many of Atlanta's other Unionists,
happy to honor one another as the city returned to commercial success.
Two years before his death, Markham had earned Sherman's enmity and

garnered national news coverage after giving an interview alleging that the March to the Sea had been "an afterthought." Markham had served on a committee of leading citizens who in September 1864 asked Sherman to reconsider his expulsion order, and the general had responded that he planned to hold Atlanta until the end of the war and could not feed the citizens. Consequently, when Sherman and his army left Atlanta, Markham concluded that plans had changed. Sherman denied Markham's allegation and the story, calling it "trash," and several newspapers picked up the exchange.[13]

Although Markham helped his only son escape to the North in 1863 to keep him out of harm's way, less fortunate Americans experienced a level of destruction and death that would have been unimaginable when the war began. Experts now estimate that as many as 752,000 soldiers and 50,000 civilians died, creating what historian Drew Gilpin Faust has called "a new relationship with death" in a "republic of suffering." In 1865, groups of white women in the South began decorating the graves of fallen soldiers, with seventy such groups forming in a very short time. In Georgia, this process began in the city of Columbus when Mary Williams appealed to the public to spend one day annually in offering floral tributes on "the graves of our martyred dead." Williams hoped that this tradition would be "handed down through time as a religious custom of the South."[14]

In June 1866, ALMA formed to decorate graves at City Cemetery (later renamed Oakland Cemetery) east of the downtown area. Several thousand Confederate soldiers were interred there, including men who had died in hospitals and others who lost their lives fighting in the Atlanta Campaign. Prior to the event, women placed a notice in the *Atlanta Daily Intelligencer* about the need to honor the dead "of *our* country," a reference to the defeated Confederacy and probably an effort to inform the public that the group would not be honoring the more than one hundred Union soldiers who had died in Atlanta's military hospitals during the war and been interred at the cemetery.[15]

Historian Thomas J. Brown has called Confederate Memorial Day ceremonies "the most dynamic early vehicle for Confederate remembrance." Ladies memorial associations led the way among white southerners. From the beginning, these groups had a political intent. Before ALMA had decorated its first grave, it sponsored a June 14, 1866, lecture by Robert Alston (1832–79), who had served as an officer in the cavalry of partisan ranger John Hunt Morgan. Alston paid homage to the South's "fallen heroes" who fought for "the preservation, in its original purity," of the Constitution. He castigated "the Radical majority which now rules our land," a reference to federal Reconstruction policy. Though Radical Republicans in Congress had not yet wrested control of Reconstruction policy from President Andrew Johnson, Alston feared "this march of fanaticism." By appearing under the auspices of a women's organization, southern political partisans like Alston could say what they liked while pretending to be nonpartisan. So effective was ALMA at hiding its political intent that General George Meade, at that time the commander of the U.S. army detachment in Atlanta, attended one of its wreath-laying ceremonies.[16]

The notion of a Lost Cause, including the theme of southern defeat by the North's larger armies and superior industrial might, emerged over many years, but one of its earliest and most important promoters was Edward A. Pollard (1832–72), former editor of the *Richmond Examiner*, who published *The Lost Cause: A New Southern History of the War of the Confederates* in 1867. According to Pollard, the South had fought for noble ideals that later generations must remember. This image of the Confederacy gained many adherents, including former Confederate general Jubal Early (1816–94), who in 1873 became editor of the *Southern Historical Society Papers*, an influential publication with a wide following. Early wanted to present a white southern interpretation of the Civil War's causes, battles, and outcome as a bulwark against northern writers who might present a pro-Union, pro-emancipation interpretation.[17]

Early was also responsible for elevating Lee's reputation and legacy. The general had been a beloved figure in the Confederacy, but his stature suffered after he surrendered to General Ulysses S. Grant in April 1865. Many white southerners subsequently preferred to exalt the memory of General Stonewall Jackson, who had died, undefeated, at the peak of his military success in 1863, at least until Lee died in 1870. An outpouring of grief at his passing resulted in a greater willingness to view Lee as a figure to be venerated, and Early aided that process. In a speech on the second anniversary of Lee's death, Early emphasized Lee's brilliance as a general, arguing that Lee had not been defeated but rather had been overwhelmed by the Union's manpower advantages, industrial might, larger network of railroads, and more extensive government infrastructure. As Gary W. Gallagher has pointed out, this interpretation denied any credit for northern victory to Grant and other Union commanders, and it largely ignored the

Western Theater of the war, where Confederate defeats in Tennessee and Georgia were difficult to interpret in heroic terms.[18]

Atlantans played their own role in the emerging narrative of Robert E. Lee and the Lost Cause. In the late 1860s, members of ALMA, like their counterparts in other memorial groups, began raising funds for a monument to honor Confederate dead. Like other ladies memorial associations, ALMA chose to place its monument at the local cemetery and that monument, like others constructed in the first decade after the war, was funereal—an obelisk, the ancient symbol for eternal life—rather than the representation of a Confederate soldier. In October 1870, when Lee died in Lexington, Virginia, ALMA members quickly organized a cornerstone-laying ceremony, eager to pair Atlanta's wartime legacy with that of the South's greatest wartime leader.[19]

The ceremony took place on the same day that Lee was laid to rest in Virginia. Atlanta businesses and factories closed for the day, and an estimated five thousand citizens—believed to be the largest crowd ever gathered in the city—met at the Capitol on Marietta Street before walking in a solemn procession to the cemetery. One of the marshals in the parade was a former slave, Roderick D. Badger, now an upwardly mobile businessman. Following the marshals were members of fraternal organizations, students from Oglethorpe University, members of the General Assembly, representatives of Fulton County government, the mayor of Atlanta, and members of the city council. The principal speaker was Confederate major general John B. Gordon (1832–1904), who had known Lee well and spoke about him with genuine conviction. "Lee was never really beaten," Gordon claimed, ignoring Gettysburg and other instances where Lee had fallen short, "Lee could not be beaten! Overpowered, foiled in his efforts he might be, but never defeated until the props which supported him gave way."[20]

In 1874, after stonemasons completed the monument to "Our Confederate Dead," Atlantans gathered for a second ceremony on what would become known as Confederate Memorial Day, April 26, the date on which the last major Confederate army in the field had surrendered. With Georgia now "redeemed" from Reconstruction and federal soldiers gone from the South, African Americans were not included in the procession. At the time of its completion, the Confederate monument was the tallest structure in Atlanta.[21]

Many ALMA stalwarts had previously staffed Atlanta's two organizations of female benevolent volunteers during the war, including Maria Westmoreland, founder of the Ladies' Soldiers' Relief Society, and Eugenia Goode Morgan of the rival Atlanta Hospital Association. Although the middle- and upper-middle-class white women who made up ALMA did not defy gender norms in most instances, they did take over leadership of the organization from men early on. John P. Logan served as the first president of the organization, but women held the office after that. ALMA members not only drew attention to Confederate valor but also kept careful records to document their own contributions. The artifacts enclosed in the cornerstone for the Confederate obelisk, for example, included a picture of General Lee, a flag never touched by the hand of a Yankee, coins, newspapers, and the names of ALMA members. The group further memorialized itself by writing an official history and by putting up a small monument in the 1930s. The Atlanta group communicated with other women's organizations across the South, sometimes raising money to help sister organizations.[22]

In addition to decorating graves, ALMA raised money to disinter the bodies of Confederate soldiers from shallow mass graves in and around Atlanta and reinter them at City Cemetery. Because of the logistics and cost involved, ALMA limited its effort to reburying soldiers from a ten-mile radius of the city.[23] Over time, ALMA's efforts took on a quasi-official status. Atlanta's mayor issued an annual proclamation asking residents to "unite with the Ladies of the Memorial Association in doing honor to our martyrs, whose life-blood washed upon the altar of our liberties," as one mayor put it. Because festivities generally took place in the afternoons, businesses closed for a "half holiday," while banks shuttered for the entire day. Hotels and boardinghouses cut their prices for those traveling to Atlanta, and the city's luxury hotel, the Kimball House, often hosted out-of-town speakers free of charge. The *Constitution* frequently printed news stories about ALMA, at times couching its language in religious terms, including one reference to the "holy duties" of Atlanta's "patriotic ladies." The *Constitution* wanted to remind each Atlanta woman that those buried at Oakland had died "in her defense."[24]

Fundraising represented an ongoing challenge for ALMA. Efforts to seek a significant amount of money from the Georgia legislature failed, although it did make a token contribution of "one day's pay" in 1868. The Atlanta City Council appropriated five hundred dollars in 1871, and the city donated the land on which the Confederate obelisk was constructed. Beginning in the 1880s, the city council contributed two hundred dollars annually for the upkeep of Confederate graves. For the most part, however, ALMA raised money through individual contributions and social gatherings, such as strawberry festivals and skating parties. One fundraiser featured a traveling company led by "Madame Jarley." The performers presented a tableau of wax figures that included Caesar; Nero; Mary, Queen of Scots; and Jack Horner with his Christmas pie; music was provided by a "colored band." At the annual celebrations on April 26, collection boxes at the cemetery garnered modest sums.[25]

Twenty years after its efforts began, ALMA completed a registry of the names of soldiers interred in the Confederate section of the cemetery, replaced rotting wooden headstones with marble ones, and added new sod. Because the precise location of twenty-three hundred Confederate graves within the cemetery could not be determined, ALMA erected two twelve-foot marble shafts with the names of those men.[26]

The organization next focused its efforts on commemorating the three thousand unidentified Confederate dead interred at the cemetery. ALMA erected a monument based on the Lion of Lucerne, a famous Swiss statue honoring soldiers who died defending the life of Marie Antoinette. Made from the largest piece of quarried stone ever excavated in the United States to that time, with "Unknown Confederate Dead" chiseled on its base, the Lion of Atlanta lies on a Confederate flag and has a stake driven through its back. At the 1894 dedication ceremony, Colonel John Milledge, the designated marshal of the event and husband of ALMA president Fannie Milledge, spoke of "the martyrs and patriots who sleep their last sleep here." Milledge also emphasized the civilian theme by drawing attention to Sherman's expulsion of civilians from the city and its burning and destruction. When he gave the signal, Fannie Milledge drew a curtain aside to reveal the impressive monument. While a band played "Dixie," the assembled crowd applauded and cheered for several minutes. Congressman Henry H. Carlton, a Confederate veteran and the designated "orator of the day," offered praise for ALMA's efforts during the past thirty years, including the reburial effort and its work in replacing headstones.[27]

Although ALMA continued to play an important role in annual celebrations of Confederate Memorial Day, it lost some of its influence in the planning of these events in 1886, when Confederate veterans in Atlanta organized as the Confederate Veterans Association of Fulton County.

Thereafter, ALMA took charge of floral arrangements and often selected the chaplain for the occasion, while the Confederate Veterans Association selected the speaker. Women did not publicly express any resentment over this change but later resumed their previous role when the veterans, their numbers dwindling, relinquished the task in the twentieth century.[28]

Charter members of the Confederate Veterans Association of Fulton County included John Milledge, the *Constitution*'s William A. Hemphill (1842–1902), and former mayor William Lowndes Calhoun (1837–1908), the son of Atlanta's wartime mayor and an officer in the 42nd Georgia in the war. Calhoun became the group's president and offered effusive praise for ALMA and enthusiastic support for the Lost Cause. At the organization's April 1888 annual meeting in Atlanta, Calhoun invoked the U.S. Constitution in explaining secession but showed greater willingness than many southerners to acknowledge slavery's role: "The people of the Southern States believed that [their] most sacred rights had been infringed; that class of property which constituted our wealth had been endangered." Calhoun believed that the Confederate Veterans had a duty to act as a brotherhood, to "revive and cherish the memories of that great contest," and to proclaim to their descendants that "we were not traitors."[29]

In the post–Civil War period, veterans formed a unique brotherhood of men, especially in the South, where the overwhelming majority of white men served in the military. In Fulton County, more than 85 percent of men aged between fifteen and fifty served in the army, exceeding the average for Confederate states. Thousands of southern soldiers returned from the war with disabilities, including wounds, disease, and amputated limbs. The presence of veterans with prosthetic limbs became common in towns and cities across the postwar South. In the absence of government help for veterans' medical, psychological, and economic needs, members of the Confederate Veterans Association of Fulton County set up a relief committee to help its indigent and disabled members and lobbied for the creation of a Confederate veterans home in Georgia, an effort that would take far longer to achieve than any of them imagined. The group also held an annual memorial service to honor those who had died over the preceding year.[30]

No African American presence at Confederate Memorial Day celebrations was recorded in Atlanta's daily newspapers after 1874. The city's blacks and whites remembered the war in ways that reflected their differing views of events.

In the immediate postwar period, African Americans celebrated the Fourth of July, a holiday largely ignored by white southerners during and after the war. July 4, 1867, marked the beginning of the Republican Party in Georgia, and African Americans celebrated with banners, one of which read "The Birth of Liberty, July 4th, '76, The Death of Slavery, July 4th, '67." Georgia's Republicans were a biracial coalition of African Americans, prewar Unionists, and yeoman whites from North Georgia and the Wiregrass region of South Georgia. However, this version of the Republican Party was short lived in Georgia, and July 4 evolved into a social celebration for blacks.[31]

Instead, "Emancipation Day" became Atlanta's major celebration of the Civil War and freedom in the black community, a role it also played in many other African American communities across the South. The date varied from place to place: in Virginia, for example, many African Americans celebrated April 9, when Lee surrendered to Grant at Appomattox Courthouse, whereas freedpeople in Texas celebrated Juneteenth (June 19), when slaves in the Southwest learned of their freedom. But in many places in the South, including Atlanta, January 1 became the central celebration of freedom, marking the day when Lincoln signed the Emancipation Proclamation. Emancipation Day festivities often took place in local churches and included a reading of the proclamation by a prominent member of the community along with speeches and music. Oral communication at black celebrations was important because illiteracy remained an ongoing problem. Sometimes the festivities began with a parade, including the Emancipation Day celebration in Atlanta on January 1, 1884. Bishop Henry McNeal Turner (1834–1915), a bishop in the African Methodist Episcopal Church and a fiery polemicist, gave the keynote speech, insisting that "the devil in hell would not make the distinctions against the negroes, that are made in this county."[32]

Throughout the South, Emancipation Day speeches were occasions to educate the community about political issues. The white press often covered these events warily. In their study of Charleston, Ethan J. Kytle and Blain Roberts point out that the city's *Daily News* referred to "much inflammatory matter" at one Emancipation Day meeting. At Atlanta's Lloyd Street Methodist Church in 1890, audience members passed resolutions condemning recent lynchings in Jesup, Georgia, and Barnwell, South Carolina. The Jesup lynchings caused particular fear because they occurred within the state. Jesup was a community in South Geor-

gia where African Americans found employment in turpentine distill-
eries and sawmills. In a Christmas Day 1889 event that came to be known
as the Jesup riot, a racial confrontation led to the death of deputy marshal Matthew Barnhill and another white man, possibly at the hands of
Bob Brewer, whom the *Atlanta Constitution* labeled a "colored desperado." Brewer eluded capture by escaping into the nearby Florida swamps,
and a retaliatory mob lynched three African Americans—William Hopps,
Peter Jackson, and William Fluid. In addition, the vigilantes terrorized
Hopps's mother, Martha, invading her home in the middle of the night,
stripping her naked, and whipping her. By early 1890, blacks—including Martha Hopps—began abandoning Jesup. Speakers at Lloyd Street
Church called on Atlanta's white churches and the white news media to
"denounce these outrages, in the name of the constitution of the state,
and of the United States."[33]

Emancipation Day festivities also focused on a positive message of racial advancement, especially when celebrations took place at black colleges
and universities. January 1 held particular meaning in the black community because in slavery times, January 1 had been "Heartbreak Day," when
slaves whose owners had rented them out separated from their families
and communities to begin a new annual lease. In 1897, the *Constitution*
reported that "every negro in Atlanta" celebrated the thirty-fourth anniversary of Emancipation. Bishop Wesley Gaines (1840–1912), a founder
of Morris Brown College, gave the benediction, after which Clark Atlanta
College students provided choral music. President Richard R. Wright
(1855–1947) of Savannah State University offered an inspiring speech
highlighting the importance of raising children with proper values so that
they would lead upright lives as adults, a message that resonated with the
"racial uplift" philosophy of Booker T. Washington, president of Tuskegee Institute in neighboring Alabama. In 1903, the Reverend Henry H.
Proctor (1868–1933) of First Congregational Church took the pulpit at
Ebenezer Baptist Church with a speech that focused on climbing out of
poverty. "One white man on Wall street could buy us out twice," he declared. Proctor wanted audience members to work hard and acquire skills
that would enable them to earn money.[34]

Although ministers provided leadership in Emancipation Day festivities, women also played important roles. At Atlanta University in 1894, a
student named Mattie Freeman Childs took the podium in a speech called
"The Progress of Colored Women Since 1863": "Suddenly snatched from

the cursed bondage of slavery, placed in the blessed light of freedom, with
God as helper, we have patiently and arduously toiled upward, and tonight
we can look in the face of any man and boldly say, 'We are rising.'" Childs
concluded that "Never before in the history of America has woman occupied so high a position as she does now in this glorious Nineteenth Century." She called for equality of the genders, insisting that "Almighty God
in his infinite wisdom did not make one sex inferior to another."[35]

In the decades following the Civil War, black and white writers produced dramatically different interpretations of the war that gave special
attention to the home front. In *The Black Side* (1894), the reverend Edward R. Carter (1856–1944) of Friendship Baptist Church recounts Atlanta's history before, during, and after the conflict. Born in slavery in Athens,
Georgia, and taught to read as a child, Carter became a shoemaker after
the war, then moved to Atlanta in 1879 to attend Atlanta Baptist Seminary
(later Morehouse College). He became a pastor the following year and in
1882 accepted the call to serve Friendship Baptist Church, a congregation
founded in 1866 after freedmen left the white First Baptist Church to form
their own congregation. Carter's ministry at Friendship Baptist spanned
more than six decades and lasted until his death. According to a booklet
published on the sixtieth anniversary of his ministry, black congregants
had been expelled from First Baptist in 1866 because the "changed atti-
tude, on the part of the freedmen did not accord with the mental state of
the whites, and they took steps to remove the colored members from their
church rolls."[36]

As leader of a prominent congregation, Carter understood the need to
maintain peaceful relations between the races, and he was diplomatic in
his interpretation of Atlanta's history. His view of events was much less
confrontational than that of Bishop Henry McNeal Turner who served in
the Georgia legislature during the brief period of Republican dominance
and later moved to Savannah. By contrast with Carter who was a racial accommodationist, Turner advocated black self-reliance and back-to-Africa
movements. Nonetheless, Turner wrote the introduction to *The Black
Side*, praising Carter as "grandly contributing his part in the promotion
and general advancement of our race."[37]

Carter went out of his way to extol Atlanta's virtues in *The Black Side*,
calling his adopted city "the beautiful, enterprising city of Atlanta," but he
did not gloss over its history of racial division. Carter opened by protest-
ing the "continual effort to debar and prevent the Brother in Black from

entering into any lucrative business." In his treatment of Atlanta's Civil War history, Carter was careful to express sympathy for the suffering of white Atlanta residents, acknowledging that people had been killed and wounded during Sherman's bombardment: "This was a sad picture, a pitiable scene! The loss on the white side was great." However, he also wrote that the arrival of the Union army in Atlanta had a very different meaning for African Americans: "The shells of General Sherman were the strokes of the hammer of liberty, unfastening the fetters of the accursed and inhuman institution of slavery!"[38]

Carter offered a measured interpretation of Reconstruction. During the brief period of Republican rule of the state, African Americans served in the legislature, but in 1868, white legislators voted to expel black members. Atlanta, which elected two black members to the city council during Reconstruction, did not elect another until 1965. Carter chose to focus on the positive, listing the names of Georgia's prominent black legislators during the "trying times" of Reconstruction. He suggested that race relations had been relatively stable in the 1890s and that the black man had "realized that he must act for himself." However, Carter also made his views clear, writing that blacks paid taxes in Atlanta and therefore had "the rights of a tax-payer" to have "free access to the public positions of the city." His book offers a lengthy recounting of African Americans' postwar achievements in education, business, and religion as well as individual biographies accompanied by photographs of those Carter viewed as meritorious.[39]

Mary Ann Harris Gay's memoir, *Life in Dixie during the War* (1897), offers a marked contrast to Carter's book. A white woman who lived a few miles east of Atlanta in Decatur, Gay (1829–1918) produced a volume that was a classic Lost Cause tribute, applauding Confederate valor on the battlefield and the home front. She came from a prominent family that owned farmland in Gordon County, Georgia, as well as a home in Decatur. Unmarried and thirty-two years old when the war began, she lived with her mother in a handsome federal-style home that still stands today. Gay's half-brother, Thomas J. Stokes, served in the Confederate army and died at the Battle of Franklin in 1864. Thereafter, his widow and son resided with Gay and her mother.[40]

Gay's memoir begins with a spirited defense of the institution of slavery. Thirty years after the war ended, Gay still upheld the institution's alleged virtues. Her family owned three slaves in Decatur and probably others on their rural farmland. Gay reminded her readers that slavery had at one time been legal in all parts of the American colonies and that northerners as well as southerners had profited from the institution. She held the traditional white southern view that slaves were lightly tasked and well treated and declared that "no people held in bondage ever received so many benefits." Two of the family slaves—"our ebony Confederates"—had remained loyal throughout the war, although a third escaped to the Yankees.[41]

After the war, Mary Gay identified herself as a Confederate veteran because she believed that women who nurtured and nursed soldiers deserved that distinction, and her memoir is filled with references to her energetic and efficient support for Confederate soldiers. She knitted, sewed, and frequently traveled into Atlanta, sometimes even walking the seven-mile distance, to donate clothing and "edibles" to soldiers and to nurse the wounded at the Fair Ground and Empire Hospitals.[42]

The memoir's most arresting moments describe what Atlantans had begun to call "the dark days of '64" when Union soldiers occupied Decatur and Atlanta and expelled civilians from Atlanta. Gay praised one Union officer who expressed sympathy for her aged mother and for her ill and dying slave and sent a tray of food but had nothing but contempt for the "diabolical" Sherman, whose men constituted a "ruthless, Godless band." Moreover, Gay laid blame for starting the war squarely on the North, declaring the Republican Party the "Abolition party" "founded on falsehood and hate."[43]

Gay's discussion of Atlanta and Decatur after their capture reminded readers of their tribulations after the Union army began the March to the Sea. The expulsion of civilians from Atlanta had left hundreds of people "dumped out upon the cold ground without shelter," while Gay and her family in Decatur had shelter but no food and had to resort to picking up kernels of corn left behind by Kenner Garrard's federal cavalry. In the coming months, Gay scavenged the battlefields around Atlanta for minié balls, exchanging lead for something to eat.[44]

After the war, Gay earned a living by selling Bibles, sometimes traveling as far away as Texas, so she knew something about marketing. She published Life in Dixie during the War in Atlanta, initially asking buyers to contact her directly to purchase a copy. She also sold the book on her sales trips. The book's growing popularity, fueled by nostalgia for the Lost Cause and aided by an introduction from the popular writer Joel Chandler Harris, led to multiple reprintings. The Atlanta Constitution called Gay's volume "a conspicuous success" and gushed that it imparted "perfect truth." Local reviewers picked up on the theme of the "dark days of '64," and Gay became a local celebrity. More than any previous source, her book focused attention on the plight of civilians in Atlanta and Decatur and the role of southern women in coping with wartime adversity. Gay later helped to raise money for a statue to Confederate vice president Alexander Stephens in his hometown of Crawfordville, Georgia, following Stephens's death in 1883. Gay's name was so closely associated with that of Stephens that when she died at the age of ninety in 1918, her obituary suggested that the two might have been sweethearts in their youth.[45]

Many other Atlanta women offered reminiscences about the home front in a series of newspaper interviews published in the *Atlanta Journal* in 1909 and 1910. These women—members of the Atlanta Pioneer Women's Society, founded in 1909—carried Gay's themes of endurance, resilience, and survival into the twentieth century and enlarged her narrative with multiple stories of their own.

The Pioneer Women filled a vacuum created by the lack of surviving physical reminders of war and the lack of public and private records. Long before Sherman's army arrived in Atlanta, African Americans had begun liberating themselves by running away, but slaves, most of them illiterate, left few records, and sites where slaves were auctioned in Atlanta did not survive the war. The white women and children who worked in the Confederate Arsenal or produced hand-stitched garments for the Confederate quartermaster did not write testimonials about their wartime travails, and the workshops that once comprised the arsenal were destroyed by Sherman's burning. Atlanta's Unionists, some of whom played roles during Reconstruction, did little to promote their legacy in public after Reconstruction ended.[46] In the absence of alternative sources, the Pioneer Women became central figures in chronicling Atlanta's wartime past. They did not discuss the wartime conditions that led to destitution for the city's needy citizens, child labor in Atlanta's Confederate Arsenal, or the 1863 bread riot. They also did not discuss the presence of Unionists or the gradual breakdown of the institution of slavery. By the early twentieth century, the role of Unionists, poor whites, and enslaved Atlantans had begun to recede into the shadows of public memory.

The Atlanta Pioneer Women's Society provided a female counterpart to the all-male Pioneer Citizens' Society of Atlanta, which had been created a few years earlier. Membership in the women's group was restricted to white women who lived in Atlanta before the Civil War or were descended from an antebellum resident. By 1910, the organization had 150 members, many of whom, like founder Eugenia Goode Morgan (1844–1924), were active in ALMA. The Pioneer Women's Society held monthly meetings and an annual gathering to memorialize their newly deceased members. Although the Pioneer Citizens published a book of biographical essays about themselves, it contains surprisingly little information about their Civil War activities; perhaps these men did not want to call attention to their lack of military service in the war. While the Confederacy's soldiers had fought for a losing cause, many of Atlanta's Pioneer Citizens had been making money from contracts with the Confederate government to produce military goods. Some of them paid others to fight in their place or joined the militia or other volunteer units, unlikely to see much actual fighting.[47]

In contrast, the Pioneer Women's Society wanted the record of their wartime activities to be passed down to future generations. They gave interviews to their historian, journalist Lollie Belle Wylie (1858–1923), who published them in the *Journal*. In defending the Lost Cause, Morgan led the way by praising the "noble struggle of the brave soldiers," with Leila Sisson adding that the South was "subdued [but] never conquered!" Most of the women recorded stories of Atlantans' ability to cope with adversity. Delia Foreacre could not afford to purchase coffee, so she made a substitute out of sweet potatoes mixed with chicory. Mary Rice recalled paying the outlandish sum of twenty-five dollars for a handkerchief and kept it after the war as a memento. Callie Goode Torbett, a child during the war, remembered that all the girls wore homespun dresses because machine-made cloth was too scarce.[48]

Pioneers also wanted to record their efforts to help wounded soldiers in Atlanta's Confederate hospitals as well as to acknowledge the special role played by Martha Winship (1813–82). Although her home in Atlanta was burned by Sherman's soldiers and she did not return to live in the city after the war, Winship had been the city's most indefatigable wartime nurse. Organizer of the Atlanta Hospital Association, she and her twelve vice presidents and countless volunteers arranged donations of food, scheduled shifts of nurses, and organized fundraising events that doubled as social occasions designed to keep both soldiers and civilians focused on Confederate victory. Among the Pioneers, the Battle of Chickamauga also evoked strong memories. So many soldiers flooded the city in September 1863 that women were asked to deliver enormous quantities of food to the hospitals. Lula Cozart made "soup by the gallons," aided by her slave,

Marm Silvery. Since military hospitals could not handle the multitude of wounded men, medical authorities asked women to take soldiers into their homes. Sarah Massey nursed five men in her home and remembered proudly that only one of them died.[49]

The women's most vivid collective memory was the bombardment of the city in July and August 1864. Many citizens who had the means to do so had departed before General Sherman ordered his artillery to take aim at Atlanta, but the two thousand or so frightened civilians who remained were trapped and literally forced underground. Francina Austell lived in a rudimentary but commodious bombproof filled with straw and covered with logs. Cornelia Venable, however, stayed in tighter quarters—a tiny backyard shelter that had only enough room for the children to lie down; the adults had to sit up. Lucy Kicklighter recalled, "It is impossible to describe to any one who has never heard the whizzing and bursting of these shells the terror the sound carries."[50]

The Pioneer Women also focused on the narrative of Atlanta's subjugation by Sherman and his army. When a federal officer took Kicklighter's home as his headquarters, she hoped it might be protected; however, "with the burning of Atlanta our home went, too." Homes that survived often bore the effects of shelling. Frances Blackburn found an unexploded bomb in her chimney. Torbett's family counted seventeen places where shell fragments had struck their house. Many women reacted emotionally when they saw the damage to their city: "It made me very sad to realize the calamity that had overtaken our thrifty, courageous city," Venable recalled. "We returned home to find our house in ruins and city a heap of ashes and debris." Lula Haralson and her family traveled back to Atlanta by boxcar "to take up the broken thread of our lives." Forced to accept rations from the federal army, they subsisted on a diet of field peas and fatback.[51]

Most Pioneers sidestepped discussions of African Americans after the war, but a few offered comments that provide clues about the aftermath of slavery. Augusta Moore witnessed a procession of freedpeople holding a mock funeral to symbolize the end of bondage. Led by a man robed in white and carrying an open Bible, the procession included a wagon carrying a miniature coffin. "We buryin' Slavery, we is," one participant told Moore. Lucy Lumpkin Wilson was astonished to learn that a family slave, Bob, was elected to the Georgia legislature from Macon County after the state's 1868 constitution enfranchised black men. When the legislature was in session in Atlanta, Robert Lumpkin boarded with the family of his former owner, "quartered with the servants in our back yard." Massey had doubted the existence of the Ku Klux Klan during Reconstruction, believing it to be "a myth of the negroes," until her African American servants told her about the death of a black infant, when a preacher intoned, "Thank God, it gone to heaven, where no Ku Klux can ever come." By and large, however, Pioneers focused on Atlanta's wartime resilience and its rapid rebuilding after the war, with several using the term "Atlanta Spirit" to describe the city's renaissance. One article described Winship as "the mother of the Atlanta Spirit, so much talked of now," while another article explained that "amid the ashes of ruin . . . Hope awakened and grew strong."[52]

Women's efforts to remember the war continued in the twentieth century, but shifts in Atlanta's commemoration began as early as the 1870s, when the city's political leaders began taking modest steps toward reconciliation with the North. Lost Cause rhetoric remained prominent, but a warmer tone infused Confederate Memorial Day speeches, Fourth of July orations, and Gordon's political activism. Deeply invested in promoting the city's commercial growth, Atlanta's leaders understood that good relations with the North would be good for business.

One of Robert E. Lee's nephews, Fitzhugh Lee (1835–1905), a former Confederate cavalry general, traveled from Virginia to give a reconciliationist oration in Atlanta on Confederate Memorial Day in 1879. The younger Lee offered the expected comments about honoring and remembering the sacrifices of those who gave their lives for the Confederacy and about how the federal government had declined to help maintain Confederate cemeteries, leaving that work to female volunteers. But Lee also declared that all surviving veterans, both those who had worn blue uniforms and those who had worn gray, would one day stand before God's judgment and cited Massachusetts senator Benjamin Butler and Georgia senator Benjamin Harvey Hill as figures promoting a united country that would become "what our forefathers intended it should be, the 'glory of America and a blessing to humanity.'"[53]

Some communities in the former Confederacy refused to celebrate the nation's birthday, with Vicksburg, Mississippi, bombarded and subdued as Atlanta had been, refusing to hold official celebrations until after World War II. Atlanta, however, resumed the quasi-official practice of celebrating July 4. City festivities in 1875 included a military procession, a thirty-eight-gun salute, and a band playing appropriate music. The *Constitution* suggested that the day's events recalled an earlier era, before the Civil War, when "everybody, white and black, old and young, turned out en masse to see the military parade." With the city substantially rebuilt and white political dominance restored a decade after Appomattox, Atlantans were again willing to consider themselves part of the United States.[54]

The keynote speaker at these commemorations was Alexander Stephens (1812–83), who was joined on the dais by current governor James Smith (1823–90); wartime governor Joseph E. Brown (1821–94); and Lucius Gartrell (1821–91), who had represented Atlanta in the U.S. Congress before the war and in the Confederate Congress during the conflict. Despite his advancing age and obvious frailty, Stephens had not lost the ability to command an audience. The former Confederate vice president noted the ninety-ninth anniversary of the Declaration of Independence as well as the centennial of Georgia's decision to take armed action against the British. Regarding the Civil War, he offered a measured interpretation: "If we of the south committed error, either in judgment or policy, in our attempt to withdraw from the union," it was done in the name of saving "the principles of the constitution," the same goal for which the North had fought. According to Stephens, therefore, both sides had been fighting for what they perceived as valid constitutional principles.[55]

Though Stephens's 1875 address made no mention of slavery, fourteen years earlier, shortly after being named Confederate vice president, he had declared the peculiar institution the "cornerstone of the Confederacy." In the wake of the South's defeat, Stephens attempted to distance himself from that statement, insisting in 1881, for example, that he had merely been paraphrasing U.S. Supreme Court justice Henry Baldwin, who had claimed that slavery was the cornerstone of the U.S. Constitution. Stephens also alleged that the only difference between it and the Confederate Constitution was the latter's protection of slavery in the western territories.[56]

The process by which Atlantans resumed the celebration of July 4 was by no means linear. In 1876 the *Atlanta Constitution* editorialized that "it is quite natural that we should not feel very enthusiastic either over the Fourth or the [national] Centennial, so long as we are politically proscribed and a great political party constantly seeks to deny us the equality of citizenship." The *Constitution* believed that the South's salvation lay in the election of a Democratic president in 1876. Although Republican Rutherford B. Hayes defeated Democratic candidate Samuel J. Tilden, the contested election resulted in a political compromise that led to a formal end to Reconstruction and the withdrawal of federal soldiers from the South.[57]

Georgia's John B. Gordon served as a congressional negotiator of that compromise. A former general under Lee, Gordon had emerged as one of the state's leading politicians and its principal spokesman for both the Lost Cause and sectional reconciliation, touting both for the remaining forty years of his life. Because he never held an independent command, he could bask in the glow of wartime nostalgia but could not be blamed personally for Confederate loss. In addition, Gordon was an ambitious businessman who sought closer ties to the North for economic reasons.

Born in Middle Georgia and raised in the North Georgia mountains, Gordon was the son of a minister and remained a fervent Christian throughout his life. He attended the University of Georgia, where he earned high grades, but left before graduating to marry Fanny Haralson (1837–1931) from a politically connected family in LaGrange, Georgia. Before the war, Gordon practiced law in Atlanta, invested in mining interests, and purchased slaves. Twenty-nine years old and an ardent secessionist at the outbreak of hostilities, Gordon enthusiastically volunteered for the Confederate military, forming a company of mountain men from Georgia, Alabama, and Tennessee and suggesting that they call themselves the Mountain Rifles. His men had other ideas, however, and chose to become the Raccoon Roughs. Because Georgia had already filled its quota of volunteers, the company became part of the 6th Alabama Infantry Regiment.[58]

Gordon distinguished himself in battle, revealing a talent for boldness and for motivating the men who served under him. One soldier claimed that Gordon "makes me feel like I could storm h—ll." Gordon also revealed both personal courage and an impressive steadfastness in combat. He and his men experienced serious fighting for the first time at Seven Pines, May 31–June 1, 1862, but his talents did not become fully apparent until the Battle of Antietam a few months later. Having risen to the rank of colonel, he held his men steady despite being shot twice in his right leg, then in his left arm, and again in his shoulder. Only when a fifth ball hit him in the face, barely missing his jugular vein, did Gordon fall unconscious. His bravery on the war's bloodiest day earned him a promotion to brigadier general.[59]

By the end of the war, General Lee had made Gordon a corps commander in the Army of Northern Virginia. When Lee's forces became boxed in by Grant's much larger army in April 1865 and the Confederate leader decided to surrender, he selected Gordon to play a prominent role.

At Appomattox Courthouse, Virginia, on April 9, 1865, Gordon rode at the head of his corps with an expression of dejection until he encountered the Union forces, when he

> instantly assumed the finest attitude of a soldier. He wheeled his horse ... touching him gently with the spur, so that the animal slightly reared, and as he wheeled, horse and rider made one motion, the horse's head swung down with a graceful bow, and General Gordon dropped his swordpoint to his toe in salutation. By word of mouth General Gordon sent back orders to the rear that his own troops take the same position.... That was done, and a truly imposing sight was the mutual salutation and farewell.[60]

His role in the surrender provided Gordon with a wealth of material for speeches after the war. As historian Elizabeth Varon has pointed out, Gordon and other southerners drew different lessons from the Appomattox experience than did northerners. For northern partisans, Confederate surrender represented the triumph of right over wrong; for their southern counterparts, including Gordon, Appomattox represented the triumph of superior numbers over an honorable enemy. In their eyes, Grant accentuated the notion of an honorable enemy by granting lenient surrender terms, including his personal guarantee that there would be no prosecutions of former Confederate leaders. Gordon and other white people in the South interpreted Grant's generosity to include a willingness to let the South reconstruct itself as white leaders chose.[61]

Because the vast majority of white southern men had served in the military, Confederate veterans were honored members of Atlanta society. But Gordon was a special case. In 1861, he was a young man who volunteered for military service without formal military training; by 1865, he was a major general who had won the praise of Robert E. Lee. After the war, Gordon chose to be photographed in profile because the left side of his face had been disfigured by the wounds he received at Antietam; however, his entire face was clearly visible to those who saw him speak, providing a visceral, tangible symbol of Confederate sacrifice.[62]

Like numerous white people in the South, Gordon suffered extensive financial losses in the war. Fighting and the destruction of the railroads rendered his mines inoperable. Gordon tried several alternative business ventures: a timber business, an insurance company, and an educational publishing house. The timber business led Gordon and his family to live briefly in coastal Brunswick, Georgia. At first the business did well, and Gordon grasped the need for economic ties between North and South, but ultimately it failed as a consequence of fluctuations in timber prices. He moved his family permanently to Atlanta in the late 1860s, purchasing two hundred acres of land a few miles east of downtown and building a white-columned mansion, Sutherland.[63]

Gordon's leadership ability, oratorical skills, and Confederate pedigree led to his interest in politics, and he won election to the U.S. Senate in 1872. Already a rising star in the Democratic Party, he had testified before Congress the previous year at a hearing regarding Ku Klux Klan activities in the South. Although Gordon's biographer, Ralph L. Eckert, has written unequivocally that the former general "occupied a prominent position within the Klan," Gordon told Congress that he had no knowledge of or involvement in the KKK. Gordon also expressed his outrage over federal occupation of the South after the war: "If the programme . . . at Appomattox Court-House had been carried out—if our people had been met in the spirit which we believe existed there among the officers and soldiers, from General Grant on down—we would have had no disturbance in the South." As a senator, Gordon earned the appreciation of white southerners for his behind-the-scenes role in crafting the compromise that resulted in the end of Reconstruction.[64]

In 1878, Gordon advocated for sectional reconciliation when he led a southern delegation from Congress to the city of Boston. In an address before the Commercial Club, he argued that the Civil War had been fought over differing interpretations of the Constitution before conceding to northerners that "it was in another sense a war over slavery." Two days later, Gordon told an audience of politicians including the governor of Massachusetts and the mayor of Boston that he supported the "elevation of the black race" but insisted that the white race was "superior in intelligence." He went on to tell the audience that "the industrial question" was the greatest issue facing the country and added a subtle jab at the North, where a railroad strike the previous year had crippled the region, by noting that the South had no conflict between labor and capital. By and large, both speeches emphasized sectional reconciliation. Gordon wanted audiences to know that Appomattox had ended the war and that southerners accepted the outcome. Acknowledging New England's Republican strength and the South's support for the Democratic Party, he nonetheless ended with a strong call for national unity: "The causes that divided us are gone . . . the interests which now unite us will unite us forever." Gordon's speech was covered by the national press as well as the *Atlanta Constitution*, which reprinted his words.[65]

Gordon won reelection to the Senate a few months later, delivering a victory speech that he clearly tailored to a much different audience than had listened to him in Massachusetts. Rather than emphasizing national unity, he now focused on the need for unity within the Democratic Party, which was experiencing an internal insurgency led by Dr. William H. Felton (1823–1909) and his politically savvy wife, Rebecca Latimer Felton (1835–1930). Since 1874, Felton, an "independent" Democrat, had represented Georgia in the U.S. House of Representatives. Continuing to join his reputation to that of Robert E. Lee and the Lost Cause, Gordon capped his reelection by asking listeners what they would have thought of him if he had responded to Lee's instruction to drive the enemy from the field by hesitating and claiming to be "an independent confederate." Gordon also compared the wartime fighting to the battle to wrest political control from Republicans during Reconstruction: "You captured first the outposts and then the picket line, and the main works and at last Georgia was ours." As the crowd cheered, Gordon stressed that there could be no turning back.[66]

In 1889 Gordon became president of a new organization of former Confederate soldiers, the United Confederate Veterans (UCV). Following an initial meeting in New Orleans, the UCV quickly incorporated existing veteran groups throughout the South, including the Confederate Veterans Association of Fulton County. Its organizers immediately identified Gordon as the best candidate to serve as the group's "commander," and Gordon, always happy to promote himself, obliged. In accepting the post, which he held until his death in 1904, Gordon made clear that the UCV was not a neo-secessionist organization. Gordon declared that the group was "social, literary, historical and benevolent" and that politics would not be discussed at its meetings; however, he also averred that no group was better prepared to safeguard "the just powers of the federal government, [and] the equal rights of the states" than ex-soldiers of the Confederacy. Although Gordon served as the UCV figurehead in Atlanta, George Moorman served as adjutant general and handled the organization's day-to-day operations.[67]

The UCV attracted members by keeping dues low and publishing a popular magazine, *Confederate Veteran*. As Gaines Foster has pointed out, the UCV inaugurated a new era in the Confederate veterans' movement. Unlike the earlier *Southern Historical Society Papers*, the *Confederate Veteran* was an inexpensive publication featuring human-interest stories about soldiers, battles, and civilians (including Mary Gay); it avoided the kind of lengthy constitutional interpretations and military analyses that characterized its predecessor. By the turn of the twentieth century, the UCV had 1,800 chapters across the South and close to 160,000 members.[68]

The activities of Fulton County's UCV "camp" included organizing celebrations of Robert E. Lee's birthday; fundraising for monuments in Richmond, Virginia, the former Confederate capital; and sending flowers for a monument near the site of Camp Douglas, a prisoner-of-war camp near Chicago where thousands of Confederates had died. The Atlanta camp also vetted publications about the war, endorsing an 1894 edition of the *Encyclopedia Britannica* that did not "attempt to sully the South's Fair Name." Atlanta veterans also joined thousands of others at reunions such as an 1895 encampment in Houston, Texas, that prompted the *Atlanta Constitution*, which claimed to have a higher circulation among Confederate veterans than any other southern daily, to proclaim, "Long live the memories that bring the war-worn heroes in gray together this year at Houston."[69]

Creation of the UCV in turn spawned two organizations to serve the next generation, the Sons of Confederate Veterans and the United Daughters of the Confederacy. But as some white Atlantans clung to the Lost Cause, including an interpretation of the war that ignored the internal divisions that affected civilians and completely omitted African Americans, sectional reconciliation gained a new leader when the young and dynamic Henry W. Grady took center stage as a journalist, political insider, and visionary for a New South with Atlanta at its center.

# CHAPTER 2

# The New South

**B**ARELY A DECADE AFTER the Civil War ended, a young Atlanta journalist, Henry W. Grady (1850–89), joined a conversation about interpreting the city's Civil War past and suggesting a path for its economic future. Grady wanted Atlantans to forget their wartime internal divisions as well as to reconcile with the North, because the North's financial investment was the only viable path to ensure the South's economic success. Both positions placed him at odds with Lost Cause hard-liners. By the time he died at age thirty-nine in 1889, Grady had achieved fame regionally as editor of the *Atlanta Constitution* and nationally by taking his message of a New South grounded in economic development to distinguished audiences in the North. Although Grady's message left an indelible mark on his city, the specific causes he adopted in Atlanta achieved mixed success. They included attempts to rehabilitate the reputation of General James Longstreet, welcome General William T. Sherman when he visited the city, arrange for the joint burial of Union and Confederate dead at a local cemetery, and create the city's first monument to a Civil War figure. The 1895 Cotton States Exposition represented the high point of Grady's legacy, focusing attention on sectional reconciliation but failing to eliminate the Lost Cause from public memory. Booker T. Washington's opening address started a national conversation about the war's legacy and the future of race relations.

Born in Athens, Georgia, in 1850, Henry Woodfin Grady, the eldest of Ann and William Grady's seven children, had personal knowledge of the human toll of the Civil War. William, an upwardly mobile entrepreneur who had a partial interest in a store, a factory, and a sawmill and owned five slaves, joined the 25th North Carolina when Henry was eleven and died of wounds sustained in battle three years later. William Grady's death left his widow and children in reduced economic circumstances, a situation experienced by thousands of others across the South as well as the North.[1]

Undercurrents of tension were present in the Grady household during the war. By early 1862, Ann Grady apparently was frustrated by her husband's absence and wanted him to come home, because he wrote to her, "I am determined to fight till the victory is ours and if I fail I want my sons as soon as they are old enough to take my place in the army." Moreover, he pointed out, if he resigned his commission, he might be drafted into the army as a private. While he was gone, Ann Grady endured the deaths of four of her children. Though her oldest son survived, he was undoubtedly affected by the loss of his siblings and aware of his mother's unhappiness.[2]

In the summer of 1864, Major William Grady, now in command of the 25th North Carolina, was among the more than one hundred thousand Union and Confederate soldiers stationed in the trenches near Petersburg, Virginia, a vital rail center south of Richmond. Hoping to avoid the kind of lengthy siege that had characterized the Vicksburg Campaign the preceding year, General Ulysses S. Grant authorized a risky plan that involved tunneling under the Confederate lines. On July 30 the Union forces detonated a bomb in the tunnel, surprising the southern troops, instantly killing around three hundred men, and creating an enormous crater. Grady led his regiment in fierce fighting to regain control of Confederate trenches, with one lieutenant later writing, "In retaking the works the fight was hand to hand, with guns, bayonets, and swords, in fact anything a man could fight with." Grady was wounded in the fighting and died of his injuries a few months later.[3]

Fortunately for the Gradys, in 1863, while on furlough from his regiment, William had bought a fine home on Prince Avenue in Athens, and his family moved there in July 1865. William Grady had also purchased a 338-acre farm, and Ann Grady sold the land parcel by parcel to support her three surviving children and send Henry to the University of Georgia.[4]

While studying at Georgia and later the University of Virginia, Grady joined debating societies and gained both a love for rhetoric and a competitive streak. After he left Virginia, a chance meeting with an old friend from Athens led to an opportunity to write for the *Atlanta Constitution* on a temporary basis. In 1869, at age nineteen, he joined the staff of Georgia's *Rome Courier* as associate editor. Less than a year later, Grady borrowed money from his mother to purchase the *Rome Commercial* and the *Rome Daily*. Writing in the 1880s, Grady reflected, "I have never seen a day when I regretted my [career] choice."[5]

In 1871, Grady married his childhood sweetheart, Julia King, and the following year, they liquidated his assets in Rome and moved to Atlanta, where he and two other men ran the *Atlanta Herald* newspaper. A morning paper, the *Herald* competed for readership with the better-known *Constitution*, but Grady was optimistic about his prospects, believing the *Herald* to be "a *good* paper & I feel that I will now do well." However, the Panic of 1873 squeezed many businesses, and Citizens Bank of Atlanta, controlled by former governor Joseph E. Brown (the subject of criticism in the *Herald*'s editorials), called in loans against the newspaper. Grady had difficulty supporting his wife and their newborn son, borrowing money from his mother, who eventually sold her home in Athens to keep the paper afloat. But all of those efforts came to naught, and the *Herald* ceased publishing in 1876.[6]

Nonetheless, Grady had built a name for himself as a journalist in Atlanta. On March 14, 1874, he wrote an article on "The New South" in which he suggested that the region should embrace commerce and industry as a path toward economic modernization. Although Grady certainly intended for the region to remain grounded in white supremacy, he asked white southerners to stop idealizing the plantation South and the war that had been fought to preserve it. As the son of an entrepreneur who had invested in business as well as land, Grady understood the importance of economic diversity; as the son of a Confederate soldier who had given his life for the cause, Grady had the moral standing to tell Atlantans to focus on the future: "For many generations the South got along well enough, with its monopoly on cotton growing, its labor maintained at the simple cost of food and shelter, and its society organized on principles of pure aristocracy"; however, "all that is changed." Grady cited the model provided by Columbus, Georgia, which had built textile mills staffed with white employees. He claimed that good wages benefited workers and that the mills produced significant profits to owners and investors. But commercial success would require a trained labor force and capital investment, and the latter meant making peace with the northerners who had money to invest. In return, as historian Stephen Prince has written, Grady's vision "offered Yankees an ally, an investment opportunity, a stabilized sectional relationship, a reunited nation." Grady never claimed to have invented either the term *New South* or the idea, which was promoted by several other leading journalists in the region, but he soon became its most articulate promoter.[7]

At the invitation of his friend Evan Howell (1839–1905), who had recently purchased a significant interest in the *Atlanta Constitution*, Grady joined its staff as a reporter, and he eventually became its editor and part owner. The *Constitution* was the most important newspaper in the state and one of the most important in the South. He covered important political stories, including the contested presidential election of 1876, and for the first time met his old nemesis, Brown. Grady had learned his lesson: to be a person of influence in Atlanta, he needed to make the members of the city's power structure his friends rather than his enemies. He and Howell quickly aligned themselves with Brown and Georgia's other influential politicians, John B. Gordon and Alfred H. Colquitt (1824–94), in what became known as the Atlanta Ring. These men represented the state's dominant voices during the 1880s. Although Grady considered running for political office, he remained in a behind-the-scenes role until his death in December 1889.[8]

Grady knew that his vision of a New South would resonate in a city founded as a transportation and commercial hub, but he did not want to offend those who revered the Lost Cause. He needed to sell the New South as a natural extension of the Old South. Grady had published an 1870 article in the *Rome Commercial* in which he called Robert E. Lee "the greatest man the world ever saw" but subsequently demonstrated a willingness to look critically at the war and its leaders. Grady wanted southerners to honor fallen soldiers while demystifying the Confederacy. He wrote a series of stories in the mid- and late 1870s in which he asked Confederate leaders and their wives why the South had lost the war, a question that flouted Lost Cause orthodoxy by acknowledging defeat. One of the men Grady interviewed was Robert Toombs (1810–85), a prewar U.S. senator from Georgia who had served as a Confederate secretary of state and general. Although Toombs refused to take a postwar oath of allegiance to the U.S. government, he remained a figure of importance in Georgia politics, and he believed that the Confederacy had failed because it relied on conscription, which demoralized the army. Toombs also blamed President

Jefferson Davis's decisions regarding military commanders, though Grady neglected to tell his readers that Toombs had never liked Davis and because he wanted the Confederate presidency himself.[9]

Grady also interviewed Stonewall Jackson's widow, Anna, and praised the general, whose "memory [is] in every heart." According to Anna Jackson (1831–1915), her husband had been motivated to fight by a belief in state sovereignty rather than support of slavery, and he believed that the South should have pursued a more aggressive military strategy, especially at the Battle of First Manassas in 1861. General Jackson loved and admired Lee but had written that his "only fault is that he is too slow." Lost Cause proponents considered criticism of Lee to be sacrilege, and Anna Jackson must have received a backlash when her comments were printed, because she complained in a letter to Grady that "I was incautiously led into answering too freely the multitude of questions. . . . I did not intend to publish a deprecatory word of any other public officer." She asked newspapers that reprinted Grady's piece to reprint her letter alongside it.[10]

In 1881, Grady wrote an article in which he compared Davis and Grant and found the former Confederate president superior to the former U.S. chief executive. Davis, incarcerated for two years following the Confederate surrender, never found it easy to make a living. After leaving the White House in 1877, Grant traveled around the world, then returned to the United States and cofounded an investment firm that went bankrupt. In response to his financial struggles, wealthy New Yorkers raised money to support him. According to Grady, however, Davis largely eschewed handouts because there were so many needy widows and children of dead soldiers.[11]

Grady also wrote a favorable review of Davis's two-volume, 1,279-page *The Rise and Fall of the Confederate Government*, published in 1871. Davis attributed southern secession to the abstract principle of states' rights rather than to slavery, a formulation historian James M. McPherson has called the "virgin birth theory of secession: the Confederacy was not conceived by any worldly cause, but by divine principle." In the words of another historian, David W. Blight, Davis's tome constitutes "perhaps the longest and most self-righteous legal brief on behalf of a failed political movement ever done by an American." Contemporary southern reviewers nonetheless praised the volume, with Grady hailing Davis for having written a "remarkable book."[12]

But after paying homage to Davis, Grady again veered away from the views of Confederate hard-liners, noting the former president's reversal of his assessment of General James Longstreet's actions during the Gettysburg Campaign. In the immediate postwar years, Davis had hailed Longstreet (1821–1904), Georgia's highest-ranking Confederate general and commander of Lee's 1st Corps, as a "good soldier in a good cause." In his memoir, however, Davis alleged that Longstreet had failed to follow Lee's orders to attack at daybreak during the battle's pivotal second day and that the error had been a key factor in the Confederate defeat. Grady disputed Davis's interpretation, noting that "to my mind" Longstreet had successfully rebutted that allegation, including in a testimonial published in the *Constitution* purportedly by Longstreet but actually written by Grady and based on conversations with the former general. Historians debate whether Longstreet carried out Lee's attack on July 2 skillfully, but there was no order to attack at daybreak.[13]

Grady's defense of Longstreet placed him at odds with many former Confederates who followed Jubal Early's writings in the *Southern Historical Papers* in making Longstreet the scapegoat for Lee's defeat in Pennsylvania. But Grady did not budge. Longstreet cemented his negative reputation among hard-core Confederates by becoming a Republican—a Scalawag—and by accepting a postwar patronage position from President Grant, a friend since the two men had attended West Point together. Moreover, Longstreet had published an article in the *New Orleans Times* urging the South to cooperate with Reconstruction and look forward, not back. Grady agreed with Longstreet, writing that "the wisdom of his advice [had] been proved," but most white southerners did not. Longstreet was ostracized—in Grady's words, subjected to "considerable abuse"—before retiring to his hometown, Gainesville, Georgia, where "he is restored to his old place in the hearts of his people." Grady exaggerated. Lost Cause proponents ostracized Longstreet for the rest of his life.[14]

In addition to his newspaper writing, Grady organized public events in support of his New South effort. He wanted to shine a national spotlight on Atlanta as a place where business was booming and residents had not only accepted Confederate defeat but reconciled with their former enemies. In 1879, he arranged for Sherman to visit the city that he had subdued and then torched fifteen years earlier, undoubtedly hoping that the visit would bring positive publicity. During his brief stay, Sherman toured

Fort McPherson, southwest of the city, and fifteen hundred Atlantans turned out to watch a seventeen-gun salute honoring the general while he reviewed several companies from the 18th Infantry. Asked by Howell to comment on the rebuilt city, Sherman praised its progress and especially the "appearance of enterprise and thrift that is admirable." However, Atlanta's failure to attract immigrants placed it at a disadvantage when compared with western cities such as those in California.[15]

Sherman returned two years later to attend the Atlanta International Cotton Exposition. Designed to encourage growth of the textile industry, the exposition was also intended to convince northerners that the South had put the war behind it and deserved northern investment. Grady and the *Constitution* supported the effort, and he probably invited Sherman after the two men ran into one another in New York late in 1880. Aware of the negative way many white people regarded the general, Grady published an article in the *Constitution* that was designed to soften Sherman's image. Praising him as "a great man" with "tremendous energy and courage," Grady cited Sherman's belief that he had not burned Atlanta "as a city" but rather had torched only those buildings used in the war effort. Nevertheless, the *Constitution* had to tamp down rumors that there would be a "Sherman Day" as part of the festivities. Instead, Sherman attended the fair on Mexican Veterans' Day. He did not intend to speak but did so when pressed by a group of veterans. Demonstrating his ability to represent the reconciliationist perspective, Sherman declared, "I have come this morning to look upon these buildings where once we had battle-fields." He earned applause by saying that "so far as I am concerned, I am just as friendly to Georgia as I am to my own native state of Ohio." According to the *Constitution*, "Sherman left Atlanta delighted with his visit." African Americans left with little; other than a single "Freedman's Day," the fair included no participation by African Americans.[16]

In 1886, Grady's efforts to honor Confederates while promoting internal and sectional reconciliation came together in one grand event: the unveiling of Atlanta's second Civil War monument and the first honoring a leader, a statue of the late senator Benjamin Harvey Hill. Hill might have seemed an unlikely choice for a statue in postwar Atlanta, having opposed secession and urged Georgians to wait and see what kind of president Abraham Lincoln might be. In 1870, he again alienated Georgia's white voters when he urged cooperation with congressional Reconstruction. But Hill also served in the Confederate Senate and supported President Jefferson Davis, including his controversial centralizing of the government in Richmond. Although Hill had initially demonstrated a willingness to cooperate with Reconstruction, he eventually settled into a more mainstream role as an advocate for the white South. Hill shared Grady's belief in a New South freed from "failure in the past," and Grady wanted to heal Atlanta's internal divisions. Other cities took a less conciliatory approach. The year after Grady unveiled the Hill statue, South Carolinians honored John C. Calhoun with an enormous bronze image in Charleston. A staunch defender of slavery who had died a decade before the war started, Calhoun's statue depicted him in a defiant pose, as a stalwart champion of the Old South. Grady's counterpart in Charleston, Frank Dawson of the *News and Courier*, embraced the concept of a New South but did not share Grady's willingness to put the Old South in the past. A Confederate veteran, Dawson published articles with unequivocal Lost Cause themes from the 1870s until James Hemphill took over in 1889 and continued the tradition.[17]

Grady orchestrated an immense pageant to unveil the Hill statue at the corner of Peachtree and West Peachtree Streets, with himself as master of ceremonies. The star of the show was the former Confederate president, seventy-seven years old and in declining health. Grady hoped that the event would demonstrate that the South was putting the war safely in the past by simultaneously honoring Davis and a prewar Unionist and New South supporter as well as promote the election of John B. Gordon to the governorship. Gordon had resigned his Senate seat in 1880 to pursue business ventures, but when they failed, he returned to politics and sought to keep the focus on his martial accomplishments rather than on allegations of corrupt business practices. Grady wanted to keep Atlanta's rival, Macon, from placing its favorite son, Augustus O. Bacon, in the governorship.[18]

Adoring crowds greeted Davis from the moment he arrived in Atlanta on what the *Journal* called a "day which will long be remembered." Davis seemed "deeply touched by [the] mark of love and esteem" shown to him by the crowds. Accompanied by his daughter, Winnie (1864–98), whose clothing, hairstyle, manners, conversational skills, and dancing ability were praised in the Atlanta press, Davis kissed babies, greeted matrons, and honored veterans. On the day of the dedication, the crowd was estimated at more than fifty thousand. Grady rode in a carriage along with Davis and members of the monument association. On the dais, Gordon appeared with his arm around the aging politician and announced, "He is our president and we intend to call him so" for the rest of his life. Davis spoke briefly, beginning, "You have heard of the lost cause. It is not lost. It will live again. It is not dead, but sleeping. Truth can never die." Understanding that his words could be interpreted as neo-secessionist, Davis invoked women's remembrance of the Lost Cause in an apparent effort to neutralize his comments. "No cause can be lost while the fair women of the land smile upon it."[19]

In the midst of the festivities, General James Longstreet made a dramatic and unexpected arrival, riding up on horseback and wearing a dress uniform. The men who had served under him in Lee's 1st Corps instantly recognized him and continued to respect him despite his vilification by Lost Cause hard-liners. To the cheers of the crowd, Longstreet dismounted and strode to the platform, where he embraced Davis, though the two men had become enemies during Reconstruction. A small in-ground stone marker at the site recalls this "historic reconciliation," although the statue of Hill was subsequently moved to the Georgia Capitol.[20]

At the end of the event, Grady introduced Winnie Davis, using the appellation "daughter of the Confederacy," which Gordon had bestowed on her when the train carrying the Davis party stopped in West Point, Georgia, before reaching Atlanta. Her 1886 appearances made Davis a figure of adoration within the former Confederate states, a role that may have adversely affected her personal life. A few months after her Atlanta appearance, she met and fell in love with New York attorney Alfred Wilkinson, who not only was a Yankee but also was the grandson of an abolitionist. Their relationship sparked a public outcry among southerners, and the couple eventually parted, though Wilkinson's financial struggles may have been a factor. Winnie Davis never married. She returned to Atlanta on several ceremonial occasions during the 1890s. Perhaps most notably, in 1893, three years after his death, she accompanied her father's remains on a long rail journey from New Orleans to Richmond for reburial in the former Confederate capital. As the funeral train pulled into Atlanta, a large crowd gathered: people "wanted to see the casket and they were anxious to catch a glimpse of Miss Winnie," the *Constitution* reported. She again came to the Georgia capital for a veterans' reunion in 1898 but became ill, and she died a few months later at the age of thirty-four.[21]

As Grady had planned, the unveiling of the Hill statue presented the image of a city where Civil War figures were venerated, wartime divisions were forgotten, and the New South was transcendent, but national media coverage of these events as well as others in Montgomery and Savannah also had unintended consequences. Northern audiences expressed indignation at Jefferson Davis's tour and his rhetoric. A surge of anti-Davis sentiment led a crowd in Albany, New York, to sing "We'll hang Jeff Davis to a Sour Apple Tree," while a crowd in Ohio hanged Davis in effigy. The *New York Times* called the public tour "the most serious error into which the South has been led for years," and the *Los Angeles Times* reported "a feeling of indignation." No paper was more scathing toward Davis than the *New York Tribune*, which called the former Confederate president an "arch-traitor" who "goes from city to city preaching anew Calhoun's doctrine of secession." The *Tribune* expressed outrage that southerners would make a martyr of a man who had contributed to the deaths of several hundred thousand people at a time when the region was beginning to emerge from "desolation and poverty." To a degree that Grady had not anticipated, his efforts at reconciliation met with opposition. This trend affected both the North and the South, according to Caroline E. Janney, whose scholarship focuses on the "limits of reconciliation." Janney has noted that "the Lost Cause had proved unbelievably successful in rallying white southerners," but "even as Unionists promoted reunion, they were not necessarily calling for reconciliation."[22]

Grady's ongoing efforts to rehabilitate Longstreet's reputation statewide had mixed success. On January 15, 1888, the *Atlanta Constitution* ran a lengthy story allegedly written by an "Ex-Confederate" that pointed out Longstreet's close relationship with General Lee and his role in many of the war's most important battles, including the wound he received at the Wilderness that rendered his arm useless. The article also noted the fact that although Longstreet had allied with the Republican Party, other prominent Georgians, including Brown and Hill, had also done so. The author acknowledged that Longstreet had criticized Lee's generalship on several occasions since the war but argued that Davis was also guilty on this count. The *Constitution* offered to forward to Longstreet contributions intended to ameliorate the reduced circumstances in which he now found himself. In 1897, after the death of his first wife, Longstreet remarried; his second wife, Helen (1863–1962), became his fervent supporter. The *Constitution* printed an article in which she defended his military record against the arguments of his critics.[23]

During the 1880s, Grady faced additional roadblocks in his efforts at reconciliation when he lent his support to an organization that promoted the joint burial at Westview Cemetery of unidentified Union and Confed-

erate soldiers killed during the Atlanta Campaign. Atlanta's municipal
Oakland Cemetery had run out of space, and the city opted not to build
another cemetery. Westview, a private cemetery, occupied ground where
the Battle of Ezra Church had been fought on July 28, 1864. The group,
the Battle Monument Association of the Blue and the Gray, had started
in Richmond when a former Confederate soldier began raising funds for
a facility to house disabled veterans. Atlanta organizers, including Evan
Howell, who served as the group's president, initially limited membership
to veterans, a "fraternity" of men who had "tested each other's courage and
devotion on the battlefield," and quickly adopted a different goal.[24]

Within a few weeks of its incorporation in 1885, the Battle Monument
Association expanded its membership to include sons of Confederate veterans, and Grady became a vice president, with the *Constitution* noting
that his father had been "mortally wounded at Petersburg, Va., while gal-
lantly leading his command at the fearful mine explosion." As honorary
vice presidents, the Atlanta chapter selected Sherman and General Joseph
E. Johnston. President Grover Cleveland (1837–1908) and General Philip
Sheridan (currently commanding the U.S. Army) endorsed the "noble object" of burying Union and Confederate soldiers together. However, as humorist Bill Arp pointed out, since the federal government refused to provide Confederate veterans with pensions, burying them with "honor" was
something of a hollow gesture: "If our soldiers deserve a monument they
deserve a pension."[25]

The Battle Monument Association of the Blue and Gray apparently
failed to raise enough money for their joint burial at Westview, one of numerous "cracks in the plaster of national unification," as historian John
Neff has written. Westview Cemetery had stipulated that in exchange for
a plot of ground, the organization needed to raise ten thousand dollars—
an enormous sum of money for that time—to beautify the space within
five years. The *Constitution* never reported the disbanding of the group
but did report that three local businessmen, among them William Lowndes Calhoun of the Confederate Veterans Association of Fulton County,
had begun raising money for a statue marking Confederate burials at the
cemetery. On this occasion, the cemetery required only that the organizers
erect a statue costing at least five hundred dollars, a much more manage-
able amount. The Confederate monument, sculpted in Italy, depicts a soldier holding a rifle and stands atop a base featuring crossed swords on one
side and the inscription "Erected by the Confederate Veterans of Fulton

County" on another. In the words of the *Atlanta Constitution*, the monument presides over burial space "made sacred by the blood of [General John Bell] Hood's heroes."[26]

Undeterred by the failure of the monument association, Grady took his case for sectional reconciliation and northern investment in the South directly to the northern business community. In December 1886, he traveled to New York City to address a dinner at the iconic Delmonico's restaurant hosted by the New England Society of New York in honor of the 266th anniversary of Pilgrims' landing at Plymouth Rock. Grady was the guest of John H. Inman, a Confederate veteran from Tennessee who had moved north after the war and made a fortune and whose brother, Samuel (1843–1915), was an Atlanta businessman and friend of Grady. Grady, the first southerner ever invited to address the group, spoke to an audience of 360 that included J. P. Morgan, Henry Flagler, and Sherman, who offered a toast to President Cleveland.[27]

Grady began his speech by quoting Ben Hill, whose statue had been unveiled in Atlanta a few months earlier: "There was a South of slavery and secession—that South is dead. There is a South of union and freedom—that South, thank God, is living, breathing, growing every hour." Grady wanted his audience to know that southerners accepted the war's outcome, even joking that Sherman was "considered an able man in our parts" although "a careless man about fire." Grady had been preceded at the podium by a Brooklyn minister, Dr. T. DeWitt Talmage, who suggested that the typical American had yet to appear. Using this statement as an entry point, Grady suggested that Lincoln was the true American who represented the best of the North and the South—"the sum of Puritan and Cavalier." In Lincoln's "ardent nature were fused the virtues of both, and in the depths of his great soul the faults of both were lost."[28]

Although the speech was an effort to curry favor with northern business leaders, Grady also wanted to address white southerners, and he counted on press coverage of the event to achieve that goal. Grady described the South as "misguided, perhaps, but beautiful in her suffering," and declared that the region had "nothing for which to apologize. She believes that the late struggle between the States was war and not rebellion; revolution and not conspiracy." He ended with a reference to his father's wartime sacrifice, thereby sending a clear message to white people of the region: "Not for all the glories of New England . . . would I exchange the heritage he left me in his soldier's death." Nevertheless, Grady said, "I am glad . . . that human slavery was swept forever from American soil" and that "the American Union was saved from the wreck of war."[29]

Grady wanted northern audiences to understand the devastation caused by the war. The returning veteran "finds his house in ruins, his farm devastated, his slaves free, his stock killed, his barns empty, his trade destroyed, his money worthless, his social system, feudal in its magnificence, swept away." And yet, Grady claimed, "this hero in gray" did not despair. Instead, he moved forward to rebuild the region's farms and businesses. Atlanta now constituted "a brave and beautiful city," and northerners should help the South grow economically through the textile and iron manufacturing industries even as the region's cotton crop continued to supply New England's mills.[30]

Grady then turned to a question on which his northern listeners sought reassurance: "But what of the negro?" Grady insisted that when Lincoln issued the Emancipation Proclamation, "your victory was assured, for he then committed you to the cause of human liberty, against which the arms of man cannot prevail." Grady lauded the loyalty of the wartime slaves who had "guarded our defenseless women and children" and acknowledged that black men had fought for their freedom. And after the war, he claimed, relations between the races had become "close and cordial." African Americans had received "liberty and enfranchisement" along with "the fullest protection of our laws," and they as well as whites could now take advantage of public education. Economic advancement was available to any black who was willing to work with white people.[31]

Grady's speech made him famous. When he finished the address, members of the audience rose to their feet, waving handkerchiefs and hats, cheering and applauding. When he appeared in his hotel lobby the next morning, he received an ovation. The New York Times, which had disparaged Jefferson Davis's tour a few months earlier, reported that "he had touched his hearers deeply" with his declaration of "brotherly feeling" between North and South. Harper's Weekly described Grady's speech as "one of the most striking that have been delivered by any citizen of a Southern State since the war. It was very eloquent." Harper's liked Grady's simple message: "The war is over," and the South was looking forward instead of backward. The New York Evening Post hailed "a most notable address" filled with "eloquence," while Frank Leslie's Illustrated Newspaper gushed that Grady had "swept his audience by storm" and noted that the speech had been reprinted in newspapers across the nation.[32]

Indeed, newspapers in every part of the country reprinted the speech, with many papers noting Grady's clean-shaven, boyish looks and unprepossessing style; some of them printed Grady's image alongside the story. He was now the nation's preeminent advocate for a New South. In acknowledging Grady's sudden fame, newspapers also reported rumors that the "silver tongued Grady" might make a good vice presidential running mate for Cleveland in 1888. Other newspapers echoed the New York press in highlighting Grady's emphasis on putting the war behind the nation. According to the *New Orleans Times-Picayune*, "It was the most patriotic and thoroughly national speech that has been made since the war." The *Milwaukee Daily Journal* called on both sides to share the "sentiment of brotherhood" suggested by Grady's speech instead of the "bloody-shirt patriots of the north" and the "irreconcilables of the south."[33]

When Grady returned to Atlanta at ten o'clock on Christmas Eve, he was greeted as a conquering hero. A delegation met him at the passenger depot while a band played "Yankee Doodle." Grady told a cheering crowd at the Kimball House hotel that it was the best Christmas he had ever enjoyed. The *Constitution* noted Grady's "triumph" and declared that "the people of Atlanta knew that he nobly acquitted himself."[34]

However, Grady's claims also provoked some skepticism, with several newspapers focusing on African American voter suppression and exclusion from juries in the South. Two damning critiques of Grady came from the *St. Louis Globe-Democrat* and the *New York Freeman*, both of which discussed the leasing of convicts—most of them black—for labor in mines, factories, and plantations. According to the *Freeman*, prisoners had been tortured and worked to death, while the *Globe-Democrat* condemned the practice as "evil."[35]

Without question, Grady's rosy picture of race relations did not match reality. In Atlanta's public schools, blacks could not advance beyond the primary level. Many black voters were disfranchised by poll taxes. Although two black men served on the city council during the brief period of Republican rule during Reconstruction, nearly a century passed before another African American was elected. Entertainment venues, hotels, and restaurants were strictly segregated. The police force employed no black officers. And Grady looked the other way as his allies Gordon and Brown earned riches by taking advantage of the convict lease system. Whether or not Grady truly believed, as he wrote in an 1882 editorial, "Where to Draw the Line," that "the negro is entitled to his freedom, his franchise, to full and equal legal rights," he also stated unequivocally, "social equality he can never have." Moreover, "he does not have it in the north, or in the east, or in the west."[36]

On December 23, 1889, three years to the day after he boarded a train for his return trip to Atlanta and two weeks after the death of Jefferson Davis, Henry Grady died. A few days earlier, he had given another speech to a northern audience, this one in Boston. He touched on many of the same themes from the earlier address, ending the speech with a rousing call for sectional unity and northern investment in the South. Grady's frenzied schedule also included a visit to Plymouth Rock and a stop in New York, where he met with dignitaries and gave several interviews to journalists. By the time he arrived home in Atlanta, a head cold he contracted before leaving Atlanta had become bronchitis. Pneumonia set in, and he died surrounded by family, friends, and colleagues from the *Constitution*. Thousands attended his funeral, held on Christmas afternoon. President Cleveland telegraphed his condolences to Julia Grady. The *Constitution* described him as the "intellectual leader" of the South and sadly declared, "There is no man left to take his place."[37]

In its coverage of Grady's death, the viewing of his body at the Grady home on Peachtree Street, and the funeral at First Methodist Church, the *Constitution* emphasized African Americans' alleged admiration for Henry Grady. According to the paper, an "old negro woman" had stopped to view his casket; a few minutes later, an adult lifted up a young black boy so that he could see Grady's face. But Grady's claims regarding race relations in his recent speech in Boston had provoked far more negative press than his earlier oration. Newspapers from Maine to California disputed the sunny picture he painted, acknowledging his oratorical skills but challenging his interpretation of southern life. The *Boston Congregationalist* took Grady to task for suggesting that African Americans "must forever remain on that lowest plane of social serfdom." The *Chicago Daily Inter Ocean* reported that leading white politicians in the South did "everything in their power to make life a burden" for African Americans. The *San Francisco Daily Evening Bulletin* questioned Grady's suggestion that blacks received adequate funds for public education, while Maine's *Bangor Daily Whig and Courier* dismissed the entire lecture as "eloquent but valueless" and the *Indianapolis Journal* called it "twaddle." Local African American college students took note: in January 1890, the *Atlanta Uni-*

*versity Bulletin* printed the *Boston Pilot*'s critique that Grady supported "suppression of the legitimate rights of the Southern blacks."[38]

Twentieth-century historians continued the criticisms of Grady. Writing in 1937, Paul H. Buck called the 1886 speech "a bundle of platitudes made trite by endless repetition." Many others, including C. Vann Woodward, subsequently picked apart the idea that Grady's New South sought to bring prosperity and justice to all the region's citizens. Writing in the 1970s, Paul Gaston concluded, "Rich in paradoxes, the New South creed also had an ironic outcome. Designed to lead the region out of poverty . . . , the expectations were unrealized, and the South remained the poorest and economically least progressive section in the nation." Far from bringing equal opportunity for African Americans, New South promoters presented a facade of racial harmony to the North while telling white audiences at home about Anglo-Saxon superiority.[39]

Eulogizing Grady, Arp suggested that "Georgia has followed Grady wherever he dared to go," and it continued to do so after his death. In 1895, business leaders, including Grady's journalist friends Howell and William Hemphill, organized the Cotton States and International Exposition, which would bring northern audiences to Atlanta. Much larger than the fairs Atlanta had hosted in 1881 and in 1887, the 1895 fair bore Grady's unmistakable imprint, with organizers and participants repeatedly invoking his memory from the advance publicity (the *Constitution* noted "Grady's stirring sentiment") to the opening (the paper's review of the event cited "the lamented Grady") to the Reverend J. W. E. Bowen of Gammon Theological Institute, an African American who spoke at the opening of the Negro Building and quoted Grady's 1889 Boston speech.[40] The 1895 fair represented the high-water mark of Grady's New South vision, and organizers devoted substantial effort to the way that the Civil War and sectional reconciliation were framed.

The Cotton States Exposition was one of several late nineteenth-century southern fairs and organized by men who hoped to boost their region's economy. Atlanta's boosters wanted to highlight the city's commercial dynamism and alleged racial progressivism as well as promote economic growth in the aftermath of the Panic of 1893. In addition, they sought political unity in the face of threats to Democratic Party dominance from the Populist movement and the resurgence of the Republican Party in the South.[41]

The 1895 fair had a number of precedents. The phenomenal success of
London's 1851 Crystal Palace Exhibition led Americans to imitate its for-
mat, showcasing industrial and agricultural advancement. Philadelphia's
1876 Centennial Exposition set a standard for American fairs. In addition
to Atlanta's two efforts, New Orleans and Louisville also hosted fairs in the
1880s. Running from September 18 to December 31, the 1895 Atlanta Exposition was the first in a new series of southern fairs that also included
Nashville and Charleston. With two hundred thousand dollars appropriated by the U.S. government, additional money from private investors,
and labor from a chain gang supplied by Fulton County, fair organizers
hired an architect from New York who designed a series of Romanesque
buildings on land owned by the Piedmont Exposition Company. The fair
had six thousand exhibits, some local, some from other states, and still
others from foreign nations including France, England, Italy, Mexico, Ar-
gentina, China, Egypt, and Turkey. After the fair closed, the land on which
it was situated and the artificial Lake Clara Meer became Atlanta's popular Piedmont Park.[42]

Fair organizers were keenly aware that drawing northern and international business investment to Atlanta required presenting race relations in
a positive light. Proponents hoped to emulate Chicago's success in drawing
millions of visitors to the 1893 Columbian Exposition but avoid the negative publicity that resulted when Chicago planners' refusal to allow African Americans to mount exhibits prompted a boycott organized by anti-
lynching crusader Ida B. Wells (1862–1931). Consequently, when Bishop
Wesley Gaines of the African Methodist Episcopal Church and black businessman Henry A. Rucker (1852–1924) contacted Samuel Inman regarding "race representation" at the fair, Inman enthusiastically endorsed the
idea, as did the *Atlanta Constitution*. An integrated board of commissioners was created to coordinate black involvement and hired a young journalist from Virginia, I. Garland Penn (1867–1930), to serve as president
of the "Negro Department" and charged him with constructing a building to display exhibits. Two African American contractors supervised the
building of the structure. Furthermore, the 2nd Battalion of Colored Infantry marched in the opening parade—last in the line of military units
but ahead of civilian participants in carriages. Even more noteworthy, fair
organizers invited Booker T. Washington (1856–1915) to speak on opening
day. It was the first time that an African American had ever received such
an invitation in the South, and his speech represented unprecedented visi-

bility for a black orator. He was introduced by Rufus Bullock (1834–1907), Georgia's Republican governor during Reconstruction.[43]

Washington's speech is the best-remembered event of the Cotton States Exposition. The president of Alabama's Tuskegee Normal and Industrial Institute, Washington "spoke for the negro," as the *Constitution* put it. Born into slavery and educated at Hampton Institute, he was already a prominent man, but his speech catapulted him to greater national fame, much as Grady's speech had done nearly a decade earlier. Washington pointed out that one-third of the southern population was black and thanked fair organizers for the prominent role that they had given to African Americans. Washington also praised African Americans for their economic progress over the preceding three decades and urged them to "cast down your bucket where you are," suggesting that individuals work their way up the economic ladder "in agriculture, in mechanics, in commerce, in domestic service and in the professions." Turning to the issue of race relations, Washington reassured white people, "In all things that are purely social we can be as separate as the fingers, yet one as the hand in all things essential to mutual progress." When Bullock shook Washington's hand at the end of the speech, the facade of a racially united New South inspired cheers from the audience of twenty-five thousand.[44]

Newspapers across the country agreed with the *Constitution*'s assessment that Washington's speech—"the most remarkable address ever delivered by a colored man in America"—was "the hit of the day." The *New York Tribune* hailed Washington's "wisdom and good sense." The *Boston Globe* noted that black and white listeners were equally approving of the speech. The *Washington Post* called Washington's words "interesting and significant." W. E. B. Du Bois—later a critic of Washington—sent a telegram praising the speech. However, others in the black community immediately took a dimmer view: one speaker at the Bethel Literary and Historical Society in Washington, D.C., disagreed with Washington's suggestion of the inferiority of his race.[45]

When the Negro Building officially opened on October 21, another round of speeches, poems, and music took place. An ode read by D. Webster Davis and a speech by the Reverend J. W. E. Bowen (1855–1933) echoed Washington's theme of self-help. To demonstrate that African Americans had rejected the notion of government aid to disadvantaged people, Davis wrote, "We've left for aye our rude estate, to shape our lives by rule / And banished reconstruction's dream—'forty acres and a mule.'" According to the *Atlanta Constitution*, Bowen "asked that the negroes of the south and the people of the south be left to settle their own problems in their own way," but Bowen also showed a willingness to go beyond Washington's accommodationist perspective when he suggested that African Americans deserved "equality of opportunity" and "civil justice." Charles Collier (1848–1900), a white Atlanta businessman and president of the fair, followed with a speech reminding listeners that the Cotton States Exposition was the first fair with a dedicated building for African Americans. The Atlanta University chorus ended the festivities by singing the doxology, and the Reverend Edward R. Carter gave a benediction. The *Constitution* estimated the audience at fifty-five hundred, among them about five hundred white people. The *Constitution* had already reminded black visitors that they could dine at a restaurant in the Negro Building and find lodging in several locations in the city, including the Hotel Howell on West Mitchell Street, but the paper did not mention—because everyone of both races would already have known—that African Americans were not welcome in white restaurants and hotels either inside or outside the fair.[46]

The Negro Building gave African Americans a public space in which to showcase their achievements and challenge racial stereotypes. Prominently situated near the Jackson Street entrance to the fair, the commodious structure featured exhibits by individual southern states that highlighted successful black-owned businesses, scientific inventions, and works of art and music. Many artworks featured an emancipationist theme, including W. C. Hill's life-sized sculpture of a former slave with broken manacles to symbolize the end of bondage and the words "Chains broken, but not off" to symbolize the ongoing struggle. Because black women were not welcome as exhibitors at the fair's Woman's Building, their work appeared in the Negro Building. Accomplished sculptor Edmonia Lewis contributed a bust of U.S. senator Charles Sumner, a champion in the antislavery and civil rights movements. Black colleges and universities presented exhibits highlighting educational and professional achievements by African Americans. From time to time, the Negro Building hosted "congresses" of different professions, religious groups, women's organizations, and military companies. The Negro Building provided an opportunity for African Americans to frame a narrative that focused on emancipation and the accomplishments of black people after the war despite pervasive discrimination.[47]

Although total attendance at the fair neared one million, the number of black visitors is unknown. Teacher Millie McCreary brought her students from Atlanta Baptist Seminary four times, including three trips to the Negro Building. Alonzo Herndon (1858–1927) issued a special invitation encouraging black barbers to attend the fair on "Negro day," December 26, and referred to "our quota," an indication that leaders tried to recruit African American attendees. Herndon, who had become Atlanta's wealthiest black man via barbershops and business investments, was well known to both black and white Atlantans.[48]

Sectional reconciliation was a priority of the fair's organizers. "Blue and Gray Day" during the opening week featured veterans from across the United States in a carefully choreographed event timed to follow the dedication of the Chickamauga battlefield in North Georgia as a national park. Organizers hoped that veterans who traveled to attend the festivities at Chickamauga would then journey on to Atlanta. On Blue and Gray Day, Confederate veterans were encouraged to wear white badges, while former Union soldiers wore red. Formal festivities in the auditorium began with music—"Dixie," the "Star-Spangled Banner," and "Tramp, Tramp, the Boys Are Marching." On the platform Republican governors Levi Morton of New York and William McKinley of Ohio sat on either side of General Longstreet, who was greeted by cheers from the audience when he gave a speech that focused on patriotism during the Mexican-American War. McKinley (1843–1901), a Union veteran, promoted sectional reconciliation in an address that betrayed his 1896 presidential ambitions with its reference to "a grander civilization for our common country." Departing from the carefully stage-managed presentation of a South that had lost its bitterness, Captain W. D. Ellis, speaking for Confederate veterans, told the crowd that he hoped to "see the day when the federal government, *our* government, will take the old veterans of both sides into its protecting care and treat them all as wards of the nation." Perhaps realizing that he had crossed a line with this reference to the absence of Confederate pensions, Ellis backtracked, claiming that he had not meant "pecuniary aid" but instead was referring to "lofty paternal love."[49]

Another means by which Atlanta's fair organizers promoted sectional reconciliation was encouraging special ties between their city and Chicago. A rail city that had burned in 1871 and risen even stronger from the ashes, Chicago had some obvious parallels with Atlanta, and the commercial success and status of the nation's second-largest city provided Atlanta with inspiration. On November 10, six special trains brought several hundred Chicagoans to the exposition's "Chicago Day." Newspapers covered the visit in detail, including the arrival of Illinois governor John P. Altgeld, Chicago mayor George Swift, and Potter and Bertha Palmer, wealthy citizens and Chicago fair backers. George F. Stone, secretary of the Chicago Board of Trade, made a speech that emphasized commercial connections between the two cities. The *Constitution* marked the day with a salacious illustration of Chicago and Atlanta as women, naked except for strategically placed banners reading "The World's Fair 1893" and "Exposition of 1895." The two smiling women hold hands beneath a banner proclaiming "Friendship" and surrounded by images of fire and of the rebuilt cities.[50]

Organizers of the Cotton States Exposition initially did not plan to include a building devoted to the Confederacy; on the contrary, they wanted to downplay the war aside from the appearance of veterans and the theme of reunion. According to the *Atlanta Journal*, fair organizers believed that northern visitors might find Confederate symbols off-putting and sought to avoid any "stirring up of the old memories." However, Helen Plane began a chapter of the United Daughters of the Confederacy in Atlanta shortly before the start of the fair and appealed to the "exposition people." Perhaps deeming it unwise to refuse the request, they constructed a small "Confederate Relics Hall" in a far corner of the exposition grounds. The building's star attraction was the cradle in which the infant Jefferson Davis had allegedly been rocked. The building's staff included Elizabeth Kirby Smith, daughter of Confederate general Edmund Kirby Smith, who told the *Atlanta Journal* that "all the northern visitors have been most kind" and that some had donated to the Confederate Veterans' fund.[51]

In addition to its exhibits, the 1895 exposition also included a midway with a Ferris wheel (an innovation developed for the Chicago World's Fair just two years earlier), a water slide, an Indian village of thirty Sioux from South Dakota, and a notorious act involving "coochee-coochee dancers." Several midway exhibits also featured depictions of Africans and African Americans that undermined the positive images created by the Negro Building. An allegedly realistic "Dahomey Village" showed "primitive life," with partially dressed West Africans preparing meals and washing clothes. Another scene, the "Old Plantation," featured black people pretending to be slaves, evidently happy in their servile state. In the words of the *Atlanta Constitution*, an "old colored mammy" plied a loom, "jes' spinnin' away . . . same lac I used to do fo de war." When President Cleveland stopped at the Old Plantation, "old antebellum mammy" welcomed him as "massa president." But the woman who played this character was able to use the faithful slave stereotype to her personal advantage. After hearing her describe herself as the seventy-five-year-old mother of twenty children, one of whom died while serving his master in the Civil War, a northern governor gave her a nickel and then passed a hat until it was filled with coins, giving "mammy" a significant purse.[52]

In the end, the fair was a curious mixture of Old South and New. Financially, the fair barely broke even; it did not lose money, but it brought no return for its investors. More to the point, the visitors included thirty-five hundred journalists and editors who trumpeted Atlanta's New South vision around the world. Henry Grady would have loved it. After the fair closed, Collier told a journalist that "the result will go on. The good [the exposition] has done will increase with the years."[53] Yet in just over ten years, Atlanta was again in turmoil, as a race riot roiled the city and tarnished its image as a haven of reconciliation and progress.

# CHAPTER 3

# Sectional Reconciliation in a Time of Racial Tension

IN THE SUMMER OF 1898, Atlanta hosted the annual encampment of the United Confederate Veterans (UCV). A fixture of American life in the Gilded Age, encampments of Civil War veterans included Union soldiers who met as members of the Grand Army of the Republic and Confederates who met at separate summer gatherings as members of the UCV. Beginning on July 20, 1898, the thirty-fourth anniversary of the Battle of Peachtree Creek, the four-day UCV event brought close to sixty thousand soldiers, family members, and visitors to the Georgia capital to relive the glories of the Confederacy. In addition to speeches, music, earsplitting Rebel yells, and attractive young women smiling and waving, the meeting included a consistent buzz among attendees about the events playing out in Cuba. The Spanish-American War and specifically the Battle of Santiago fought earlier that month evoked Atlantans' interest. Newspapers interspersed updates about Cuba with coverage about veterans. Atlantans who once disdained any celebration of the Fourth of July now found themselves enthusiastic participants in this highly nationalistic war. By 1898, sectional reconciliation with the North was well underway, but racial healing was not, and in 1906, Atlanta's racial tensions exploded in a bloody race riot, caused in part by Thomas Dixon's incendiary play, *The Clansman*. The riot resulted in several dozen fatalities and damaged Atlanta's reputation as a broad-minded, business-friendly city.

Atlanta might have been unrecognizable to soldiers who had not seen it since 1864. By 1890, the city boasted ten railroads, including three that had been built during the preceding decade. Forty-six dry goods firms and twenty-eight grocery businesses served a population of 65,533. Atlanta's 410 industries included three major cotton mills and four cotton warehouses, the largest of which was owned by Samuel M. Inman. Other factories made agricultural implements, fertilizer, patent medicines, and beer.[1]

The city had also modernized to some degree with the addition of streetcars—two electric, two horse-drawn—street lighting, and a sewer system. The streetcar lines converged in the central business district, Five Points, which was also where street lighting was available. The sewer system served only affluent neighborhoods, and few city residents had access to safe drinking water. Poor sanitation contributed to an African American death rate that was 2.5 times higher than that for whites. In an important step toward helping its nonelite residents, Atlanta had organized a system of public schools in 1872, but African Americans could attend only segregated elementary schools and could not advance beyond the primary level. The city made few efforts to help the poor of either race, appropriating a total of just eighty-seven hundred dollars for poor relief in 1890, and that sum included money designated for pauper burials and the removal of "undesirables" from the city.[2]

The veterans reunion gave Atlanta's New South boosters a chance to showcase their city under the auspices of an Old South event. Citizens were encouraged to decorate their homes with flags and to open their homes to the aging veterans. On July 18, two days before the veterans were to arrive, organizers dedicated an auditorium, the "Confederate Tabernacle," at Piedmont Park, repurposing the structure that housed the Hall of Agriculture during the Cotton States Exposition three years earlier. With a seating capacity of eight thousand, the hall featured a portrait of Jefferson Davis flanked by paintings of Robert E. Lee and Stonewall Jackson. According to the Atlanta Constitution, the three thousand local residents who attended the dedication ceremony wanted to express "heartfelt sympathies" to Civil War veterans and similar sentiments for "the brave lads" who were risking their lives in Cuba. Attendees contributed to the Atlanta Relief Association, which raised money to help Georgians serving in Cuba. The band played "Stars and Stripes Forever" but did not play "Dixie."[3]

"Dixie" was, however, played many times during the reunion, which featured heavy doses of Lost Cause ideology. During a July 22 parade, "grizzled old veterans" marched through the streets as citizens cheered and bands played "the glorious strains of 'Dixie.'" John B. Gordon led the parade astride a magnificent black horse, then took a place of honor at the reviewing stand. The entire event occurred during a torrential rainstorm, yet the *Atlanta Constitution* boasted that the "veterans faced the weather and never faltered." The previous day, Gordon appeared before a cheering crowd of ten thousand veterans, whose sympathies were stirred by the sight of his "battle-scarred face."[4]

General Clement Evans (1833–1911), commander of the Georgia division of the UCV, provided the introductory remarks, followed by speeches from Mayor Charles Collier and Governor William Y. Atkinson (1854–99). When it was Gordon's turn to speak, he described Confederate veterans as a brotherhood of men defeated by "overwhelming numbers and resources." Despite being just as worthy of government support as "our heroic brothers" who had served in the Union army, Confederate veterans received no federal pensions. Gordon then shifted to less politically divisive rhetoric, declaring that Confederate reunions did not imply any fracture to the "unity of the republic" or any doubt that white people had accepted the end of slavery. After Gordon finished, Mississippi's Charles Hooker (1825–1914), a veteran, former member of Congress, and popular lecturer who was serving as "orator of the day," delivered an unabashed Lost Cause address. He spent ninety minutes revisiting the causes of the war, the war itself, and Reconstruction, sprinkling his turgid prose with references to "our dead heroes" and concluding that the South "fought not for slaves, but for Constitutional liberty." Hooker's address exemplifies what one historian has called "collective vindication" by former Confederate soldiers. They accepted defeat, even reunion with the North, but continued to venerate what they saw as the South's honor and their own version of military events.[5]

In addition to speeches, the veterans reunion offered social opportunities for old soldiers to reconnect with comrades, some of whom they had not seen in more than thirty years. Groups of Confederate chaplains, physicians and surgeons, and sharpshooters held their own smaller reunions. Veterans made excursions to Grant Park, southeast of the city center, to view the Cyclorama painting of the Battle of Atlanta, once a traveling exhibit, now a permanent fixture that had been moved from its original location on Edgewood Avenue and repaired for the occasion. Veterans of the

Atlanta Campaign recognized many of the landmarks depicted in the circular painting.[6]

African Americans played behind-the-scenes roles as hotel employees, porters, and personal servants, but racial issues garnered news coverage on several occasions. The *Atlanta Constitution* reported that a black man was badly beaten on Decatur Street after someone gave him a Confederate veteran badge and he wore it on his lapel. The newspaper implied that the victim had been duped into putting on the badge but then blamed him because he was "a very large and a very ignorant negro" and suggested that the incident taught him a lesson. In lighthearted coverage of the issue of race, the *Atlanta Constitution* focused on a social highlight of reunion week when Polk Miller (1844–1913), a Confederate veteran from Virginia, entertained a large crowd at Columbia theater with his minstrel act. According to the paper, Miller, who did not wear blackface, was "one of the funniest men that has ever attempted to depict the old southern negro in his ridiculous vein."[7]

The local Sons of Confederate Veterans (SCV) sponsored Miller's performance; one purpose of this and other annual reunions was to further the process of passing the Confederate legacy to the next generation. The SCV had been founded in 1895 by Robert A. Smyth of Charleston, South Carolina. The Atlanta chapter, the "Jefferson Davis Camp," had a visible presence at the reunion, at one point debating the criteria for membership after a motion was made to allow sons of Confederate sympathizers to become members of the group. After heated discussion, with one proponent declaring that the son of a man conscripted late in the war might be less sympathetic to the Confederate legacy than other supporters, the group voted to retain the rule that membership was open only to those descended from men who had served in the Confederate army or navy. On another occasion, members considered a proposal to change the group's name to Confederate Sons Association so that the initials CSA might be used.[8]

Women were present in many capacities. The United Daughters of the Confederacy (UDC), which had been founded in 1894 and was led by its indefatigable president, Helen Plane (1829–1925), appeared to be everywhere during reunion week. As Karen Cox has pointed out, the UDC supplemented the work of the ladies memorial associations by focusing less on remembering the dead in favor of vindicating the Confederate legacy. At the veterans reunion, the UDC sponsored a "grand reception" at the city's premier hotel, the Kimball House, on July 22. The group publicized the names of women who served as sponsors of each state division of veterans, and each sponsor had attendants known as maids of honor—pretty young women dressed in white whose images frequently appeared in Atlanta's newspapers. Miss Hedwig Penzel, for example, was described as a "beautiful young woman who will be sponsor of the Arkansas division." Gaines Foster has written that "a ritual presentation of virgins to veterans . . . assured the soldiers that the women of the South loved them despite their defeat and thereby indirectly affirmed their manhood." At the Kimball House reception, UDC members wore gray ribbons, and young people wore white ribbons as members of the Children of the Confederacy. Formed in 1896 as an auxiliary of the Atlanta UDC, the Children of the Confederacy began when fifteen children met at the YMCA and later incorporated as the Julia Jackson Chapter, taking its name from Stonewall Jackson's only surviving child. Georgia eventually had eighty-five chapters around the state.[9]

The widows of prominent Confederates participated in the reunion. At a session held in the Confederate Tabernacle on July 21, Anna Jackson, widow of Stonewall Jackson, was joined by the widows of Generals A. P. Hill and George Pickett. Veterans cheered the women, who followed protocol by bowing but not speaking. However, at the reunion's concluding session, Hallie Alexander Rounsaville (1864–1964), president of the Georgia UDC, gave a speech in which she promised that "the principles for which [veterans] fought can never die" as long as "the record of your glories and your faith survives." Rounsaville's statement encapsulated the UDC's mission. The UDC supported the resolutions made at the conclusion of the reunion, including an organized effort to preserve the Confederate White House in Montgomery, Alabama, where Jefferson Davis lived before moving to Richmond, and resistance to public use of the term *War of the Rebellion* in favor of War between the States.[10]

The Confederate reunion attracted an enormous crowd—the largest ever seen in the city, according to the *Constitution*. In one week, 350 trains brought visitors to the city, and close to sixty thousand people were believed to have participated—more, Atlantans bragged, than had attended the reunion in Nashville the previous year.[11]

For all of the Confederate hoopla, a strain of nationalism also pervaded the proceedings. Atlantans were keenly interested in the progress of the Spanish-American War, which began in April and lasted just ten weeks.

Southerners cheered the appointment of Joseph Wheeler, a former Confederate cavalry commander who had fought in the Atlanta Campaign, as major general of volunteers. Veterans were thrilled to learn about Wheeler's exploits and about the Spanish army's use of smokeless powder, a remarkable innovation. During the reunion, Atlanta newspapers printed interviews with wounded U.S. soldiers being treated at Fort McPherson, located a few miles south of the city. A small number of Spanish prisoners held at the base became a source of great curiosity, and they met with a delegation of reunion attendees. The *Constitution* reported that the prisoners "were acquainted with the records of the gallant confederate veterans." Meeting at the Confederate Tabernacle on July 22, the anniversary of the Battle of Atlanta, the UCV and SCV passed a resolution pledging "loyal support of confederate veterans throughout the south to the prosecution of the war with Spain" and volunteering to serve "in any capacity in which they might be needed."[12]

The Spanish-American War represented *the* turning point in national reconciliation. Volunteer soldiers from the North and the South trained together at Camp Thomas, located on the site where Civil War soldiers had clashed at Georgia's Chickamauga battlefield in 1863, and soldiers killed in Cuba were buried together, no longer separated into Union and Confederate cemeteries. President William McKinley, whose popularity soared after the war ended in August, visited Atlanta a few months later as part of a national "Peace Jubilee" tour.[13]

For Atlantans, the presidential appearance took sectional reconciliation to a new level. Speaking before the Georgia Legislature on December 14, McKinley declared that sectional lines no longer defined the United States. He spoke of Americans' shared love and loyalty to their country, as demonstrated by the recent war. And then McKinley astonished members of the audience when he declared, "The time has now come . . . when in the spirit of fraternity we should share with you in the care of the graves of the Confederate soldiers." The *Atlanta Constitution*, which called the speech "remarkable," noted that the Republican McKinley's magnanimity was all the more noteworthy because he had not received the votes of most southerners. Wallace Reed, who in 1889 published the first history of Atlanta and wrote occasionally for the *Atlanta Constitution*, spoke for many when he praised the former Union officer for his "epoch-making speech" that would mean "a great deal to the millions of Americans in the region who, for more than a generation, have felt that they were under the ban

because they or their fathers proved in the sixties that they had the courage of their honest convictions." McKinley's visit included a parade during
which he reviewed U.S. troops from the 15th Pennsylvania and the 3rd
New Jersey regiments. Wheeler and his command also marched, followed
by Union veterans in the Grand Army of the Republic. Two additional
remnants of Atlanta's Civil War past, members of the Gate City Guard and
the Atlanta Rifles, also participated.[14]

As Atlanta entered the new century, the twin themes of Confederate
celebration and American nationalism marched forward in tandem. The
UCV held annual memorial services for deceased veterans. In 1930, the
forty-first such occasion, a service took place at Park Street Methodist
Church to honor a surgeon, a cavalryman, an artilleryman, and a member
of the Georgia Cadets. By the end of the decade, few Confederate veterans
remained, and the UCV, joined by the SCV and the UDC, focused attention on other forms of commemoration.[15]

Part of the UDC's charge was to support Confederate veterans and their
widows. Meeting with other state UDC groups in Little Rock, Arkansas, in
1910, Helen Plane and Mildred Rutherford (1851–1928) proposed the construction of a facility to house Confederate widows and indigent women.
However, their emphasis on "women of refinement," as opposed to all
Confederate women, led to heated discussion and the proposal's rejection
by a majority of the delegates. The 1922 state UDC meeting, held in Decatur, discussed creating a home for needy Confederate women, as several
other southern states had done. Although Georgia never constructed such
a facility, the state UDC did support a home for soldiers called the Confederate Soldier's Home of Georgia, with the UDC's state president serving
on its board of trustees. The UCV and the SCV also provided assistance.[16]

In spite of the work of all three organizations, the Confederate Soldier's
Home of Georgia in Atlanta was plagued by mishaps from the beginning.
Part of a region-wide movement to provide housing for indigent veterans, the effort was fueled in part by resentment that the federal government subsidized veteran homes in the North but provided no subsidies
for former rebels. The Georgia home won the backing of a powerful broker in 1889, when Henry Grady led a fundraising campaign, but he died in
December of that year. Grady's colleagues from the *Atlanta Constitution*,
Evan Howell and William Hemphill, joined the effort, as did Confederate
veterans William Lowndes Calhoun, Clement Evans, and John Milledge.
But divisions between the Atlanta Ring and Georgia's agrarian interests,

which feared the city's growing power, hampered planning for a home. Although a cornerstone was laid on Confederate Memorial Day in 1890 (with not only Gordon and Longstreet but their fellow generals Joseph E. Johnston and Edmund Kirby Smith in attendance) and the building was completed the following year, the Georgia Legislature refused to appropriate money to fund its operations. In the ensuing years, various proposals to fund the home through philanthropic efforts were debated and rejected, and at one point the UDC tried to purchase the structure.[17]

The 1898 veterans reunion finally broke the political logjam, as the presence of so many former Confederates called attention to the plight of the state's aging warriors. The legislature agreed to appropriate money to fund the institution, and on June 3, 1901, birthday of the long-deceased Jefferson Davis, the Confederate Soldier's Home accepted its first residents— forty men representing twenty-six Georgia counties. Calhoun praised the many individuals who had supported the decade-long effort and offered special thanks to members of the UCV, SCV, UDC, and Children of the Confederacy for their refusal to give up. Three months later, however, the building burned to the ground. Undeterred, the facility's loyal promoters moved the residents to a hotel and appealed to sympathetic members of the Georgia Legislature, received an appropriation to rebuild, and completed a new home by 1902. By the time it was razed in 1967, it had housed twelve hundred veterans and become an Atlanta fixture. The UDC maintained ties with the home by organizing parties, paying veterans' burial expenses, and covering the medical expenses of veterans' children.[18]

Confederate heritage groups served as important players in commemoration efforts, but Gordon was Atlanta's most visible reminder of the Civil War and an enthusiastic proponent of sectional reconciliation. Gordon retired from politics in 1890 and devoted the remainder of his life to speaking and writing about the Civil War. His speech "Last Days of the Confederacy" inspired both Union and Confederate veterans, who responded to its mix of pathos, nationalism, and humor. A relentless self-promoter, Gordon always focused on his own wartime role, that of Robert E. Lee, and the common soldiers on both sides, making few references to other Confederate officers.

Although Gordon framed the speech as a narrative of Confederate surrender at Appomattox, its focus was "the spirit and character of the American soldier and people." Gordon alleged that history had no parallel to the "heroism, devotion, and self-sacrifice which was exhibited by those American boys in blue and gray from '61 to '65." He paid homage to the Lost Cause by stating that Confederate soldiers never lost confidence in Lee's "infallibility." Gordon held audiences' attention with humor: when Lee sent word that there would be no last attempt to break through the federal lines at Appomattox, Gordon's efforts to surrender were hampered by the fact that "there [was] not a white shirt in the entire army," a line that always brought laughter and applause. Gordon had to attach an old rag to a pole. He closed the speech with a message of nationalism, describing the United States as "an unbroken brotherhood from sea to sea."[19]

Gordon delivered the speech dozens and possibly hundreds of times, garnering positive responses from veterans on both sides of the Mason-Dixon Line. Historian Nina Silber has noted that Americans in the Gilded Age welcomed "a culture of healing and unity" as a reassuring diversion from the political corruption and social and labor unrest that characterized the era. Selwyn Owen, chief justice of the Ohio Supreme Court, described Gordon's address as "an oratorical wonder": he had heard it twice and hoped to hear it again because "it is fervent in its patriotism and full of the spirit which is destined [to] wipe out that fast fading dead line between the sections." On at least one occasion, Gordon delivered the speech to an audience of African Americans, accepting a 1902 invitation from Booker T. Washington to speak at Tuskegee. Speaking to an enthusiastic audience of eighteen hundred students, faculty, and area residents, Gordon played up the faithful slave narrative, praising the bondspeople who "befriended and cared for the wives and sisters of the Confederate soldiers" and declaring his appreciation for the plantation spirituals sung for his benefit by Tuskegee students. In David Blight's view, Gordon and Washington represented "a kind of racial reconciliation unique to the South; wrapped in ceremonial paternalism, promoted officially by Tuskegee."[20]

Gordon was also the star of the show when Atlanta hosted a Blue-Gray Reunion in 1900. In the aftermath of the Spanish-American War, organizers predicted that a meeting of Confederate and Union veterans would be appropriate and popular. The *Atlanta Constitution* reported that "throngs of veterans" attended the July event but made no estimate of a specific number, raising the possibility that the event had greater significance for its symbolism than its actual attendance. The reunion featured a meeting of soldiers at the site where Union general James McPherson (1828–1864) had died and a series of speeches accompanied by a barbecue the next day. At the McPherson site, Confederates ceded the occasion to General Oliver

Otis Howard (1830–1909), who had replaced McPherson as commander of the Army of the Tennessee. Howard did not mention his role as head of the Freedmen's Bureau after the war but instead focused on the importance of sectional reconciliation. Speakers at the barbecue included Albert D. Shaw (1841–1901), commander in chief of the Grand Army of the Republic, who lauded the "one ideal of American citizenship," criticized those who would keep alive "sectional teachings" about the causes of the war, and praised Lee for his belief that sectional teachings must not continue. Despite his declaration that "both sides were in the right," Shaw provoked Gordon's ire. The former general responded by acknowledging the sympathetic reception he had received in the North but then offering a vigorous defense of southerners' justifications for fighting. To cheers from the Confederate veterans, Gordon concluded, "I never will be ready to have my children taught that I was wrong or that the cause of my people was unjust and unholy." Shaw then backtracked, agreeing with Gordon and defusing any residual tension, and "that is the way the incident ended," as the *Constitution* put it. The exchange between Shaw and Gordon reveals the degree to which sectional differences still had the potential to divide audiences thirty-five years after the Civil War ended.[21]

Although he began a conversation with a New York publisher in the 1890s, Gordon did not publish a memoir until 1903. By the turn of the century, deeply in debt and despondent over a fire that had destroyed his home and much of his correspondence, Gordon needed money. He wrote a series of articles for *Scribner's Magazine* and published his memoir with Scribner's as well. Gordon acknowledged that "slavery was undoubtedly the immediate fomenting cause" of the war but also noted theoretical debates that dated as far back as the Constitutional Convention of 1787 regarding whether the Union existed in perpetuity or with the consent of individual states. Gordon suggested that 80 percent of Confederate soldiers neither owned slaves "nor had the remotest interest in the institution." Gordon wanted Americans to forgive and forget their divisions. *Reminiscences of the Civil War* found an audience among Civil War veterans and sold well. His emphasis on the shared courage of soldiers on both sides of the war appealed to Americans interested in what he called "the distinguishing magnanimity and lofty manhood of the American soldier."[22]

Three months after his memoir was published, Gordon died suddenly at his winter home in Florida, and Atlantans turned out to honor him at a funeral procession more elaborate than that of Grady. City offices and schools closed so that citizens could watch as an immense hearse drawn by four black horses carried Gordon's casket to the Capitol, where he lay in state. After a religious service at Central Presbyterian Church across the street, the general was interred at Oakland Cemetery, with politicians, veterans, and members of Confederate heritage organizations participating in the rituals. Declared the *Atlanta Journal*, "Oakland, the City of the Dead, has gathered in another hero," as Gordon was laid to rest close to Oakland's two Confederate monuments and the graves of thousands of others who had fought for the Confederacy.[23]

Georgia's other famous Confederate general had died exactly one week earlier. James Longstreet succumbed to pneumonia at the home of his daughter in Gainesville. The *Athens Banner*, like many other Georgia papers, sidestepped Longstreet's role as a Scalawag—"forgetting all that transpired just after the war"—and chose instead to remember the "brave and devoted soldier." The *Atlanta Constitution*'s coverage of Longstreet's death included a story defending his actions at the Battle of Gettysburg written by his second wife, Helen, who spent the remaining six decades of her life defending his war record. The *Atlanta Journal* printed a more personal account of the two generals by Henry D. Capers, a resident of the Confederate Soldier's Home of Georgia. As colonel of the 12th Georgia artillery battalion, Capers had served under Gordon, an "intuitive military genius" who was audacious in battle. Longstreet, in contrast, had a more "cautious and painstaking" style and a superior sense of timing: when he acted, "it was terrific in effect."[24]

In May 1907, Atlantans gathered for the unveiling of an equestrian statue of Gordon in front of the Georgia Capitol, making him the third Georgian, after Ben Hill and Henry Grady, honored with a public monument. The erection of the statue, which became the first monument at the Capitol, was the work of the Gordon Monument Commission, which had begun fundraising following his death and received small contributions from across the nation, including some from northern businessmen who heard Gordon speak or admired what they read about him in the newspapers. The owner of a drill company in Cleveland, Ohio, sent fifteen dollars and a note describing Gordon as "beloved by the people, both North and South." The owner of a hardware business in Elmira, New York, contributed five dollars because Gordon's memory "should be held sacred for the part he has taken in healing the sectional feeling between the North & South." The Georgia Legislature also provided monies. At the unveiling, Gordon's widow and children posed for a photograph in front of the statue, which was the work of sculptor Solon Borglum.[25]

Gordon remained Atlanta's most famous Confederate long after his death, and his family protected his reputation against real or imagined efforts to sully it. Fanny Gordon survived her husband by nearly thirty years, never passing up an opportunity to promote his legacy. Following her demise, the Gordon children and grandchildren assumed this role. When local historian Allen P. Tankersley (1906–57) began studying Gordon's career in the 1930s and 1940s, Gordon's grandson, Hugh Gordon Jr., pressured the Harvard-trained historian to downplay the general's role in the Ku Klux Klan in what would become *John B. Gordon: A Study in Gallantry* (1955).

When Tankersley provided a draft of the work, Hugh Gordon objected to its characterization of the general as closely allied with the Klan, claiming that he had supported the early Klan when it was a "protective organization" but had not backed the excesses of the later Klan. In particular, Gordon objected to Tankersley's chapter title "Grand Dragon of the Realm of Georgia." In 1947, Gordon told Tankersley that "there is not a word" in any surviving document that "warrants the assumption that [Gordon] was the head of the Ku Klux Klan in Georgia."[26]

Tankersley replaced the offending chapter title with the more benign "The Ku Klux Klan." He also softened his analysis, suggesting that Gordon met with KKK founder Nathan Bedford Forrest "in all probability" and that it was "commonly believed" that Gordon led the Klan in Georgia "though no person who could have known the fact directly has ever publicly revealed it." Tankersley also noted that when testifying before Congress in 1871, General Gordon "showed an intimate knowledge of the purposes and organization of the Klan, but surprising ignorance of the names of its members." The changes placated Hugh Gordon, who wrote to Tankersley, "I congratulate you heartily for what you have done. I believe that it will fill a great need in the records of our Southland."[27]

No other Atlantan equaled Gordon's stature as a public figure promoting both the Lost Cause and reconciliation; however, Myrta Lockett Avary (1857–1946) added a feminine voice to the conversation. Like Gordon, she was not a native Atlantan. Born on a Virginia plantation in 1857, she moved to Atlanta in 1884 when she wed James Corbin Avary, a promising young physician and Fulton County coroner. The *Atlanta Constitution* described the bride as "quite literary in her tastes" and the author of "pretty poems." After the death of the Avarys' infant son, their marriage appears to have been troubled. Myrta Avary later claimed that her husband had a drinking problem and used morphine, and she left Atlanta and moved to New York to pursue a literary career.[28]

Ambitious, energetic, and talented, Avary nonetheless learned that women writers had a difficult time supporting themselves in New York City. She wrote for a variety of publications, often anonymously, and found her work for the *Christian Herald* especially fulfilling, but she gave up on New York in the late 1890s after a variety of leading newspapers and magazines rejected her attempts to obtain a permanent position. However, she had made valuable contacts among reformers, editors, and most importantly publishers and returned to Atlanta with a book contract from D. Appleton Company.[29]

In the first decade of the twentieth century, Avary's literary career took off. She established her residence in Atlanta, legally separated from her husband, and published *A Virginia Girl in the Civil War* (1903), allegedly the true story of a woman and her husband who served in the Confederate army. Like Gordon, Myrta Avary was motivated by money. Although she kept her husband's name and welcomed the veneer of respectability brought by being a married woman (technically at least), she needed to support herself, and the best way to do so was to sell books, not short articles, for which she received minimal pay. Avary sensed that there was a market for books that promoted sectional reconciliation: "My life, my northern friendships, enabled me to meet this mood [of reconciliation] with sympathetic comprehension." She could also use her pen to present a positive portrait of her region. In *A Virginia Girl*, Avary presented Yankee troops not as evildoers but as chivalrous soldiers. As a result, "my little book was welcomed warmly, almost gratefully, by Northern press and people." Although the reconciliationist elements of the book appealed to northerners, Avary's book attracted white southern readers because it offered a nostalgic view of the war. Her publisher advertised the book in the *Atlanta Constitution* using a quotation from Clement Evans: "The book has taken me over the scenes and places with which I was made so familiar" in military campaigns with Generals Lee and Jackson.[30]

Two years after her first book came out, Avary and Isabella Martin edited and published the first edition of Mary Chesnut's Civil War diary under the title *Diary from Dixie*. Chesnut's diary ultimately became one of the most influential first-person accounts of the Civil War ever published.

Avary understood that Americans, North and South, would be attracted to Chesnut, a "well-born and high-bred" South Carolina plantation woman whose husband served as a military adviser to Jefferson Davis. During the couple's residence in wartime Richmond, Mary Chesnut (1823–86) knew many of the Confederacy's iconic leaders, and her sophistication and skill as a writer made her narrative a compelling tale. Chesnut had intended to publish her diary but died in 1886 without having completed it, and Martin, a friend of Chesnut's, took on the project. On a 1904 research trip to the South, Martin met Avary, who contacted Appleton, helped edit the diary, and coauthored the introduction. To accentuate the portrayal of slavery as a benign institution and to soften Chesnut's image with a northern audience, Martin and Avary worked to illustrate how well the Chesnuts purportedly treated their slaves. For example, according to Martin and Avary's introduction to the diary, James Chesnut "was borne to his grave amid the tears and lamentations of those whom no Emancipation Proclamation could sever from him." Despite some editorial tussles with Appleton, Avary and Martin won accolades for *Diary from Dixie*, and the book sold many copies.[31]

Like Gordon, Avary veered from Lost Cause orthodoxy to only a limited degree. One year after publication of the Chesnut diary, Avary wrote *Dixie after the War*, which presented white southerners as victims of a war that left them financially devastated and a Reconstruction period that was characterized by government corruption and chronic difficulties getting previously enslaved blacks to work for wages. Avary dismissed the possibility that the Ku Klux Klan posed a threat to black southerners: ("I never saw a Ku Klux; my native Virginia seems not to have had any") and instead presented the Klan as an instrument of good. According to Avary, "A few [African Americans] who had been making themselves seriously obnoxious observed terrified silence and improved demeanour" in the presence of KKK night riders. Avary praised ladies memorial associations for remembering the sacrifices made by southern men during the war but paid homage to sectional reconciliation by adding that Confederate veterans when visiting the North had been received with "unsparing . . . honour and hospitality."[32]

Even Mary Gay, a staunch supporter of the Lost Cause, acknowledged sectional reconciliation with her 1907 book, *The Transplanted*, telling the story of an antebellum Mississippi gentleman who marries a Boston woman. Like Avary's works, *The Transplanted* romanticizes the Old South, thereby helping to soothe the nerves of southerners in an era of economic and social change by reminding them of their rural past. Both Avary and Gay made money peddling nostalgia for the South's rural heritage with the assistance of commercial publishing and mass distribution.[33]

Atlanta's African Americans did not allow Confederate interpretations of the war, including faithful slave narratives and laudatory versions of Confederate military history, to go unchallenged. Henry A. Rucker, born a slave in Washington, Georgia, was owned by William King of Athens when hostilities broke out. After the war, King's daughter Julia married Henry Grady and moved to Atlanta. Rucker, too, moved to Atlanta, where he attended the public schools, studied at Atlanta University, and later became an important figure in the Republican Party. In 1897, President McKinley appointed Rucker collector of internal revenue, a patronage position he continued to hold under the administrations of McKinley's Republican successors, Theodore Roosevelt and William Howard Taft. When Rucker died in 1924, his *Atlanta Constitution* obituary emphasized the "deference and consideration" he maintained toward his former owner and his role in "bringing about friendly and cordial relations between the races." In fact, Rucker's appointment had rankled Atlanta's white men, with the *Constitution* reporting in 1901 that Rucker's reappointment "lands a straight arm blow at the lily white republicans of Georgia who have advanced man after man of their own number" in an effort to replace him. And Rucker clearly did not approach Gordon with "deference and consideration": at Gordon's death, Rucker declined to lower the U.S. flag on Atlanta's federal building, an incident that received coverage in the *New York Tribune* under the headline "Negro Incenses Ex-Confederates." The *Tribune* reported that President Roosevelt issued orders to lower the flag, and others across the state had complied, but Rucker did not, a small but meaningful gesture that represented a refusal to let a former high-ranking Confederate general also claim the mantle of a nationalist and patriot.[34]

But no black man challenged white Atlanta in the way that W. E. B. Du Bois did. Du Bois (1868–1963) rose to national prominence through his writing and his scholarly conferences and challenged the consensus that white people had achieved with Booker T. Washington's notion of racial accommodation.

Born and raised in Great Barrington, Massachusetts, the son of a Union army soldier who deserted late in the war and then deserted his family when his son was two years old, Du Bois attended integrated public schools before joining the student body at historically black Fisk University in Nashville, where he was exposed to southern-style racism. He earned a PhD from Harvard, paying his tuition with a small inheritance, loans, and summer jobs, and did further graduate study at the University of Berlin. In 1897, at the age of twenty-nine, Du Bois joined the faculty of Atlanta University as professor of history and economics and moved his wife and infant son to an apartment on the campus of this historically black institution.[35]

Although he was not a popular teacher, Du Bois quickly made a name for himself as a scholar, holding a series of conferences and publishing papers on topics relating to the sociology of the black family and church. But Du Bois's ivory tower existence ended abruptly in April 1899, when the lynching of a black man in a town south of Atlanta brought home the issue of white-on-black crime. Lynching was a common occurrence in the late nineteenth century. Between 1877 and 1950, forty-four hundred African Americans were killed in acts of racial violence in the South, including several hundred in Georgia, but this lynching was gruesome even by the standards of such crimes. A laborer, Sam Hose, had killed a white man in self-defense after they argued about Hose's pay and whether he could visit his invalid mother. Hose briefly escaped, but Georgia's newspapers stirred up the outrage of white vigilantes by suggesting that Hose had raped the dead man's wife, although he had not. When Hose was caught, a mob chained him to a tree, mutilated him, and burned him alive. Witnesses took home pieces of charred bone and flesh as souvenirs. Northern news outlets covered the events, with the *New York Times* alleging that four thousand people had traveled by train to witness the lynching or to visit the scene in its aftermath; still others came to Atlanta to claim reward money offered by the governor for Hose's capture. The *Atlanta Constitution* reported the size of the reward but not the lynching of Hose. Six months later, insurgents fighting the American occupation of the Philippines following the Spanish-American War nailed a placard to a tree urging African American troops to join the insurgency. Their sign, in Spanish, referred to Hose's lynching.[36]

Hose's murder led Du Bois to conclude that "one could not be a calm, cool, and detached scientist while Negroes were lynched, murdered and starved." The crisis led to new urgency in his work. On Emancipation Day 1900 he was the featured speaker at Edward R. Carter's Friendship Baptist Church. Following a reading of the Emancipation Proclamation by schoolgirl Bessie Roberts and of an original poem, "The Negro Is Rising," by the Reverend B. T. Harvey, Du Bois delivered an address, "The Problem of Negro Crime." Du Bois had been studying this issue, which became the focus of a scholarly conference in 1904, and he emphasized the need for self-protection.[37]

According to Du Bois, African Americans comprised 25 percent of all U.S. prisoners in 1890, and even in the North, black men were incarcerated in larger numbers than their white counterparts. He blamed crime rates in the black community on the legacy of emancipation, which he called a revolution that left blacks ill prepared for independent life. He concluded by urging black parents to create proper homes for their children, emphasizing training and discipline. He stressed the importance of education and implored parents to keep their children in school. He extolled the virtues of hard work and the need to lead a morally upright life, a nod to Booker T. Washington, whose emphasis on work ethic as a method of racial uplift had impressed those who listened to or read about his 1895 speech at Piedmont Park.[38]

Du Bois subsequently became less willing to share Washington's gradualist and accommodationist approach to race relations. In the late nineteenth century, voter registration among blacks plummeted in the South. In Louisiana, for example, the number of African Americans registered to vote dropped from 130,344 in 1896 to 5,320 by the turn of the century. Lynching remained a horrific reality in Georgia and throughout the region. While Washington earned national attention by publishing his memoir, *Up from Slavery* (1901), in which he emphasized personal virtues such as work ethic and religious observance, Du Bois burnished his growing reputation by publishing *The Souls of Black Folk* (1903).[39]

*Souls* begins with a memorable statement: "The problem of the Twentieth Century is the problem of the color line." Consisting of fourteen essays, the volume includes one that praised black colleges such as Atlanta University for training future leaders, a group that Du Bois later labeled the Talented Tenth. Another essay took issue with Washington's overemphasis on vocational education, a path that deterred African Americans from demanding political rights and higher educational attainment. Another essay, "Of the Dawn of Freedom," offered a spirited defense of Reconstruction. Based on an article Du Bois published in the March 1901 issue of *Atlanta Monthly*, this piece took direct aim at critics in both mainstream culture and the academic world who claimed that Reconstruction was a period in which misguided freedpeople were led astray by self-seeking Carpetbaggers and Scalawags. Reconstruction's critics included not only popular writers such as Avary but academic historians led by William Archibald Dunning and his graduate students at Columbia University, who gave academic credibility to popular notions about Reconstruction's alleged abuses. Du Bois also praised the Freedmen's Bureau, an institution often dismissed by critics as ineffectual. He defended the bureau for its sincere efforts to help former slaves as they tried to navigate the court system, open bank accounts, buy land, and gain access to education.[40]

*The Souls of Black Folk* had an immediate impact and went through several printings. Among African Americans, Du Bois was now regarded as Washington's equal as a national leader. It is hard to know how many white people in Atlanta read the book. The *Atlanta Constitution* did not review it but reprinted a review from the *New York Times Saturday Review of Books* in a recurring column patronizingly called "The Eternal Negro." White Atlantans who read the reprinted review might have been astonished to learn that the author of *Souls* firmly believed that "this social color line must in time vanish like the mists of the morning." In addition, according to the review, Du Bois suggested that Washington's leadership was based more on support from whites than from blacks. Washington's emphasis on practical education discouraged African Americans from seeking access to higher education and the chance to produce famous leaders. The review described Du Bois as asking for three things: the right to vote, "civic equality," and the right to education for black children. Du Bois formally broke with Washington at the 1905 meeting that founded the Niagara Movement and in 1909 helped to found the NAACP.[41]

Du Bois was not in Atlanta when the city erupted in violence during September 1906, but the Atlanta Race Riot forever changed both him and the city. In the South, race riots were "the bigger, bolder second cousin to lynching," as one scholar has written. The Atlanta riot played out against a background of changing racial dynamics, including an influx of rural blacks and rising crime rates that whites attributed to indolent blacks and the Decatur Street saloons. The riot was also fueled by years of racial tension exacerbated by white politicians and newspaper editors who played up instances of black "impudence" toward whites and by newspaper articles that sensationalized unsubstantiated rumors of the rape of white women by black men.[42]

In 1906, J. Max Barber (1878–1949), editor of the Atlanta-based *Voice of the Negro*, a monthly that promoted the accomplishments of African Americans and offered political and economic commentary, wrote that the rioters got their "first psychological impulse" from Thomas Dixon's novel *The Clansman* (1905). The subsequent stage version of *The Clansman* then "stimulated and presaged the gathering of evil winds." The second book in Dixon's trilogy about the Civil War era, Dixon's work presented the Klan in heroic terms—as having "overturned reconstruction rule and preserved the integrity of the Anglo Saxon race in the south."[43]

Born in North Carolina and educated at Wake Forest College, Dixon (1864–1946) became a Baptist minister and served pastorates in Boston and later New York. He became increasingly interested in social issues, lecturing on the Chautauqua circuit and developing a popular following before turning to a career as novelist and playwright. The *Atlanta Constitution* called him "a striking personality" and a "virile force in the making of American fiction."[44]

Dixon venerated the Old South and believed that the Civil War had "created the negro problem" by freeing the slaves and thus leading to "a bigger and more serious [problem] than anything it settled." According to Dixon, the "Negro Problem" could be solved in only one way, by colonizing blacks outside of white enclaves: "If the negro is not sent away there will be a race war." Dixon warned that recent educational advances by African Americans would lead to their rising expectations. The result could be racial mixing: Dixon had seen "big buck negroes" accompanied by white women while strolling along Broadway in New York City. Dixon, like most white Americans at the turn of the twentieth century, found the idea abhorrent.[45]

Dixon's New York publisher, Doubleday, advertised *The Clansman* in Atlanta newspapers as "a dramatic love-story" and alleged that the novel was a feel-good reconciliationist book, showing "Abraham Lincoln as the true friend of the South, and reveal[ing] the work and spirit of the Ku Klux Klan which, later, fell into disrepute." In reality, the novel did not promote sectional reconciliation; instead, it presented Reconstruction as a period when evildoers from the North enabled tragedy in the South, including the "violation" of southern white women, a theme explored through the character of Flora, who is abused by the former slave Gus. The KKK brought "order" out of the chaos of Reconstruction, including the capture and execution of Gus. Dixon's earlier novel, *The Leopard's Spots*, had proven popular, leading the publisher to order an initial printing of fifty thousand copies for *The Clansman*. Together, the two novels became the basis for the 1915 movie *The Birth of a Nation*.[46]

The stage play of *The Clansman* evoked controversy when it toured the South in the fall of 1905 and Dixon accompanied the fifty cast members and made personal appearances. When several members of the audience in Columbia, South Carolina, hissed, Dixon calmly offered one thousand dollars to anyone who could prove historical error in his work. In Atlanta, the play was performed five times to packed houses in late October and early November, and the audience cheered when he appeared at the end of one performance. He spoke of southern playgoers' "passionate approval" and claimed that the play had been presented in thirty cities. He suggested that the audience members who had disrupted the Columbia performance had been white, while the few black attendees, who were of course relegated to the segregated gallery, made no comments. In fact, Richard Carroll, an African American educator who saw the play in Columbia, called it "horrible" and told Dixon that he was "making 'blood' money off the negro." The *Atlanta Constitution* printed the news. Although the *Atlanta Journal's* theater critic opined that *The Clansman* lacked "depth of plot" and "does not rise to the dignity of drama," the newspaper also concluded that "one thing stands out boldly above all else—Mr. Dixon's performance has created interest bordering on the sensational and is being more widely discussed than any play that has been presented in the South in a long time."[47]

Not all of Atlanta's white residents supported Dixon; his most articulate critic was an old college friend from Wake Forest, the Reverend Len Broughton (1865–1936), now a prominent local clergyman. Broughton spoke to an audience of forty-five hundred at Atlanta's Baptist Tabernacle on November 5 and took Dixon to task for stirring up emotions on the issue of race. Broughton did not advocate racial mixing but argued against the play, earning applause and cheers from his listeners. "I call for a halt in all this wild and foolish talk about the negro," he declared. "Let the white man go on and rule this country as he is doing it now, but for God's sake, the negro's sake, and our sake, give the negro a rest from abuse and incendiarism!" Atlanta did not need a traveling troupe of pretend Klansmen to keep the peace. Broughton called the play un-American and un-Christian as well as "unsafe."[48]

Despite Broughton's efforts to rally progressive Atlantans, many whites echoed Dixon's racial fears, which were stoked by business and civic leaders who enforced racial segregation and increasingly sought to discourage black voting. Working-class whites felt threatened by evidence of a rising black middle class. In 1906, fifty black businesses clustered in the downtown area, including Alonzo Herndon's chain of barbershops; the medical office of William F. Penn, a Yale graduate; and the headquarters of Barber's *Voice of the Negro*, which had a circulation of fifteen thousand. Atlanta's black colleges and universities—Atlanta University, Atlanta Baptist College, Spelman College, Clark College, and Morris Brown College—enrolled two thousand students.[49]

Adding to racial fears, an unending stream of newspaper stories in the summer of 1906 alleged crimes by black men against white women. Among the most sensational was the story of Ethel Lawrence, a woman in her twenties, and her teenaged niece, Mabel. The two women were allegedly attacked by a black man, who slashed Ethel's face and inflicted minor cuts on Mabel. The local Hearst paper, the *Atlanta Georgian*, decried the treatment of the Lawrences and the failure to bring the perpetrator to justice. "No crime in Fulton county in years has so stirred up the people as the attack on Miss Lawrence and Miss Mable Lawrence." In response, the *Voice of the Negro* condemned the "masked hatred" of the *Georgian*'s editor.[50]

The riot began on the evening of Saturday, September 22, 1906, after several days on which newspapers published stories alleging crimes against women. The *Atlanta Journal* claimed that blacks "had been guilty of the boldest assaults on white women." As a crowd of white men gathered in the city center, Atlanta's mayor attempted to reason with them, urging them to go home. Ignoring his entreaties, the mob, which numbered in the thousands, began its rampage. For the first time in its history, two riot calls were rung on Atlanta's fire bell that night. Policemen were called out, and authorities later summoned help from the militia, but law enforcement was not up to the task, and some witnesses faulted police for failing to act decisively.[51]

Throughout the night, marauding groups of white men attacked blacks indiscriminately. On Peachtree Street, a black man was beaten to death, while a mob attacked an ambulance as it carried a badly injured man to the hospital. The ambulance driver eluded the mob by laying a quick whip to the horses. Doctors and nurses worked through the night to treat the injured, with some victims choosing to stay in the hospital because they were afraid to leave. Thirteen-year-old Lucy Rucker, the daughter of Henry Rucker, spent the night on the floor of the family home with her mother, terrified that the mob would attack their residence in the city's Sixth Ward. Her father and brother had gone out to see what was happening and hunkered down in the post office building. But Lucy and her mother "didn't know what had happened to them, and we found that [whites] were butchering people, taking them off streetcars, just killing them." At the corner of Marietta and Forsyth Streets, a black man traveling alone leaped from the trolley and attempted to run for his life but was beaten to death. Another black man sought protection inside a store, but the mob beat down the door and killed him. The bodies of three dead men were piled at the base of the statue on Marietta Street erected in honor of Henry Grady, who had proudly told northern audiences twenty years earlier that the South had no race problem.[52]

Sunday, September 23 began peacefully but ended in more deaths. With a strong military presence in the city, African Americans who had not fled the downtown area were identified as "idle negroes" and arrested. Most black Atlantans, however, prepared for further violence. Residents of the Darktown neighborhood near the black commercial corridor of Auburn Avenue collected weapons and extinguished streetlights; other African Americans sought shelter near the black college campuses. South of the city center, in the Brownsville community, police looking for troublemakers arrested several black men on Sunday night, leading to a confrontation in which two black men were shot and killed. On Monday, several black men died after encountering soldiers searching for guns in Brownsville, but by Tuesday morning the riot had ended.[53]

At least twenty-five black men and one white policeman died in the Atlanta Race Riot, and property damage in the downtown area was extensive. Nevertheless, African Americans took pride in the fact that they had defended themselves, preventing the mob from entering their neighborhoods after Saturday. Du Bois rushed back from Alabama with "a Winchester double-barreled shotgun and two dozen rounds of shells filled with buckshot. If a white mob had stepped on the campus where I lived I would without hesitation have sprayed their guts over the grass. They did not come." A few weeks later, Du Bois published an emotional essay in which he poured out his anger about the riot and condemned Washington's accommodationist approach, calling it a failure. Du Bois's dissatisfaction grew as he lost patience with a city that billed itself as the center of the New South yet refused to allow black patrons to use its new public library, the region's largest. In 1909, Du Bois made history by reading an essay defending Reconstruction before a community of scholars attending a meeting of the traditionally all-white American Historical Association. The following year, he left Atlanta and moved to New York as director of publicity and research for the fledgling NAACP.[54]

The riot prompted considerable soul-searching in the black community. In the October issue of the *Voice of the Negro*, Barber asked, "Where are our friends?" While acknowledging that "the Negro race has friends in the [white] South," including Atlanta, Barber deplored the white leaders' failure to stop mob rule, writing, "We simply plead for decency, fair play and protection." The riot also revealed the limitations of a strategy of racial uplift, long the goal of local African American civic and religious leaders who encouraged black educational and economic empowerment for elites and preached to nonelites about the need for sobriety and upright behavior. But such efforts had not prevented the rioting.[55]

Atlanta's entrepreneurs and politicians understood the damage that the riot had done to the city's reputation as a business-friendly, progressive metropolis. Historian William Link has pointed out that "Grady's vision of a New South" was so "tattered and frayed" after the riot that it was rarely invoked after 1906. City leaders created a Committee of Safety, an effort supported by the *Atlanta Constitution* on the grounds that "our women" required protection after suffering from "nervous prostration": one woman had supposedly succumbed to "fright." The newspaper also acknowledged that the riot had tarnished Atlanta's reputation, with "friction between the races in Atlanta . . . at a tension unknown since reconstruction," and called for the hiring of new policemen to supplement an inadequate force of fifty-seven. The city's white clergymen said very little except to call for an end to violence. White Atlantans blamed the riot on black Atlantans despite the lack of evidence that white women were ever in peril. For good measure, the *Constitution* reprinted excerpts from many other southern newspapers that shared its editorial perspective.[56]

In December, with rumors spreading that another riot was about to begin, Atlantans created a biracial civic league. White members included prominent businessman George Muse and Charles T. Hopkins, a lawyer and member of the Chamber of Commerce. Black members included clergymen Edward R. Carter and Henry Proctor as well as Du Bois. Though the white and black members did not meet together, the civic league helped some of the fifty-nine black defendants arrested after the September riot by hiring a defense attorney to represent them. On Sunday, December 9, about two hundred of the city's white and black clergy delivered sermons supporting law and order, and Washington spoke at Carter's Friendship Baptist Church in the afternoon, urging interracial cooperation. Despite these efforts, African American leaders chafed at whites' ongoing efforts to blame all blacks for lawless behavior and at the city's refusal to add black members to the police force.[57]

Atlanta's business and political elite acknowledged *The Clansman's* role in sparking the riot by refusing to allow the play to return in 1907. In an article focused on the efforts of African Americans in Columbus, Georgia, to stop the play from appearing there, the *Atlanta Constitution* reported that Dixon's work had been "interdicted" in Atlanta. Moreover, according to the paper, *The Clansman* "should be unceremoniously placed under the ban by every township in the south."[58]

On October 10, 1911, a group of Atlantans gathered at Piedmont Park for the unveiling of the Peace Monument, erected by the "Old Guard" of the Gate City Guard. The oldest and most respected local ceremonial militia unit, the Guard played a small role in the Civil War when it was involved in a July 1861 skirmish near Staunton, Virginia. At some point, the Guard was cut off from other Confederate units, leading to a series of increasingly desperate efforts, with soldiers scaling a mountain to avoid capture and abandoning equipment, including a magnificent flag hand-sewn by Atlanta's women. After the soldiers had gone several days without food, a mountaineer fed them and helped guide them to safety. The Guard then disbanded, although some of its members joined other regiments and fought in the war. Its inglorious wartime record was subsequently forgotten by a public that chose to focus on the Guard as Atlanta's first unit to join the Confederate army.[59]

The Gate City Guard reconstituted itself after the war, and in 1879 forty members led by Colonel Joseph F. Burke and accompanied by Mayor William Lowndes Calhoun toured several northern states, stopping in Baltimore, Philadelphia, and New York, among other cities, and wearing their distinctive blue uniforms and tall hats with white plumes. The Guard's "peace tour" was controversial among some locals, who expressed concern about reopening the "old scars of the war." The 7th New York Regiment entertained the Guard in New York City, including a banquet at its armory, and paraded with the Georgia unit before a cheering crowd. For the unveiling of the Peace Monument in 1911, the Gate City Guard played host to northern militia units.[60]

The monument features a bronze angel standing over a kneeling Confederate soldier who is surrendering his weapon. The angel holds an olive branch. Praised by the *Atlanta Constitution* as a goodwill gesture and a "display of broad Americanism," the statue symbolizes sectional reconciliation while ignoring African Americans, who did not constitute part of "broad Americanism" in the eyes of Atlanta's civic leaders. On the day of the dedication, thousands of Atlantans braved a driving rainstorm to attend the ceremony. Speeches by Burke and several northern politicians reinforced the belief that the statue marked a milestone in the effort to end sectional division and a feel-good moment for white Atlantans eager to erase memories of the race riot that had sullied their city's reputation.[61]

Confederate Memorial Day ceremonies continued in the new century. In April 1907, seven months after the riot, white residents gathered at Oakland Cemetery for the annual memorial service. Fanny Gordon, loyally preserving her husband's wartime memory, sat next to the pastor of Ponce de Leon Baptist church, who gave the invocation. The Atlanta Ladies Memorial Association, again in charge of the event, chose the speaker, journalist, and former legislator John T. Boifeuillet, whose long oration framed the war as a "struggle for truth and right." Although the association claimed that thousands watched the annual parade preceding the festivities, the *Constitution* estimated the crowd only at "many, many hundreds."[62] Given the modest turnout, proponents of Civil War memorialization must have wondered how the Confederacy would be remembered in the twentieth century.

A member of the United Daughters of the Confederacy lit the Eternal Flame of the
Confederacy in December 1939 as part of the festivities surrounding the premiere
of *Gone with the Wind*. Not visible in the photo is the large hole at the base of this
lamppost caused by a Union artillery shell that ricocheted and killed a free black
man, Solomon Luckie, in 1864. Until 2017, most Atlantans ignored Luckie's story.
(LBMPE-026a, Lane Brothers Commercial Photographers Photographic Collection,
Special Collections and Archives, Georgia State University Library)

John B. Gordon (1832–1904) became Atlanta's most important
spokesman for both the Lost Cause and sectional reconciliation.
(Hargrett Rare Book and Manuscript Library, University of Georgia Libraries)

An estimated sixty thousand
people participated in the 1898
Confederate reunion held in Atlanta.
(Hargrett Rare Book and Manuscript
Library, University of Georgia Libraries)

Reu. Edward R. Carter

FRIENDSHIP BAPTIST CHURCH

ATLANTA · GEORGIA

In 1894, the Reverend Edward R. Carter (1858–1944) published
*The Black Side: A Partial History of the Business, Religion,
and Education of the Negro in Atlanta* celebrating African
Americans' freedom as the result of the Civil War.
(Archives Division, Auburn Avenue Research Library on African American
Culture and History, Atlanta-Fulton Public Library System)

Mary Ann Harris Gay (1829–1918) explored civilian hardship on the home front in *Life in Dixie during the War*, published in 1897.
(Georgia Archives, Vanishing Georgia Collection, image DEK-418-85)

Myrta Lockett Avary (1857–1946) wrote about the Lost Cause and sectional reconciliation in a series of books published in the first decade of the twentieth century.
(Kenan Research Center, Atlanta History Center)

The statue of Benjamin Harvey Hill unveiled in 1886 was Atlanta's first monument to a figure of the Civil War era. Although the event attracted a huge crowd, it also provoked controversy in northern publications. (*Harper's Weekly*, May 8, 1886)

The
# CITY BUILDER
OCTOBER 1925

RESURGENS

1847

1865

ATLANTA, GA.

The Spirit of Atlanta

As this 1925 Chamber of Commerce publication attests, many Atlantans regarded Henry W. Grady (1850–89) as a visionary leader long after his death. (Kenan Research Center, Atlanta History Center)

Gutzon Borglum (1867–1941) with a model for his carving of Robert E. Lee on Stone Mountain. In 1915, the United Daughters of the Confederacy hired Borglum for the project, and Borglum convinced them to include multiple Confederates. (Kenan Research Center, Atlanta History Center)

For the public unveiling of Robert E. Lee's head on Stone Mountain in January 1924, Gutzon Borglum carried ninety-five-year-old C. Helen Plane (1829–1925) to the staging area. As president of the local chapter of the United Daughters of the Confederacy, Plane had hired the sculptor a decade earlier. (Stuart A. Rose Manuscript, Archives, and Rare Book Library, Emory University)

Margaret Mitchell (1900–1949, *center*) attended the December 1939 premiere of *Gone with the Wind*, which brought Hollywood royalty (*left to right*) Vivien Leigh (1913–67), Clark Gable (1901–60), David O. Selznick (1902–65), and Olivia de Havilland (1906–) to Atlanta.
(LBMPE1-023a, Lane Brothers Commercial Photographers Photographic Collection, Special Collections and Archives, Georgia State University Library)

Thousands of spectators thronged Loew's Grand Theatre for the first showing of *Gone with the Wind* on December 15, 1939. Loew's did not admit African American patrons, and the movie's black actors were not invited to the premiere.
(LBMPE2-004a, Lane Brothers Commercial Photographers Photographic Collection. Special Collections and Archives, Georgia State University Library)

Commercial artist Wilbur G. Kurtz (1882–1967) became twentieth-century Atlanta's most prominent advocate for preserving historic Civil War sites. (Kenan Research Center, Atlanta History Center)

Emory University professor Bell Irvin Wiley (1906–80) played a prominent role locally and nationally during the Civil War centennial. (Stuart A. Rose Manuscript, Archives and Rare Book Library, Emory University)

The Reverend William Holmes Borders (1905–93) gave his first Emancipation Day address in Atlanta in 1938. In 1970, he offered the benediction at the unveiling of the Confederate carving. (AJCP353-071e, *Atlanta Journal-Constitution* Photographic Archives, Special Collections and Archives, Georgia State University Library)

When President Richard Nixon (1913–94) canceled plans to attend the 1970 dedication of the Stone Mountain Confederate carving, Vice President Spiro Agnew (1918–96) served as his substitute. While Agnew spoke at the dedication, students filled the streets of downtown Atlanta to protest the U.S. invasion of Cambodia. (*Atlanta Constitution*, May 10, 1970)

Atlanta's first two African American mayors, Maynard Jackson (1938–
2003, *left*) and Andrew Young (1932–), grappled with the preservation
of the city's Civil War history and memory. Jackson supported efforts
to preserve the Cyclorama painting of the Battle of Atlanta, and Young
endorsed a plan to preserve the Margaret Mitchell House.
(AJCP432-040b, *Atlanta Journal-Constitution* Photographic Archives,
Special Collections and Archives, Georgia State University Library)

# CHAPTER 4

# The UDC and the Struggle over Stone Mountain

A T THE DAWN OF THE NEW CENTURY, the United Daughters of the Confederacy (UDC) took a leading role in Atlanta's Civil War commemoration. The city held another Confederate reunion in 1919, but with each passing year, fewer gray-bearded men remained to attend these functions. While members of the Atlanta Ladies Memorial Association tended the graves of Confederate dead, members of the UDC focused on shaping wartime memory for a twentieth-century audience. Dolly Blount Lamar (1867–1955), who served as Georgia's UDC division president in the 1910s, wrote about the organization's interest in erecting monuments to preserve "historical truth and spiritual and political ideals." Atlanta's UDC focused on a series of bronze tablets to remember the Atlanta Campaign as well as on a Confederate carving at nearby Stone Mountain. The effort began as an individual tribute to Robert E. Lee but evolved to become a national project and the largest memorial to the Lost Cause. Lamar conceded that "every such enterprise [of monument building] seems to be accomplished only after a fight." Although most fights were settled quickly and internally, the Daughters engaged in a deeply divisive and ultimately unsuccessful public battle to maintain control of the Confederate carving they helped to create.[1]

After 1890, the Lost Cause "entered its most highly organized and institutionalized phase," as one historian has put it. Many young white men honored their fathers by joining the Sons of Confederate Veterans (SCV). Both the Spanish-American War and later the First World War provided opportunities for the descendants of Confederate soldiers to prove their martial valor and thus show themselves worthy of the sacrifices of their wartime forebears. Southern white women, some with mothers who had been active in the ladies memorial associations a generation earlier, sought their own public outlet in the UDC. The Atlanta group's membership peaked during the 1920s, when it became the city's leading Confederate heritage group. For white men and women in the South, Confederate memory continued to play a meaningful role in their lives well into the twentieth century. In her 1940s memoir, Katharine Du Pre Lumpkin (1897–1988), who was born in Macon, Georgia, in 1897 and lived in several locations in Georgia and South Carolina, recalled her childhood and the multigenerational nature of Confederate commemoration at that time. Members of Lumpkin's family participated in the United Confederate Veterans (UCV), the UDC, and the SCV, while younger members, including herself, joined the Children of the Confederacy. "Thousands of families showed such a devotion," Lumpkin wrote. "It was a lusty movement and fervently zealous. I chanced to know it at the peak of its influence."[2]

Atlanta's 1919 Confederate reunion represented only the second time it had welcomed members of the UCV. After the death of John B. Gordon, the UCV lacked the visibility and unity it had enjoyed under his leadership. Gordon had chosen Stephen D. Lee as his successor, but Lee's death in 1908 provided an opening for Atlanta's Clement A. Evans to take the position until his death three years later. By 1919, none of the Confederacy's important military figures remained alive, and leadership of the UCV had passed to K. M. Van Zandt of Texas, who had played a relatively minor role in the war. Nathan Bedford Forrest, grandson and namesake of the Confederate general and Ku Klux Klan founder, served as head of Georgia's SCV and general secretary for the reunion. Atlanta's business leaders appealed to citizens' sense of civic pride in fundraising for the event, noting that more than twenty years had passed since Atlanta had hosted the UCV and that Richmond, Birmingham, Nashville, Chattanooga, and Memphis had each hosted at least two reunions, while New Orleans had hosted four. The chair of the reunion's finance committee, G. F. Willis, also pointed out that reunions boosted the economies of their host cities.[3]

In many ways, the UCV's twenty-ninth meeting was a typical reunion, including speeches and a parade through downtown Atlanta that featured soldiers delivering rebel yells and local people cheering and clapping. The *Atlanta Constitution* estimated that ten thousand soldiers attended the event but made no attempt to estimate the size of the crowds, probably an indication that they were not as large as past events. The *Atlanta Journal* suggested that "thousands" attended. In keeping with the theme of sectional reconciliation and in light of America's recent victory in World War I, city streets featured "the blending folds of the Stars and Stripes and Stars and Bars, forgetful of the differences of the sixties," as the *Constitution* put it.[4]

In other ways, the reunion reflected changing norms. Veterans traveled from Atlanta's rail stations in automobiles, not carriages, and some parade participants also rode in cars. The grand ball at the auditorium featured traditional dances, including the quadrille and Virginia reel. An *Atlanta Constitution* reporter suggested that young people watching from the balcony might have marveled at these old-fashioned steps given their own propensity for jazz music and modern dances.[5]

By the early twentieth century, members of the UCV, understanding that their numbers were dwindling rapidly, expected that the SCV would take over the leadership role in Confederate commemoration; however, that role was assumed by the UDC. Although the SCV gradually built its numbers, the UDC grew even faster, nearing eighty thousand members by 1912. Founded by Helen Plane in 1895, the UDC's Atlanta chapter had 668 members by 1900. Two decades later, the organization's three Atlanta-based chapters boasted a combined membership of 1,702, the largest of which had 1,499 members and in 1922 purchased a house to use as a headquarters. Unlike the SCV, the UDC did not require that members be descended from a Confederate soldier but instead asked that they be related to a male or female Confederate and devote themselves to the memory of those who fought, the role played by southern women, the creation of "truthful history" of the war, protection of historical places, and the care of needy veterans and their families. In addition to such broad membership requirements, the Daughters found new recruits by tapping into traditional notions of female volunteerism, the popularity of women's clubs and civic organizations, and the growing number of college-educated women seeking an expanded public role. Although UDC women used a public forum to advance their agenda and believed that women had the right to express civic ideals in public, they also upheld traditional gender roles, believing that women should emulate their Confederate forebears in their sense of duty and in deferring to men.[6]

The Atlanta UDC encouraged its members to engage in work of the national UDC, including prizes it bestowed on children for the best essays on a variety of topics such as "Mammy in the Old Plantation Days." The image of the faithful slave was a hallmark of Lost Cause ideology, and mammy was a centerpiece of that genre. Allegedly devoted to her white "family," mammy was often a caricature that bore little resemblance to the actual slave women who cared for children, cooked, and managed white households. Yet the mammy figure appeared in the oral traditions of southern families, in memoirs, in fiction, in paintings, and in vaudeville acts and movies. Local chapters also gave awards, including the "Cross of Honor" essay contest, which was presented to Dorothy Bosworth in 1925. Like many UDC winners, she was a young woman from a prominent Atlanta family. The *Atlanta Constitution* featured her picture but failed to offer any details about her essay.[7]

Georgia's UDC was one of the few state chapters to advocate both for Confederate commemoration and for helping the underprivileged. By supporting the Rabun Gap School in the North Georgia mountains, the Georgia UDC made an important contribution to educating some of the state's poorest white children. In 1907, it raised funds to build a dormitory at Rabun Gap and named it for Francis Bartow, the Savannah congressman who died leading Confederate soldiers at the 1861 Battle of Manassas.[8]

The Atlanta UDC, however, focused primarily on creating memorials to highlight the city's Civil War heritage and cast it in a Lost Cause perspective, echoing the focus of the broader UDC, which pledged more time and resources toward the construction of monuments than did any other Confederate heritage organization. In 1919–20, the Atlanta chapter unveiled a series of historical markers, including six bronze tablets at the Georgia Capitol commemorating key moments in the Atlanta Campaign: "Transfer of Command" from General Johnston to General Hood, "The Battle of Peachtree Creek," "The Battle of Atlanta," "The Siege of Atlanta," "The Battle of Ezra Church," and "The Evacuation of Atlanta." State historian Lucian Lamar Knight composed the inscriptions, which were presumably approved by the Daughters.[9]

The tablets, which still adorn the Capitol grounds, contain information about the campaign, albeit with some embellishment. "The Battle of

Atlanta" identifies the city's strategic importance as a supply depot that made it a "prize of war" for the Union army. "The Evacuation of Atlanta" alleges that with the "fall" of Atlanta, "the Confederate Citadel," the Confederacy itself fell. In reality, although Atlanta's capture played a critical role in ending the war, Confederate surrender did not occur for another seven months. Knight and the UDC saved their most emotive language for "The Siege of Atlanta" and "The Evacuation of Atlanta." The siege was "veritably a reign of terror. . . . [W]omen and children were exposed to this leaden hail of the inferno." The shelling undoubtedly frightened civilians, but relatively few people—perhaps two dozen—died during the weeks of bombardment. Sherman's decision to expel civilians from the city after its surrender was and remains controversial: Knight and the Daughters called it "his merciless order" and claimed that "a few days thereafter, he reduced the city to ashes." In fact, Sherman destroyed a significant portion of the city but probably less than half as he was leaving it two months later. The Daughters did not commemorate Reconstruction or the business elite's success in securing Atlanta as the site for both the state's constitutional convention and its new Capitol.[10]

The Atlanta Daughters' most ambitious project involved the Confederate carving on Stone Mountain, and it was primarily the work of two individuals: the UDC's Plane, who proposed erecting a statue of Lee at the base of the mountain, and the sculptor she hired, John Gutzon de la Mothe Borglum (1867–1941), who convinced her to include a multitude of Confederates in a grand composition.

Caroline Helen Jemison had deep connections to the Old South and the Confederacy. Born on an Alabama plantation in 1829, she attended Wesleyan College for women in Macon, Georgia. In 1854 she wed William F. Plane and resided with him on a farm in Baker County, where they owned considerable acreage and six slaves. With the outbreak of war, William Plane joined the Baker County Fire Eaters, part of the 6th Georgia Volunteers under the command of Alfred Colquitt. At the Battle of Antietam, Captain Plane was wounded and captured, and he died while in the hospital. His last words, dictated to a surgeon's assistant, expressed love for his family and a willingness to die for the cause of southern independence. Helen Plane never remarried. She spent the next several decades managing her family's finances and raising children, including her son and the orphaned children of her half-brother. In the 1890s, she joined the UDC. Although she was part of the wartime generation and thus older than many Daughters, she nonetheless founded the Atlanta chapter, resolute in her wish to draw public attention to a cause for which her husband had fought and died. A close friend described Plane as "vigorous and highly opinionated. She was a person for whom the War between the States had never ended." At her insistence, the 1895 Cotton States Exposition included a Confederate Relics Hall. She served as first president of the UDC's Georgia Division in 1895–96 and thereafter held the title of honorary president.[11]

Plane was not the first person to suggest a carving on Stone Mountain, but her vision, determination, and organizational skills made it happen. In 1914, when she was eighty-five years old, she created a committee of the Atlanta UDC chapter to sponsor the project and then convinced Samuel Venable (1856–1939) of the Venable Brothers Granite Company to deed one side of the mountain for a Confederate carving. In 1915, she invited New York–based sculptor Gutzon Borglum to Georgia to view the site. The world's largest granite outcropping, Stone Mountain has a domed shape that made it a popular picnic spot with residents of Atlanta and DeKalb County, and its smooth, relatively flat side made it ideal for carving.[12]

Plane launched the project at a time when Civil War monument building was very popular. In the South, Confederate heritage groups enshrined the Lost Cause by erecting statues that glorified soldiers' sacrifice in the context of increasing concerns about preserving the place of white people in the region's social hierarchy. Monument building was also popular in the North. In the late nineteenth century, Americans took great inspiration from Civil War leaders, much as the World War II generation inspired late twentieth-century Americans. Washington, D.C., received a spate of new monuments honoring Union generals John A. Logan (1901), Ulysses S. Grant (1902), William T. Sherman (1903), George B. McClellan (1907), and Philip Sheridan (1908) as well as a monument to the Grand Army of the Republic (1909). Sheridan's statue, a bronze that depicts him astride a magnificent horse with his arm outstretched, rallying his troops during the 1864 Battle of Cedar Creek, dominates Sheridan Circle, a tree-lined area in Northwest Washington. The figure projects action, power, and triumph. The dedication ceremony on November 25, 1908, included President Theodore Roosevelt, veterans of the Civil War and Spanish-American War, and the monument's sculptor—Gutzon Borglum.[13]

Visiting Stone Mountain in 1915, Borglum was impressed by its beauty and size and the challenge of carving it, but he was especially drawn to the idea of producing a grand narrative. Borglum knew that he and other sculptors had captured images of individual heroes of the Civil War, and he received positive press not only for his Sheridan monument but also for several sculptures of Abraham Lincoln. But Stone Mountain offered Borglum the chance to create something much more impressive. As he told the Atlanta UDC in 1917, "I saw something I had been dreaming of as a sculptor all my life, an opportunity to produce a great epic of a people" and to do so on a massive piece of "virgin stone, not spoiled and not mutilated." Borglum believed that Americans had not done enough to celebrate their history through fine arts. He informed the *New York Times* that he wanted to "build a memorial to a cause, without singling out an individual." Although Plane and the UDC suggested a carving of Lee at the base of the mountain, Borglum proposed a series of mounted men to fill a mountain scarp that was far too immense for a single figure. A group of Confederates, including Lee, would appear to ride across the massive granite wall. Borglum told *Scientific American* that he wanted to represent "Lee and his army moving, as if alive." Borglum assured Plane that the project could be accomplished at reasonable cost and would be completed within eight years.[14]

In many ways, Borglum seemed like an unlikely choice to become Stone Mountain's sculptor, for he had no ties to the Confederacy. Born in Idaho territory to a Mormon, polygamous union (his Danish-immigrant father had children with two women who were sisters), he was educated in San Francisco and at the École des Beaux Arts in Paris, where he found additional inspiration by visiting the studio of acclaimed sculptor Auguste Rodin. Borglum remained in Europe for many years before establishing his North American studio. Although Lincoln became and remained Borglum's favorite American hero—he named his only son after the sixteenth president—Borglum came to regard both the Union and the Confederate narratives as important. His seemingly contradictory loyalties can be explained in part by his status as a westerner born after the Civil War as well as by his desire to win commissions as an artist. Borglum identified with the Republican Party and its Progressive wing, which venerated Lincoln as a paragon of honesty and statesmanship. But as a romantic, Borglum believed that soldiers on both sides displayed commitment, courage, and military valor, and his interest in celebrating Civil War heroism corresponded with the national trend toward sectional reconciliation. Plane never doubted her decision to hire Borglum, describing him to the *Atlanta Constitution* in 1915 as "the greatest American sculptor" and adding that "he combines with the genius of the artist the patriotic appreciation of what the confederate war has meant to the south, and always will mean." Plane must have been reassured to learn that several years earlier, Borglum's brother, Solon (1868–1922), had sculpted the equestrian statue of John B. Gordon that was placed in front of the Georgia Capitol.[15]

At a meeting with Plane, now the designated president of the Stone Mountain Memorial Association (SMMA), and UDC members, Borglum laid out his specific plan. He would carve Lee, as Plane desired, but he would be on horseback, and the sculptor suggested adding equestrian statues of Stonewall Jackson and possibly Joseph E. Johnston, a sure sign that Johnston's failure to protect Atlanta from General Sherman in 1864 had been forgiven. Borglum also wanted to include groups of infantry, cavalry, and artillery—scores of figures in all. And he would cut into the base of the mountain to create a room dedicated to the UDC to be used by its members for meetings and storage for archives. It would contain an allegorical stone sculpture of a white southern woman to commemorate Confederate womanhood, thereby giving Georgia women a monument to match those erected to Confederate women in South Carolina (1912) and North Carolina (1915). Borglum's grand vision appealed to the Daughters' belief that the Confederacy represented a noble cause led by heroic people, but speakers at the ceremony launching the project, May 20, 1916, emphasized sectional reconciliation. Borglum spoke of "the greatness of the American people," while Judge Emory Speer referenced President William McKinley's commitment to caring for Confederate graves and President Theodore Roosevelt's emphasis on Confederate valor.[16]

Although Plane and Borglum now shared a vision for the mountain and the Atlanta chapter pledged five thousand dollars to fund it, neither the Georgia UDC nor the national group endorsed the plan, believing it too ambitious and costly. At its 1915 annual convention, the Georgia UDC voted against Plane's resolution to provide financial support for the mountain; later that year, the national UDC reached a similar conclusion even though Borglum spoke at the organization's annual gathering in San Francisco. He reported to Plane that the UDC was "heavily obligated" and unwilling to undertake any new work "until their accounts were cleared." Borglum tried to reassure the Daughters that the Venable family would not charge them for use of the mountain, and he suggested that Plane should pursue aid for the project from the State of Georgia. In 1916, the UDC national president again warned Borglum that the organization would not support the project "directly or indirectly," though Plane scored a small victory the following year when the UDC agreed to give the Confederate carving "moral" support and left open the possibility of future financial aid. Plane then sought another avenue for fundraising.[17]

The movement to sculpt Confederate leaders on Stone Mountain corresponded with the rise of the Ku Klux Klan. There are varying accounts about the origins of the twentieth-century Klan, but without question Atlanta's William J. Simmons (1880–1945), a failed businessman and preacher, played a leading role. Simmons recruited men for a meeting to discuss the notion of reviving the Reconstruction-era organization. One of those men was Sam Venable, whose family owned Stone Mountain. Several factors contributed to a climate in which Simmons's followers found this notion attractive. The United States was a rapidly changing nation, with traditional rural life declining as Americans relocated to cities in search of factory and mill jobs, immigration broadening the number of Americans who embraced religious faiths outside of Protestantism, and African Americans making economic and educational progress despite white efforts to prevent such advancement. In sum, white, native-born Americans, including many in Atlanta, worried about their changing world. As historian Nancy MacLean has written, "Declaiming against organized blacks, Catholics, and Jews, along with the insidious encroachments of Bolshevism," the Klan "put itself forward as the country's most militant defender of 'pure Americanism.' It stood for patriotism, 'old-time religion,' and conventional morality. . . . The message took." As Imperial Wizard of the Klan, Simmons moved into the Imperial Palace, a mansion on Atlanta's Peachtree Street.[18]

The climate of ethnic and racial prejudice contributed to the lynching of Leo Frank (1884–1915) in Marietta, Georgia, in August 1915. Born in Texas and raised in Brooklyn, New York, Frank, who was Jewish, was serving as the manager of an Atlanta pencil factory where a young female worker was raped and murdered. Frank was implicated in the murder by the factory's African American janitor and by testimony from young women employees that he had engaged in sexually suggestive behavior. Frank was sentenced to death. Many observers believed that Frank had been a victim of anti-Semitism, raising questions about the fairness of the trial that led Governor John Slaton (1866–1955) to commute Frank's death sentence to life in prison. On August 16, 1915, a crowd of vigilantes seized Frank from the state prison farm in Milledgeville and lynched him the

next day. It was a seminal moment in the state's history, garnering national publicity and painting Georgia as a place of intolerance and vigilan-
tism. President William Howard Taft called the lynching "a damnable outrage . . . that makes a decent man sick."[19]

Three months later, on Thanksgiving night, November 15, 1915, Simmons, with the permission of the Venable family, led a group of fifteen men
to the top of Stone Mountain, where they burned a cross and the Klan was
reborn. The *Atlanta Constitution* described the "impressive services" on
the mountain and declared that Simmons's "invisible empire" would seek
to bring about "the betterment of mankind." On December 4, the State of
Georgia granted a charter to the Knights of the Ku Klux Klan, an organization dedicated to promoting the interests of white Protestant men. In addition to terrorizing African Americans, who Simmons believed had become
increasingly "uppity," the new Klan opposed immigrants, Catholics, and
Jews. Like the Klan of the Reconstruction era, the new Klan's membership
was at least partially secret. Estimates vary, but the second Klan probably
included several million members nationwide and had more members in
the North than in the South as a consequence of its message of nativism,
Protestant religious values, and Prohibition.[20]

The Klan attracted close to fifteen thousand members in Atlanta and
made money by selling white robes and other regalia produced by a local factory. It sold copies of a weekly newspaper, the *Searchlight*, that combined populist support for increased wages for coal miners and public
aid for poor (white) children with a message of racism and intolerance. It
backed the deportation of "undesirable" foreigners and warned about an
international conspiracy of Jews and the menace posed by the Pope and his
followers. The *Searchlight* urged employers to dismiss Catholic employees
and exhorted Atlantans to boycott businesses owned by Catholics.[21]

The KKK showed its paramilitary side when it participated in local
marches and "klonvocations." Wearing blue capes bearing the Klan coat
of arms and shiny helmets with visors to conceal their identities, the Klan
marched in an Atlanta Labor Day parade in 1922. Speaking in Rome,
Georgia, the preceding month, Governor Thomas Hardwick (1872–
1944) argued in vain that the KKK should dispense with its masks, noting that the group had been implicated in "reports of tarring and feather-
ings, whippings and other outrages [against African Americans] around
Atlanta." Klonvocations held in Atlanta culminated in cross burnings on

Stone Mountain. In 1923, an estimated ten thousand Klansmen attended a convention in Atlanta, and a procession of twenty-five hundred automobiles clogged roads to the mountain, where Klan members prayed and then lit an enormous cross at midnight. To emphasize their pseudopatriotism, Klan members sang "America" while Old Glory flew nearby.[22]

Klan recruitment efforts benefitted locally and nationally from the phenomenal success of the film *The Birth of a Nation*. The silent film directed by D. W. Griffith (1875–1948) told the story of the Civil War and Reconstruction, breaking new ground in American cinema through its use of narrative, lighting, camera angles, and editing. Though based on the novels of Thomas Dixon, the film differs in one significant way: while the novels and stage play focus on Reconstruction, the movie also includes the war. It follows two families, the southern Camerons and the northern Stonemans, who lose sons in battle, thus emphasizing the shared suffering of both sections of the country. Both regions mourn the death of President Abraham Lincoln, represented as a friend to the South. By the end of the film, a double wedding unites the two families, leading audiences to believe that North and South are united at the end of Reconstruction. In fact, the process of reconciliation was much longer and far more ambiguous.[23]

The film is historically inaccurate in many ways, and Griffith's depiction of race made the film controversial even in 1915. In contrast to the film's depictions, although African Americans held a considerable number of seats in the South Carolina legislature, they never dominated the state; black legislators did not make legalizing interracial marriage a legislative priority; and there is no evidence to support the contention that black men commonly raped white women. And many of the black men in the film were portrayed by white actors in blackface. Yet Griffith represented the Ku Klux Klan as a heroic organization that protected white womanhood from the advances of predatory blacks. Ben Cameron's rescue of Elsie Stoneman (played by the beautiful Lillian Gish) from the evil mulatto politician Silas Lynch is one the film's dramatic highlights.[24]

*The Birth of a Nation* debuted in New York on March 3, 1915, with ushers outfitted in either Confederate or Union dress. In the coming days, sellout crowds offered rave reviews. Early reaction to the film helped to create interest in other cities, including Atlanta, where the film opened on December 6—just two days after the Klan had received its charter from the state. Moreover, President Woodrow Wilson, who was born in Virginia and raised primarily in Augusta, Georgia, previewed the film at the White House before its release, and it was shown to members of Congress and the U.S. Supreme Court at the National Press Club in Washington, D.C.[25]

African Americans tried in vain to stop the release of the film, understanding that its use of melodrama and its false interpretation of history could lead to racial hatred and even reprisals against blacks nationwide. Despite an appeal before the National Board of Censors, the NAACP failed to stop the film. In Atlanta, African American minister Henry H. Proctor asked for help from the sympathetic Evangelical Ministers' Association, but local censors ignored the clergymen and endorsed the film after viewing it in Macon. A group of white progressive ministers also appealed to Mayor James G. Woodward (1845–1923), expressing the view that the movie would lead directly to another race riot. Representing the interests of "a large number of ministers of the city," the Reverend Dunbar Ogden of Central Presbyterian Church and the Reverend C. B. Wilmer of St. Luke's Episcopal, along with a leading industrialist, John J. Eagan, asked Mayor Woodward to interdict the film. He ignored the request.[26]

Audience reaction to *The Birth of a Nation* at least partially confirmed the fears of those who had tried to suppress it in Atlanta. Although the film did not lead to rioting, it stirred up strong emotions. After attending the film's premiere, where music was provided by a thirty-piece orchestra, reviewer Ned McIntosh falsely claimed in the *Atlanta Constitution* that the film was educational and was "vindicated by historical facts." He also declared Griffith the "American Homer" and opined that the film was designed to "arouse your emotions, and it does it." Trumpet blasts from the orchestra pit signaled the big-screen arrival of robed KKK men who dashed "at breakneck speed" and ultimately "rescue[d] women and homes and civilization from an unspeakable curse." *Atlanta Journal* critic Ward Greene was equally sensational: "The negro mob grows wilder and wilder, the white-shrouded riders are tearing nearer and nearer. Then, with a mighty blast from the bugle, they sweep into the town and with a shattering volley hammer into the crowd." At the end of the premiere, many audience members rose from their seats to cheer, while audiences at some subsequent showings applauded every time the KKK appeared onscreen. Greene concluded, "There has been nothing to equal it—nothing. Not as a motion picture, nor a play, nor a book." Viewers of the film were "mellowed into a deeper and purer understanding of the fires through which your forefathers battled to make this South of yours a nation reborn."[27]

In addition to being shown twice daily during its three-week run, *The Birth of a Nation* was featured at a special December 13 afternoon matinee for one hundred men from the Soldier's Home. Plane, who admired the film and its depiction of the KKK, also arranged for a showing under auspices of the UDC, with Confederate flags sold at the event and a percentage of the proceeds benefiting the Stone Mountain carving. In advertising the occasion, one newspaper suggested that the film would help "southern women and their children to perpetuate the history, so dear to their hearts." *The Birth of a Nation* ended its run in Atlanta on Christmas Night, after breaking all of the city's records for attendance at theatrical events.[28]

Released fifty years after the end of the Civil War, *The Birth of a Nation* helped to solidify an image of the war as a conflict between sections that ended with white people patching up their differences and keeping black people in a subservient place. The promoters of Stone Mountain's Confederate carving hoped to enshrine what they saw as the nobility of the Lost Cause in a way that would further that effort, yet despite the film's success, the project struggled financially. Like the national UDC, Georgia's UDC declined to provide monetary support, and the U.S. entry into World War I in 1917 essentially halted the Stone Mountain effort, as some of Borglum's workmen entered military service and local women turned their attention toward raising money for Liberty Bonds and volunteering with the Red Cross. Assuring Plane that the project would eventually be finished, Borglum returned to his home in Stamford, Connecticut, to wait for peacetime.[29]

True to his word, Borglum returned to Atlanta after the war ended and began conferring with Plane and Venable about organizational changes. In 1919, with the enthusiastic backing of the SMMA's executive committee, Plane proposed adding a second Stone Mountain monument depicting an American soldier of the Great War. Plane insisted that the statue would represent American patriotism and thus must reflect "*all American* soldiers" regardless of region and include an eagle with its wings spread above the soldier. Plane hoped that the new monument would help with fundraising for the Confederate mountain carving. Borglum, however, rejected the idea of a second carving on the grounds that it would "conflict with the present design." With money increasingly tight, Borglum dropped plans for a UDC room at the base of the mountain, though he continued to discuss possible additions to the carving, including one that would honor the role of the Confederate navy, as well as the construction of a memorial hall.[30]

In 1923, a dramatic change in leadership occurred after the elderly Plane stepped down. Another UDC leader took her place in the short term but was then replaced as president of the executive committee by Hollins Randolph. The Virginia-born Randolph (1872–1938), a descendant of Thomas Jefferson, had moved to Atlanta in the 1890s and become a successful corporate lawyer. He was a new type of leader for the mountain, a self-assured representative of the business class who rejected the idea of women volunteers as stewards of important public projects. Tapping into Atlanta's long-standing dedication to business culture, Randolph imposed a new organizational structure on the mountain effort. Similar to Forward Atlanta, an initiative begun by the city's Chamber of Commerce in the 1920s, Randolph's plan would advertise Stone Mountain and Atlanta as destinations for tourism and business. Randolph opened an office in the Hurt Building downtown and hired a publicity director, Rogers Winter. In addition to a small executive committee, Randolph appointed fifty men and women to a board of directors. Borglum, who had a cordial relationship with Plane and Venable, quickly formed a negative opinion of Randolph, whose officious manner the sculptor and others found off-putting. Plane and Venable deferred to Borglum as Stone Mountain's artist and visionary; Randolph viewed Borglum as an employee of what was now known as the Stone Mountain Confederate Monumental Association (SMCMA). Having already invested considerable time in the mountain project, Borglum asked for and received a contract from Randolph. It called for the sculptor to finish a central group of carvings to represent Lee, Jackson, and Jefferson Davis (who had replaced Johnston as the third proposed figure) by June 1926 and to receive a payment of $250,000.[31]

Despite their uneasy relationship, Borglum and Randolph proceeded with efforts to promote the mountain carving. In 1923, Borglum arranged for Randolph and several others to meet with President Warren G. Harding during his visit to Augusta, Georgia. Randolph appreciated Borglum's willingness to use his Republican political contacts to arrange the meeting, and Harding pledged his support for the project. Randolph and Borglum also worked together to raise money. A "Founders Roll" allowed families to donate one thousand dollars and have their names carved on a tablet at the memorial hall, and among those who signed up were John B. Gordon's grandson, Hugh Gordon Jr., and William Gibbs McAdoo, a

Marietta native then living in Los Angeles. McAdoo was married to Eleanor Wilson, daughter of the former president, and had served as treasury secretary during the recent war. He had also sought the 1920 Democratic nomination for president but lost to James Cox and was weighing another presidential bid. He sent his contribution to Randolph in July 1923 along with a letter in which he invoked the Confederacy, Christian civilization, patriotism, and the "indissoluble union of indestructible states." Despite receiving the KKK's endorsement, McAdoo was unsuccessful in his 1924 quest for the Democratic nomination, losing out to John W. Davis.[32]

Although the Klan had its critics, the early 1920s represented the high-water mark of its popularity, and all of the principal players in the Stone Mountain effort were Klan members or sympathizers. Venable was a founding member and a true believer, while Plane, Randolph, and Borglum were more opportunistic in their support. Eager to maintain a position of importance in Georgia's Democratic Party, which had Klan ties, Randolph increased the Klan's visibility in the SMCMA by appointing Nathan Bedford Forrest (1872–1931), former head of the Georgia SCV and now the leader of the state's Klan, to the fifty-member board of directors. Prior to his appointment to the board, Forrest had made small financial contributions to the mountain effort, with the money coming not only from Georgia Klan donors but also from several in Kansas. Like Randolph, Plane hoped to tap into the Klan's considerable recruitment and fundraising network, dangling the possibility of a bronze statue of a Klansman at the mountain's base. Borglum, too, probably hoped that the Klan would help fund the mountain carving. In addition, he admired the group's emphasis on what he saw as traditional, rural, Protestant values, including Prohibition, and feared "imported isms"—a euphemism for radical political views. Although he had Jewish friends, Borglum held anti-Semitic views common to Klansmen. Whatever his motives, Borglum was both a member and an activist. On December 20, 1922, the *Atlanta Constitution* reported that he had called on President Harding at the White House and introduced him to the new Imperial Wizard of the Klan, Hiram W. Evans (1881–1966) of Texas. Harding himself was rumored to be a Klan sympathizer. Borglum, who had once supported Theodore Roosevelt's Progressive Party, dabbled in a variety of political movements during his long public career. Understanding his impulsive tendencies and constantly shifting political leanings, Borglum's friends wished that he would stay focused on art.[33]

The fundraising effort for Stone Mountain expanded with the creation of the Children's Founders Roll: boys and girls under age sixteen could donate one dollar and receive a bronze medal designed by Borglum. The campaign would culminate on January 19, 1925, the 118th anniversary of Lee's birth. This national campaign served the dual purpose of raising money and invoking Confederate memory. Like the Founders Roll, it attracted support from political leaders: South Carolina congressman John J. McSwain enrolled his child.[34]

By far the most ambitious fundraising campaign involved the sale of commemorative half-dollar coins. In 1924, both houses of Congress gave unanimous approval to a bill authorizing an issue of five million coins—ten times more than any previous commemorative effort—as a "memorial to the Valor of the Soldier of the South." Featuring figures of Lee and Jackson on horseback, each coin cost fifty cents to produce but was sold for a dollar, with the proceeds benefiting the Stone Mountain carving. Both the unanimous vote in Congress and the size of the issue suggest the backers' success in garnering national publicity for the project despite its associations with the Klan. Indeed, Borglum bragged to a friend that he "got a Republican Congress to strike for the South a memorial coin."[35]

Begun as a local project, the Stone Mountain Confederate carving had achieved national standing. Borglum gave interviews to local and national publications in which he expressed his artistic vision and explored the engineering challenges of implementing it. On August 12, 1923, readers of the *Atlanta Constitution* learned that the figure of Lee mounted on his horse, Traveler, would tower higher than the city's seventeen-story Candler building. *Scientific American* explained to its subscribers that Borglum used a huge projecting lamp to illuminate his design, which was painted onto the mountain at night. During the daytime, workers suspended by ropes drilled holes in rows six inches apart and used cutting tools to remove stone and create the sculpture. And before the carving had even begun, work crews had removed tons of loose boulders.[36]

On January 19, 1924, Borglum completed Lee's head and the SMCMA staged a carefully choreographed unveiling. With national attention focused on Atlanta, SMCMA leaders wanted to present an image of the city as a place of patriotism and decorum and a good place to do business. They also no doubt hoped to erase from the public mind the memories of Frank's lynching nearly ten years earlier. To that end, the invocation was given by Rabbi David Marx (1872–1962), who had comforted Frank's widow and Atlanta's Jewish community in the aftermath of Frank's death. Attendees at the 1924 event included governors and former governors from Georgia and surrounding states, and in addition to Marx, they heard Ashby Jones, pastor of Atlanta's Ponce de Leon Avenue Baptist Church. His father had been chaplain at Washington College in Lexington, Virginia, when Lee served as its president after the Civil War. In addition, Jones was known as a man of temperate views, and Randolph wanted to protect Atlanta's image by avoiding a strident Lost Cause address despite the carving's subject matter. And indeed, after praising Borglum's "genius," Jones described Lee as representing "all that was best in the Confederacy"—a man who disapproved of slavery and secession, knew when to fight as well as when to surrender, and had no bitterness after the war. In what many attendees viewed as the most poignant moment in the day's festivities, Borglum carried the frail, ninety-five-year-old Plane to the staging area. Plane gave the signal to reveal the statue, and Borglum announced, "The head of Lee is on Stone Mountain" as the crowd roared its approval.[37]

After the successful unveiling, however, the uneasy alliance among Stone Mountain principals unraveled. Although the Georgia UDC endorsed the mountain project in 1924, thereby encouraging individual chapters to lend financial support, Randolph began reorganizing the SMCMA executive committee, replacing most members of the UDC with his friends. One such ally was Mildred Lewis Rutherford, who became a vice president of the group. Rutherford, who lived in Athens, was a former Georgia Division president and historian for the national UDC. Randolph and his closest advisers, Winter and Reuben Arnold, legal counsel as well as Randolph's brother-in-law, now had firm control of the organization. Venable protested the changes by resigning from the executive committee. Borglum disliked Randolph's actions, especially his disregard for the UDC, but kept working on the mountain, turning his attention to carving Jackson's head.[38]

Money woes continued to plague the SMCMA as fundraising efforts remained inadequate. Borglum ran up debts with local companies including Beck and Gregg Hardware, Western Union, and the Black and White Cab Company and complained that he was not being paid in a timely fashion. Randolph retorted that the sculptor was not spending enough time on the mountain, probably resenting Borglum's September 1924 trip to South Dakota to discuss the proposed Mount Rushmore carving. In February 1925, Borglum met privately in Washington, D.C., with Calvin Coolidge, who had become president after Harding's death in 1923. In a statement released to the press, Borglum stated that funds for the Confederate carvings were "exhausted" and that the SMCMA had failed to keep him informed of its proceedings. Borglum advocated for the creation of a national committee to oversee the mountain, a plan he had first suggested to the executive committee in 1924. In Atlanta, Venable complained to Randolph about the salaries paid to Winter and others, while Winter wrote in his diary that Borglum and Venable were a "pair of hyenas" engaged in "a plot to destroy the whole existing administration of the Memorial." For his part, Borglum believed that Randolph and his backers were part of a conspiracy to seize control of the project.[39]

Outraged by Borglum's behavior, the executive committee voted to dismiss him. Thrilled to be rid of a man he regarded as a prima donna, Randolph planned to hire another sculptor to complete the carving using Borglum's models, but several factors thwarted this plan. First, after learning of his dismissal, Borglum destroyed his models and burned his sketches, a violation of his contract with the SMCMA. When Randolph sought a warrant for his arrest, the sculptor, in the midst of delivering a lecture to a UDC group, left the meeting and fled across the state line into North Carolina, barely evading law enforcement. Winter noted in his diary, "The city seethes with excitement over the news." The *Atlanta Journal* carried the headline, "Officers of Two States Seek Sculptor Gutzon Borglum while Armed Guards Patrol Stone Mountain Property."[40]

Second, the SMCMA waged a public relations campaign to discredit Borglum, but it did not produce the desired result. Winter quickly printed twenty thousand copies of a pamphlet, *Reasons Why It Was Necessary to Dismiss Gutzon Borglum*, that included a series of charges against the sculptor, some of them baseless or exaggerated. Winter accused Borglum of "gross neglect" of his work, "false statements to the press," and "numerous attempts to use the Memorial for personal profit." Winter distributed the pamphlet to government officials and civic groups, including UDC chapters, and the *Atlanta Journal* printed Randolph and Winter's press releases.[41]

Randolph underestimated Borglum's popularity. The sculptor had support from the Atlanta UDC, which called for arbitration between the artist and the SMCMA; from the Venables, including Sam and his sister, Elizabeth Venable Mason; and from many other Atlantans who admired the sculptor. Oglethorpe University had given Borglum an honorary degree the previous June, lauding him as "sculptor, preserver of loyalties, moulder of mountains and men." Women's clubs and civic organizations remained loyal to Borglum, who took them seriously, answered their letters, and spoke at their meetings. The *Atlanta Constitution* printed Borglum's side of the story. When the sculptor was arrested in North Carolina, he was released on bond and went home to Connecticut. Georgia governor Clifford Walker (1877–1954), unhappy over negative publicity, hoped the entire sorry mess would disappear from the headlines, privately urging Arnold and Randolph to drop the charges. They ultimately did so, but the damage had been done. One year after an opening ceremony designed to reveal Atlanta as a center for business and tourism, the city was deeply divided over the mountain, and those divisions were reported in the national media. "Chisels on Stone Mountain Cast Aside," read one headline in the *New York Times*. Another article revealed that "sober-minded citizens here have realized the harm the controversy has been doing the State and particularly the memorial cause."[42]

Two months after Borglum's firing, Helen Plane died, and her funeral became a politicized event. Eager to be seen as respecting Plane's legacy even after dismissing her sculptor and removing most members of the UDC from the Stone Mountain governing body, Randolph insisted that the executive committee and the larger board of directors attend the funeral at St. Mark's Church as a group. Members of the UDC also sat together at the service, and the Atlanta Chapter subsequently passed a resolution praising her dedication to Confederate commemoration and her work "to give to the South in perpetuity the conception of Gutzon Borglum of a panorama to be carved on the scarp of Stone Mountain." Plane was buried in Macon's Rose Hill Cemetery next to her long-dead husband, a location that prevented her grave from hosting visits by warring factions seeking to invoke her memory.[43]

Randolph hoped to end the controversy over Borglum by quickly announcing the appointment of a new sculptor, Augustus Lukeman (1872–1935). Though a resident of New York, Lukeman had been born in the Confederate capital, Richmond, Virginia, a point the SMCMA was happy to make. His previous commissions included statues of Christopher Columbus in New York and Confederate women in Raleigh, North Carolina. At the meeting where the executive committee voted to hire Lukeman, Rev. Jones, who had spoken at the dedication ceremony the previous year, and Dr. Plato Durham of Emory University had sought to postpone the decision for two weeks until one last effort was made to reconcile with Borglum. Randolph's friends voted them down.[44]

The final problem with Randolph's plan to replace Borglum involved the expectation that Confederate heritage groups would fall into line. They did not, at least initially. Borglum's firing left these groups in a bind. In May, the UCV held its annual convention in Dallas, Texas, with the Stone Mountain situation on the minds of many. Members introduced a resolution demanding representation on the SMCMA's executive committee. Randolph addressed the group, as did Borglum, now living in Texas as he pursued projects in the West. Randolph offered reassurance; Borglum insisted that "unfriendly hands have seized the great memorial." Moreover, rumors circulated that a newly designed mountain carving might include the figure of a Union soldier. In the end, the UCV compromised: its members decided to "keep hands off the Stone Mountain memorial dispute" by tabling the resolution calling for representation on the SMCMA executive committee but promised to sell coins to support the carving. The UCV condemned the idea of including a Union soldier, forcing the SMCMA to issue a press release declaring that there had never been any discussion of including Union soldiers on the mountain. Despite the UCV's endorsement of the coin campaign, the fracas over Borglum's firing clearly hurt sales: Winter admitted in his diary on May 25, 1925, that "The Atlanta coin campaign is dragging."[45]

Randolph expected UDC leaders to defer to him; instead, the Daughters went on the offensive against Randolph and the executive committee during a tumultuous state convention in Sandersville, Georgia, on October 27–29. The previous April, after Randolph refused to consider her suggestion of arbitration to resolve his dispute with Borglum, Georgia Division president Ruby Grace (1873–1939) advocated that the UDC withhold financial support for the Confederate carving until the group was satisfied with the SMCMA's management of the operation. The UDC's Atlanta chapter immediately endorsed her action, but the leadership of the SMCMA cut Grace from its board of directors until she backed down. She refused.[46]

Grace then published a pamphlet, *Reasons Why the UDC Should With Hold Funds from the Stone Mountain Association*, in which she declared that the mountain was "one of the dearest ambitions" of their organization and criticized Randolph for failing to heed the UDC's and Durham and Jones's efforts to seek a compromise with Borglum. The pamphlet also addressed legal, logistical, and financial problems. Lukeman's vision for the mountain would require more space than Venable had granted in 1916. Grace urged UDC chapters to discontinue financial support for the SMCMA until issues regarding the mountain were resolved. On the personal side, Grace expressed her feelings in a private letter: "I am sorry matters in regard to Stone Mountain have not worked out to the satisfaction of us all. I feel very unhappy."[47]

Grace began her president's report to the Georgia UDC's 1925 annual convention with updates about the Soldier's Home (now employing a nurse, with regular visits from a physician) and scholarships (forty-two thousand dollars raised in the past year), before plunging into the controversial topic of Stone Mountain. She accused the SMCMA of financial mismanagement, of failing to consult with members of the UDC, and of excluding them from the executive committee. At stake was the principle of whether the UDC could be eliminated from the commemorative effort it had begun: "The time has passed when a few big business men or smart lawyers can put the women of Georgia to picking blackberries without giving an assurance as to what use the blackberries will be put when picked." Therefore, she argued, the Daughters should not support the memorial coin campaign. According to one newspaper account, "fiery speeches on both sides" ensued. Betty Cobb of Carrollton led the opposition to Grace, arguing in favor of continued support for the coin campaign. The proceedings became "one of the bitterest fights ever seen in a U.D.C. convention" when it was revealed that Cobb was a paid representative of the SMCMA and that she had circulated an unsigned four-page pamphlet before the convention began in which she attacked Grace. Dolly Blount Lamar spoke in favor of Grace, and the motion to withhold support for the mountain carried. Grace's term as president ended with a victory for her position, which constituted both a defense of the UDC's right to a voice in the SMCMA and a direct challenge to its male leadership. Although Grace and Lamar anchored their position to their strongly held views about Stone Mountain, they showed a remarkable willingness to defy conventional gender norms. The mountain carving had provided these women and their colleagues with an empowering public role.[48]

Although Grace and Lamar had the endorsement of the Atlanta chapter and prominent UDC members around the state, their position gradually lost support from Confederate heritage groups, including their own. When the UDC held its 1926 annual state convention in Statesboro, attendees passed a resolution authorizing the Georgia Division to release money collected by individual chapters so that they could make decisions about whether to contribute to the carving. The following year, the Atlanta Ladies Memorial Association gave its support to the SMCMA, and the national SCV endorsed Randolph. Commander in chief Sumter L. Lowry used patronizing language to label Grace and her followers as "a small, willful group, most of them misled and misinformed." *Willful* had been used to describe members of a UDC chapter in Lexington, Virginia, after its members mounted a successful 1922–24 effort to stop Washington and Lee University from replacing the historic Lee Chapel with a larger auditorium-like space intended to hold Lee's tomb. Despite Randolph's victory over the Atlanta Daughters, he acknowledged the talents of his adversaries, writing to Winter that "Mrs. Grace and Mrs. Lamar . . . are smart, as you know."[49]

Grace was correct in pointing out that Randolph now had serious problems with the Venable family. On April 16, 1925, Sam Venable issued a statement that the family would not allow additional space on the mountain to enable Lukeman's plan. Moreover, the Venables' contract with the SMCMA stipulated that all carving had to be completed by 1928.[50] With a new sculptor joining the effort, how much could be accomplished in just three years?

Borglum's firing also led to divisions within the national UDC organization. Rutherford dissented vigorously from Grace and Lamar's position and accepted Randolph's invitation to run the Children's Founders Roll campaign. Rutherford was an educator and former principal of Lucy Cobb Institute in Athens, Georgia, who had founded a local chapter of the UDC and gained even more visibility and influence by serving as historian of the national UDC from 1911 to 1916. Popular throughout the South as both a public speaker and a pamphleteer, Rutherford wanted southern white women to be crusaders for the Lost Cause. For example, in one pamphlet, *Truths of History*, she emphasized the right of sovereign states to leave the Union and the alleged "missionary and educational" benefits of slavery for African Americans. Above all, she wanted UDC members to ensure that textbooks used to teach southern children presented a version of history that reflected her view of events. Confederate soldiers must never be called either "traitors" or "rebels."[51]

Even though Rutherford was a career woman who never married, she believed that women should defer to men, including leadership of the SMCMA, though she may also have taken this stand because she believed that Randolph and others were in the best position to complete the monument. Rutherford, who attended the Sandersville meeting, worked actively to undermine Grace and Lamar's position, writing to Randolph in December 1926 that she wanted other chapters of the UDC, including one in Boston, to "line up with me." Rutherford's efforts paid off. At the national UDC's 1927 General Convention in Charleston, South Carolina, Lamar was nominated as first vice president, next in line to the presidency. However, women who supported the SMCMA, led by Rutherford, nominated another Georgian. Lamar suffered a bitter defeat at the hands of a former ally with whom she had once spoken before the Georgia Legislature in opposition to women's suffrage. In the 1950s, Lamar wrote, "It was a source of sincere regret . . . that Miss Mildred Rutherford deserted us" and joined "the Randolph clique." She added, "Borglum's great vision died hard with him."[52]

With Georgians deeply divided over the future of Stone Mountain, the carving effort nonetheless continued under the leadership of Lukeman. Because Borglum had destroyed his models, Lukeman felt free to "create my own ideas and design a composition." He initially planned to retain Borglum's head of Lee, adding Lee's torso and horse along with equestrian figures of Jackson and Davis. Lukeman also intended to include two color-bearers and six additional generals. As part of its public relations campaign, the SMCMA would allow historical societies and SCV chapters in the South to select the generals as well as provide input on the new preliminary design. Behind the generals, Lukeman planned an army of carvings to represent Confederate infantry, cavalry, and artillery. A memorial hall at the base of the mountain would include the tomb of an unknown soldier and would be dedicated to women of the South. In January 1927, Randolph optimistically suggested that both the sculptor and his foreman were ahead of schedule.[53]

Although the SMCMA undoubtedly found Lukeman easier to work with than the temperamental Borglum, Lukeman was never as well-liked as Borglum had been. Borglum's affiliation with Stone Mountain lasted ten years. During intervals when he resided in the area, his wife, Mary, and two young children lived with him, and both adults were popular figures around town. At the height of the tensions over Borglum's dismissal, Winter admitted in his diary that he was fond of Mary. Lukeman never had the same connection with local people.[54]

Atlantans' tepid response to Lukeman and the Georgia UDC's schism help to explain the public's muted response to the unveiling of Lukeman's version of Lee's head on April 9, 1928, the sixty-third anniversary of the Confederate surrender at Appomattox. Cold, rainy weather soaked the decorations and dampened the spirits of some attendees. The public response may also have been tempered by the mountain's first work-related fatality—a laborer who was killed when a slab of granite hit the platform where he was working. Another complicating factor was the SMCMA's decision to remove Borglum's head of Lee from the mountain shortly before the unveiling of Lukeman's likeness, a departure from Lukeman's initial plan to keep Borglum's version. In an attempt to reduce costs, Lukeman's new plan involved smaller figures. For a time, two heads of Lee graced the mountain—Borglum's larger one wearing a hat and Lukeman's smaller, hatless one. Although Venable took legal action to stop the SMCMA's plans, Borglum's Lee was destroyed a few weeks before the official debut of Lukeman's.[55]

Like the unveiling in 1924, the 1928 event endeavored to present a positive image of Atlanta and the Confederacy to the wider world. In this instance, Randolph chose speakers to represent both the South and the North, and they focused on Lee as signifying the best of America. Discussion of the war as a conflict over constitutional principles gave way to the theme that Lee was the quintessential American hero. The speech by Marcus Beck, associate justice of the Georgia Supreme Court, made only a single reference to the Civil War, calling it "the most splendid page in our history" because it included Lee's name. In contrast, flamboyant New York mayor Jimmy Walker—known for his ties to Tammany Hall, opposition to Prohibition, and rumored affairs with showgirls—had been chosen because he headed the most important city in the North and Randolph wanted to emphasize Atlanta's equivalent role in the South. Walker's speech underscored the theme that all Americans should claim Lee: Walker was "glad to be a citizen of a country that produced a man like General Lee" and insisted that both sides had fought for principle, not for profit. Randolph chose three-year-old Robert E. Lee IV, great-grandson of the general, to signal the unveiling. The festivities included few references to Lukeman, and members of the Georgia UDC avoided the event, though the *Atlanta Journal* reported that Mary Southworth Kimbrough, a "prominent member" of the UDC from Greenwood, Mississippi, attended.[56]

While white people waged a battle for control of the mountain, black people were shut out of the discussion, though they were hired as workmen: according to Mary Borglum, her husband's foreman "depended largely on Negro labor." African Americans were excluded from newspaper coverage of the unveiling and presumably from the event itself, as they had been in 1924, though reporters noted that as Walker was boarding a train to the mountain from an Atlanta rail station, a "small darky ran in front of the cameras just as the shutters clicked," leading Walker to quip, "A total eclipse" before resuming his pose.[57]

Black visitors were not welcomed to the monument. In June 1925, Jesse O. Thomas (1885–1972), field secretary for the National Urban League, complained to Randolph that on a recent visit, he and his friends had wanted to look at the mountain through a telescope available for visitors but were told that "'Niggers' were not allowed" to use it. Thomas noted pointedly, "I am sure this is not the policy of the association since the association is asking colored people to b[u]y [commemorative] coins. Surely one could be permitted to look through an instrument at an object, his money is helping to develop." Randolph sidestepped the issue by responding that the telescope was not located on land controlled by the SMCMA.[58]

In 1928, the Venable family's contract with the SMCMA expired. At the SMCMA's annual meeting, Randolph resigned as president, recognizing that the Venables would refuse to grant more time and space while he remained its leader. Randolph was replaced by G. F. Willis, who had helped to organize the 1919 veterans reunion. Unwavering in its opposition to the male leadership of the SMCMA, the Atlanta UDC passed a resolution in November 1928 recommending that the mountain be returned to the Venables; the Venables, in turn, granted a fifteen-year charter to the UDC to finish the carving. Since neither the SMCMA nor the UDC had the money to carry out the project, the entire operation was thrown into limbo after an effort to get the State of Georgia to take over failed to make headway. In its magazine *Opportunity*, the National Urban League quoted a Pittsburgh newspaper story that celebrated the Confederate sculpture's apparent termination, calling the project a monument to "human slavery and color selfishness."[59]

Borglum never gave up his dream of finishing the carving, however. Friends in Atlanta kept him informed of developments, and he carried on a correspondence with a variety of people in the area, often projecting an image of himself as the victim of evildoers. Lukeman, who had signed on to the project in good faith, died in 1935, opening the door for Borglum's friends to try again to bring him back. In the meantime, Borglum accepted a commission to carve a statue of Alexander Stephens, one of two sculptures to represent Georgia in statuary hall at the U.S. Capitol. Under the auspices of the UDC and paid for by Hattie High (1862–1932), whose home later became Atlanta's eponymous art museum, the statue was unveiled in Washington in 1927. Judge Ernest C. Kontz, representing Atlanta's mayor, gave the dedicatory address, emphasizing that Stephens personified the "spirit of Atlanta" and "never ceased to love the Union," an ironic statement considering that Stephens had served as Confederate vice president. Many prominent members of Atlanta society attended the event, but Borglum did not. In her 1952 biography of her husband, Mary Borglum highlighted the importance of Stone Mountain in winning his contract to carve Mount Rushmore, his most recognized work. But, she added, "the sculpture into which he poured his greatest enthusiasm was undoubtedly the Confederate memorial. It had movement instead of stasis." His friends' efforts to rehire him continued until his death in 1941.[60]

The Atlanta UDC's calls for arbitration between Borglum and the SMCMA and challenge to male authority figures faded from public memory. Rutherford died in 1928, and Grace followed in 1939. Lamar moved on to a less controversial project, a memorial sculpture to poet Sidney Lanier for the Macon Public Library, for which she hired Borglum, and the bust was unveiled in 1929. Borglum did not attend. In 1934, she was elected to serve as historian for the national UDC, the same position Rutherford had held twenty years earlier.[61]

The UDC's membership peaked in Atlanta during the 1920s and then declined. It is difficult to measure the degree to which the Stone Mountain controversy played a role. On the one hand, it certainly did not help. On the other hand, UDC membership fell statewide. UDC chapters' overall membership fell from 8,129 in the 1920s to 3,775 in 1942 and 3,190 in 1960. The UDC's heyday had passed, and a new generation of Georgians would define Civil War memory in the 1930s and thereafter.[62]

Membership in the Ku Klux Klan also declined during this period, dipping from several million in the early 1920s to 350,000 in 1927 and falling further with each passing year. The Klan fell victim to its failed political efforts and the financial and political scandals of its leaders. African Americans, Catholics, Jews, working-class groups, and political progressives worked to undermine its influence. When Hiram Evans became the Klan's national leader in 1922, he moved its headquarters to Washington, D.C. Atlanta's Catholic archdiocese eventually purchased the Klan's Imperial Palace, demolished it, and constructed the Cathedral of Christ the King on the property.[63]

With the onset of the Great Depression in 1929, the Confederate carving on Stone Mountain seemed unlikely to see completion. Helen Plane's vision had fallen victim to institutional squabbling, artistic temper tantrums, sexism, and public fatigue. In the end, the project simply ran out of money—if only temporarily.

# CHAPTER 5

# Artists, Writers, and Historians of the 1920s–1930s

IN THE 1920S AND 1930S, Atlanta entered a new phase of Civil War commemoration. By 1938, seventy-five years after Gettysburg, only about ten thousand veterans of the war remained alive, and the United Daughters of the Confederacy's influence had begun to wane. A new generation of Atlantans took the lead, including the artist Wilbur Kurtz, amateur historians Franklin Garrett and Beverly DuBose, and Margaret Mitchell, a writer for the *Atlanta Journal* who began work on a novel about the war in 1926, when she was recuperating from injuries sustained in an automobile accident. Mitchell spent years meticulously researching newspapers, maps, and manuscripts, part of an effort to produce Civil War history that was "water proof and air tight."[1] She and these other Atlantans thus grounded their interpretations of the war in facts, giving their efforts greater legitimacy than those of the Lost Cause generation, who often glossed over the war's causes and missed many of its long-term consequences. Their interpretations of race, mirroring the generation in which they came of age, did not reflect the reality of slavery and postslavery race relations. And yet, to an extent she never imagined in 1936, when her novel, *Gone with the Wind*, was published, Mitchell influenced public perceptions of the Civil War. The book and especially the movie came to dominate public memory of the Civil War not just in Atlanta but also across the United States and around the world.

By the early twentieth century, most of those who had lived through the war as adults had passed from the scene, leaving only those who had been children to share firsthand experiences. Two remarkable Atlantans did so, in the process breaking new ground. At the height of the Great Depression, Sarah Huff (1856–1943) wrote stories for the *Atlanta Journal Magazine* about the human toll of war that must have resonated with people once again struggling with poverty and hardship. Born in 1856 on her family's farm three miles north of the Atlanta city center off of Marietta Road, Sarah was five years old when her father enlisted in the Confederate military, in which six of his brothers also served. Three of her uncles did not survive the conflict. Huff's reminiscences first appeared serially in the *Atlanta Journal Magazine* between 1934 and 1937 as "My 80 Years in Atlanta" and were published in book form by the Atlanta Public Schools in 1937. In his foreword to the volume, superintendent Willis A. Sutton wrote, "The greatest way to build a future is to use aright the lessons of the past." By describing her father and other soldiers in heroic terms and characterizing slaves as "darkies" who were either loyal or disloyal to their masters, Huff helped to imbue a new generation of schoolchildren with a view of the war that was reminiscent of Mary Gay's memoir published forty years earlier. But Huff's story was far from a typical Lost Cause narrative, revealing times when civilians fell victim to Confederate as well as Union soldiers and drawing conclusions about women's growing self-confidence as a result of their wartime contributions.[2]

*My 80 Years in Atlanta* uncovers the Huff family's problems with day-to-day living. Sarah Huff documented the challenges of obtaining food, clothing, and shoes since it was "impossible to buy anything" in Atlanta late in the war. After Confederate marauders stole the family's hogs, her mother brought their chickens into her bedroom for safekeeping. Sarah remembered smallpox epidemics that swept the city, including one that occurred in 1865–66, efforts to vaccinate the local population, and her family's concerns about the safety of the vaccine. She recalled the resilience of her mother and other women and how they took a larger role in church affairs after the war, even leading the congregation in prayer, something that would previously have been unthinkable.[3]

But Huff's most compelling anecdotes involve the fighting in and near the city and civilians' harrowing lives in the midst of it. She recalled the Confederate army marching down Marietta Street and the noise from the nearby Battle of Peachtree Creek on July 20, 1864. When military authorities subsequently ordered the family to leave their home, they moved to a cottage on Railroad Street, near one of the city's major thoroughfares. There, Huff witnessed "ominous, black-covered ambulances which made their slow, pain-laden way up Decatur Street" to the military hospitals following the Battle of Atlanta on July 22. Her twelve-year-old brother, John, hoping to alleviate the men's suffering, followed the wagons, fanning away swarms of black flies. "We could see the bleeding wounds and glazing eyes of the wounded," Sarah remembered, "and every ambulance left a thin trickle of blood in the dust of the street." The Huffs were among the thousands of Atlantans trapped in the city during the bombardment in July and August, and they found shelter in the basement of an abandoned flour mill owned by Richard Peters, one of Atlanta's wealthiest citizens. After five weeks, the shelling stopped, and the family fled to the town of Social Circle, where they had relatives.[4]

Huff's descriptions of the war's aftermath present a bleak picture for whites and a narrative of liberation for blacks. Her family returned to Atlanta in December 1864, after William T. Sherman abandoned the city and began his March to the Sea. Although their home remained standing, they were shocked by the changes they encountered. Packs of hungry dogs roamed the city, and Sarah and her brother walked the battlefields, picking up bullets and bits of lead to sell and counting the frozen carcasses of dead horses. One of the Huff family slaves ran away with his son, although another slave, Charlotte, stayed until after the war. Though Huff couched the slaves' departure as part of their reduced circumstances, she unwittingly testified to black liberation.[5]

By the time of her death, Huff, like Mary Gay, had become a local celebrity. Huff served as historian for the Atlanta Pioneer Women's Society, and in this capacity, her name appears on the society's monument erected in Piedmont Park in 1938. A two-sided bronze tablet attached to a boulder, the monument features the figure of a woman at a spinning wheel on one side and the words "To Honor the Atlanta Women of the Sixties and to Keep Alive the Traditions of the South" and "Lest We Forget" on the other. When her family's ninety-nine-year-old house ("Atlanta's oldest residential landmark") was demolished in 1954 to make way for a toy factory, many observers commented on the end of an era.[6]

Even more remarkable than Huff's writing is that of Sam Small (1851–1931). Born in Knoxville, Tennessee, Small moved to Atlanta with his family as a ten-year-old boy and witnessed the city's rise as a wartime boomtown. He joined the Confederate army reserve corps in the final months of the war, when he was just fourteen. His family subsequently left Atlanta, but Small returned in 1875 as a professional journalist with the *Atlanta Constitution*. Problems with drinking led him to embrace religion, and he rebranded himself as the Reverend Sam Small, became a Prohibitionist and served as a chaplain in the Spanish-American War. By the time he wrote a series of articles about Atlanta history for the *Constitution* in 1925 and 1926, Small was in his seventies, and his association with the newspaper had spanned fifty years.[7]

Small's reminiscences are notable for the clarity of his prose and the candor of his message, which took direct aim at Lost Cause interpretations of the war. Although he assumed a folksy manner, as if recounting stories to his grandchildren, Small nonetheless provided a realistic, surprisingly modern interpretation of events. In his first story, "by way of prelude," he included a picture of a slave auction house on Whitehall Street—not the symbol that most writers of the era chose to represent the Old South. Small wrote forthrightly about the war's origins: "The existence of negro slavery in the southern states, as a legalized and protected institution, was the basic cause." He noted that the prewar South included men who favored gradual emancipation, but the economic realities of the plantation system eliminated this strategy as a viable political path. Meanwhile, northern politicians instilled a free-labor message in their region's voters, and "the election of Abraham Lincoln as president in 1860 turned the scales." He also correctly noted that Unionism persisted in Georgia and especially in Atlanta during the war and that some individuals had accurately predicted that the Confederacy would not prevail.[8]

Although Small offered praise for the fortitude of Atlanta's civilians and the talents of its "wise and resourceful" wartime mayor, James Calhoun, he did not adhere strictly to the Atlanta-as-victim narrative. He acknowledged the Confederacy's internal collapse, pointing out that wartime inflation and scarcity led to difficulty obtaining food as well as soaring prices and that the number of Confederate army deserters grew as the war progressed. Small offered few details about his personal experiences, but he did mention that his family, like others, improvised by making goods they would have purchased in better times, including hats they created by braiding palmetto leaves and combs whittled from wood. He described the siege as "harassing and destructive. Homes and lives were in continuous jeopardy." During one interval of quiet, the Small family slipped away to the south and became refugees in the town of Griffin. Small denounced Jefferson Davis's decision to replace General Joseph Johnston with General John Bell Hood on the grounds that Johnston's departure emboldened Sherman.[9]

Unlike most white writers of the 1920s, Small interpreted the Reconstruction period as a time not of tragedy but of opportunity. In "Reconstruction," he wrote that "the war had demonstrated the strategic position of Atlanta in the southeastern states. . . . The work of rebuilding the city was prosecuted with energy inspired by necessity and by the faith that a new era of prosperity must follow the restoration of the national peace." According to Small, the era concluded with two important outcomes for Atlanta: its success in wresting the state capital away from Milledgeville after "one of the hottest popular contests the state had known for several generations," and the establishment of white supremacy in the postslavery era.[10] Published in the city's leading newspaper, Small's work serves as a reminder that the Lost Cause had critics even among prominent Atlantans.

Among those who tried to save the Huff family home was Wilbur G. Kurtz (1882–1967), twentieth-century Atlanta's most persistent advocate for saving local Civil War sites. His focus on mapping battlefields and careful research into wartime history, including interviews with survivors and their descendants, led to renewed interest in Atlanta's wartime past and a more precise understanding of some of the events that took place.[11]

Born in Oakland, Illinois, to a bank clerk father and a housekeeping mother, Kurtz developed an early interest in the Civil War. He grew up hearing stories about how the war had directly touched his community: Ulysses S. Grant had mustered in his volunteer regiment in 1861 just a few miles away from Oakland, and three years later, violence erupted in nearby Charleston, the seat of Coles County, when Union soldiers on leave fought a local group of Peace Democrats, resulting in several injuries and deaths. Some of Kurtz's earliest memories involved Grant's 1885 death, as not only did church bells toll to honor the former president, but Kurtz's father, George, mounted a croquet ball on a broomstick and spent an hour striking a bell as a personal tribute. Kurtz's family moved to Greencastle, Indiana, by the time he became a teenager, and there he attended Memorial Day celebrations that offered him opportunities to speak with Union veterans. Kurtz later moved to Chicago, where he took classes at the Art Institute and supported himself by working as an illustrator, engraver, and draftsman specializing in architectural drawings.[12]

Because many Civil War veterans from Indiana and Illinois had fought in the western theater, Kurtz maintained a special interest in the battlefields of Georgia and Tennessee. In 1903, he attended a Confederate reunion in Chattanooga, where he chatted with veterans and visited Chickamauga, Missionary Ridge, and Lookout Mountain, among other battlefields. From there, he traveled to Atlanta and interviewed William Fuller, the railroad conductor who helped to capture James Andrews and the Union raiders who participated in a failed 1862 attempt to sabotage the Western and Atlantic Railroad. Kurtz made the study of this event his life's work, eventually returning to Atlanta to interview survivors of the raid. During the 1903 visit, Kurtz met and fell in love with Captain Fuller's daughter, Annie Laurie, and they married in 1911. Kurtz lived in Atlanta for the rest of his life, alternating professional success as a commercial artist with periods of unemployment but always maintaining an interest in the Civil War. Despite his status as a Yankee transplant, his marriage gained him acceptance into the city's community of writers and amateur historians.[13]

During the 1920s, Kurtz painted scenes of Atlanta before, during, and after the war for corporate and private clients. Friends described him as a "quiet, unassuming man," and his paintings, including those depicting the Battle of Atlanta, have a charming quality that reflects his personality. He did not paint the hard reality of war; instead, typically working in watercolor, he produced colorful, detailed, works that often presented southern themes in ways that invoked nostalgia for bygone days. Slaves are portrayed as simple but dignified, a contrast to the cartoonish characterizations often seen in popular culture of the time. Kurtz's first major commission for a historical painting came from the Atlanta Woman's Club, which hung *The Old South* (1921) in its headquarters. The painting features an antebellum white-columned mansion with figures representing white people in a stagecoach on one side of the painting and a slave driving a wagon filled with cotton on the other. In 1927, the Atlanta Chamber of Commerce commissioned *Atlanta from the Past to the Future*, which features horses and a locomotive in the foreground and skyscrapers, highways, and an airplane in the background. These paintings presented a history of the city that elite white people held dear: the Old South as a halcyon era of serenity and order and Atlanta as a rail hub that grew to regional and national importance during and after the Civil War. Over time, Kurtz's corporate clients included Coca-Cola and Rich's Department

Store. As his reputation grew, Kurtz won commissions in other Georgia cities and in neighboring states.[14]

In 1933, the High Museum of Art held an exhibition of Kurtz's watercolors focused on Atlanta's early history, revealing the artist's careful attention to historical accuracy. In addition to depicting the arrival of the first train in 1842 and the city's first post office, Kurtz included *Weighing Cotton*, which showed a scene from Ellerslie in South Georgia. His audiences expected to see cotton in any depiction of the Old South, but Kurtz wanted to be clear that this image represented rural Georgia rather than Fulton County, where the relatively high elevation meant that cotton was not grown. The *Atlanta Constitution's* review of the exhibition called Kurtz a "genius" whose paintings deserved "a place in any art museum in the country."[15]

In addition to his artwork, Kurtz's writings strengthened his association with the war in Atlantans' minds. Kurtz began publishing articles in Atlanta's two major newspapers, the *Constitution* and the *Journal* (as well as its *Sunday Magazine*) shortly after moving to Atlanta. He initially focused on the Andrews Raid, describing both the locomotive chase and the effort to obtain the locomotive *Texas* and to display it in Atlanta. On May 7, 1911, Kurtz applauded the Atlanta City Council's recent decision to spend five thousand dollars to move and renovate the locomotive but argued that Atlanta had not done enough to preserve its Civil War past, pointing out that a monument honoring Union general James McPherson near where he died in July 1864 was one of the city's few reminders of events during that pivotal year.[16]

Kurtz later became closely associated with efforts to improve the Atlanta Cyclorama. A circular painting of the Battle of Atlanta executed by German artists in Milwaukee during the 1880s, it had originally been intended as a traveling exhibit designed for an audience of Union veterans. Before undertaking the work, the artists visited Atlanta, walking the terrain of the battle and interviewing former generals as well as Theodore Davis, who had drawn battle scenes for *Harper's Weekly* during the war. Despite their immense size and immersive quality, cyclorama paintings lost popularity during the 1890s, and Atlanta businessman George V. Gress bought the painting from its bankrupt owner and gave it to the city, along with a circus that became the Atlanta zoo. The painting had already been altered several times, and one owner had attempted to adapt it for white southern audiences. Because the Cyclorama depicts Confederate soldiers attacking before a Union counterattack, the painting does not explicitly show Confederate defeat, and to increase its appeal among white southerners, artists repainted a group of cowering Confederates as fleeing Yankees, among other changes. After initially housing the Cyclorama in a wooden structure in Grant Park, the city moved the painting to a new, "fireproof" granite, steel, and concrete building in 1921, with Georgia's governor and Atlanta's mayor attending the ceremonies to unveil the new location. The opening reception was hosted by the Atlanta Woman's Club, not the United Daughters of the Confederacy.[17]

With the onset of the Great Depression, Kurtz oversaw efforts to improve the Cyclorama under an early federal New Deal program, the Public Works of Art Project, designed to help unemployed artists. For two years, Kurtz and his team repaired damage that the canvas had incurred during its move to the new building and constructed a diorama of more than one hundred plaster soldier figures charging toward a Confederate stronghold to give the painting depth and interest. They used mirrors to create the illusion of a stream and constructed a road with wood shavings. Small pieces of wood suspended from the ceiling simulate shell explosions. One reporter wrote that "The artists spare nothing in creating a real effect." To Kurtz's delight, the federal government also allotted money to move and refurbish the *Texas*, now housed in the Cyclorama's exhibit space. When the restoration was complete, Kurtz and others organized a ceremony at which Mayor William B. Hartsfield (1890–1971) accepted a flag of the Confederacy from the United Daughters of the Confederacy and a flag of the United States from the American Legion.[18]

With corporate art commissions dwindling during the Depression, Kurtz increasingly focused on writing newspaper stories, often illustrating them with detailed maps that gave his readers a sense of both history and geography. His stories capture moments in Atlanta's wartime past, sometimes correcting factual inaccuracies that had become local myth. When writing about the Augustus F. Hurt house outside of Atlanta where Sherman had been informed about McPherson's death, for example, Kurtz corrected the popular belief that McPherson had died on a sofa by publishing the factual information that the general had been ambushed along a local road and died instantly. Kurtz also wanted his readers to know that Hurt's home had been destroyed by federal soldiers who needed the wood for their campfires, that another home had been built on the site and subsequently torn down, and that an orphanage had been constructed in its place. However, Kurtz made little effort to place his stories in the larger context of the war's causes, its overall impact on the city, or its aftermath.[19]

Kurtz researched his stories with great care. In "Dugout Home" (1932), he explored the plight of twenty-six Atlantans who shared a bombproof underground for three weeks during the Siege of Atlanta. Kurtz interviewed family member Elizabeth Willis Herren, helping to preserve a civilian story that might otherwise have been lost and, like Huff, comforting readers facing the trials of the Great Depression.[20]

In 1930, Kurtz met Beverly DuBose, a local real estate executive. They, along with DuBose's son, Beverly Jr., and Kurtz's neighbor Franklin Garrett, a public relations expert and archivist with the Coca-Cola corporation, began making weekend trips to military sites around the metropolitan area and North Georgia. Kurtz kept detailed records of their adventures, which continued for the next eight years. On a typical Saturday morning, he walked over to Garrett's home, and the two drove in Garrett's "little Ford car," stopping to pick up the DuBoses. Despite their different interests, all four men were fascinated by railroads and by military history. While Kurtz drew maps and photographed buildings, Garrett explored cemeteries, recording information from tombstones and adding information gleaned from courthouse records to create a genealogical archive about every adult white male who died in Fulton and DeKalb Counties between 1857 and 1931, regardless of economic status. The DuBoses collected relics, at times purchasing artillery shells from farmers who dug them up in their fields.[21]

Although members of the Saturday morning group did not know Margaret Mitchell (1900–1949) well during the early 1930s, they certainly knew her father, Eugene Muse Mitchell (1866–1944), and her brother, Alexander Stephens Mitchell (1896–1983), both of whom were interested in local history and were members of the Atlanta Historical Society. Founded in 1926, the society met at the Biltmore Hotel to discuss "historical papers" and organized tours of local historical sites. On November 19, 1935, Margaret Mitchell wrote to Kurtz, introducing herself as "John Marsh's wife, Stephens Mitchell's sister and Eugene Mitchell's daughter" and reminding Kurtz that they had met at a historical society event. Then Mitchell added, "In a weak moment, I have written a book and the background of the book is Atlanta between 1859 and 1872." Part of the novel concerned the Atlanta Campaign, including the Confederate retreat from North Georgia and the battles in and around the city. She admitted that she had read every article he had written as well as those written by his wife, Annie Laurie: "I know I am imposing on you and asking a great favor of you but would you read two and a half chapters of my book . . . and tell me if they are correct? You are the only real authority I know." Several months later, Mitchell brought the chapters to Kurtz's home, and he reviewed them and suggested several changes regarding military details. Kurtz never sought to claim any credit for his role in the book's creation, writing, "I never contributed any research . . . , nor did anyone else," but Mitchell became a friend and their relationship continued until her death.[22]

Mitchell's novel and the movie it inspired, *Gone with the Wind*, dominated public memory of Atlanta and the Civil War beginning in the 1930s. Historian Gary W. Gallagher has called the film "the single most powerful influence on American perceptions of the Civil War." *Gone with the Wind* was the only novel that Mitchell ever published, and it took her from a locally known writer for the *Atlanta Journal* and a member of a prominent and affluent family to an international celebrity. The city she wrote about became the subject of intense interest, and national media covered the film's 1939 Atlanta premiere, which attracted an unprecedented number of visitors to Mitchell's hometown.[23]

Mitchell had a difficult relationship with both of her parents. Eugene, a successful real estate lawyer, was emotionally distant, while her mother, Maybelle, had a strong personality and devoted much of her adult life to civic volunteerism and women's suffrage. Margaret recalled attending a suffrage meeting in Atlanta as a young child, sitting on a table next to the water pitcher and blowing kisses to audience members as her mother gave a speech. Maybelle Mitchell also inculcated in her only daughter the importance of social position and proper etiquette. At her mother's insistence, Margaret enrolled at Smith College in 1918 but raced home in January 1919 when her mother fell ill during the influenza epidemic. Maybelle died before Margaret arrived, leaving a deathbed letter with conflicting instructions for her daughter: Margaret should both care for her father and live for herself and her dreams. Margaret finished out the year at Smith but did not return the following fall, and she developed ambivalent feelings about women's appropriate role that were reflected in the characters of rebellious Scarlett and virtuous Melanie in *Gone with the Wind*.[24]

Growing up before the era of radio and film, Mitchell was part of the last generation steeped in family lore more than media culture. The stories she learned from her family and the events she witnessed during a period of racial and ethnic unrest in Atlanta made an indelible impression. Both of her grandfathers had served in the Confederate army, with Russell Mitchell fighting in multiple battles and suffering a serious wound at Antietam and John Stephens playing a less dramatic role with the Commissary General's headquarters near Atlanta. Both men prospered after the war ended, Stephens in wholesale groceries and real estate, Mitchell in the lumber business and later real estate and winning election to the Atlanta City Council in 1872. As children, Margaret and Stephens spent their summers and Sunday afternoons visiting relatives, including some in rural Clayton County who provided ties to the family's agrarian past. "I grew up when children were seen and not heard," she remembered. "I was usually scooped up into a lap . . . while the gathering spiritedly re-fought the Civil War." At other times, Mitchell was an active child, sometimes riding a pony accompanied by one or more of the aging Confederate veterans who were a presence in Atlanta during the first decade of the twentieth century. "There was still plenty of fire and dash left in the old boys," she recalled. Maybelle Mitchell believed that the rides would keep her spirited daughter out of trouble.[25]

Like other privileged white children in Atlanta, Margaret and her brother attended the April 26 celebrations of Confederate Memorial Day, occasions that Stephens Mitchell compared to ancient tribal rituals. The siblings also attended what Stephens described as "the last big Confederate Veterans Reunion" in 1919, hearing "very graphic descriptions" of wartime places and events.[26]

Margaret Mitchell came of age in an era of racial and ethnic tension in Atlanta. She was five years old during the Atlanta Race Riot of 1906 and a teenager when Leo Frank was lynched in 1915. As friends of Governor John Slaton, who commuted Frank's sentence, members of the Mitchell family came to "distrust the feelings of the lower class white people," according to Stephens Mitchell. The Mitchell siblings subscribed to attitudes about race that typified their generation and social class. They were raised with the help of African American domestics, many of whom were beloved in the household but were nonetheless paid a pittance. Margaret Mitchell's views about race intersected with her early attempts at writing. At age fifteen, she assembled neighborhood children to act out a dramatic version of *The Traitor*, the final book in Thomas Dixon's trilogy that served as the basis for *The Birth of a Nation*. Mitchell played the lead role—and got a stern lecture about copyright infringement from her father. At Smith College, she was offended when she was assigned to a history class that also included one of the few African American students at the school. The college acquiesced to Mitchell's demand that she be moved to a different section.[27]

The years immediately following her mother's death were the unhappiest of Margaret Mitchell's life. Bored with housekeeping for her father and brother, she hoped for something better. A debutante, she embraced a rebellious new persona as "Peggy" Mitchell and scandalized proper Atlanta society matrons by performing an "Apache dance" at the Georgian Terrace hotel. After seeing Mitchell's costume and watching her dance seductively with a partner, one shocked woman asked, "Did you see how he *kissed* her?" Equally outrageous, the newspaper printed a photograph of the couple in a suggestive pose. The incident resulted in Mitchell's rejection by the Junior League, a social club for affluent young women. In 1922, Mitchell defied her father's wishes and married the handsome but unstable Berrien "Red" Upshaw, creating further waves by rejecting Maybelle's Catholicism and choosing an Episcopal clergyman to preside. The marriage was short lived and abusive. Mortified to learn that her husband was engaged in rum-running, she took a job with the *Atlanta Journal Magazine* as a reporter using the byline "Peggy Mitchell" and filed for divorce.[28]

Becoming a professional writer gave Peggy Mitchell an identity. Between 1922 and her marriage to John R. Marsh in 1925, Mitchell wrote hundreds of stories. She interviewed celebrities, including Rudolph Valentino. She wrote stunt stories. For one piece, she sat in the swing used by Gutzon Borglum to carve Stone Mountain and had herself hoisted down the side of a downtown skyscraper. In 1925, she wrote biographical sketches of Confederate generals John B. Gordon, Thomas R. R. Cobb, Ambrose Ransom Wright, Henry Lewis Banning, and Pierce M. Butler Young, who had been chosen to represent the state of Georgia as secondary figures to Jefferson Davis, Robert E. Lee, and Stonewall Jackson in Augustus Lukeman's new design for Stone Mountain. According to Mitchell, Cobb, a secessionist who died at the Battle of Fredericksburg, "swept the state out of the Union and into the Confederacy by his eloquence." She offered high praise for Gordon, as well, calling him a general of "matchless courage" who also gave "thirty years of selfless service in civil life for the good of his state." Mitchell looked back on her time as a professional journalist having offered her "a liberal education" and provided her with a new set of friends, including editor Angus Perkerson and his wife, Medora,

also a journalist. When she married Marsh, who had served as a grooms-
man at Mitchell's first wedding, Mitchell left full-time employment at the
*Journal*, but her time there had been pivotal. She gained confidence as a
writer and stability in the company of like-minded friends and the loving support of Marsh, who was a writer, editor, and publicist for Georgia
Power Company. The newlyweds moved to "The Dump," a tiny apartment
at Peachtree and Tenth Streets.[29]

The circumstances under which Mitchell wrote *Gone with the Wind*
are well documented. Sidelined by an injury and using crutches, she spent
hours reading books Marsh brought home from the public library. After running out of titles for her to read, he suggested that she write her
own book. In the only autobiographical article she ever wrote, Mitchell recalled, "I chose the Civil War period to write about because I was
raised on it." She did not want to write a sentimental novel or a Jazz Age
book about "degenerate characters." Instead, she chose to write a "Victorian type" novel around the theme of survival. *Gone with the Wind* tells
the story of Scarlett O'Hara, a southern belle who confronts poverty and
loss in wartime rural Georgia and in Atlanta. Playing against the classic
stereotype of a heroine redeemed by marriage and motherhood, Scarlett
survives through her wits and "gumption." The character of Melanie rep-
resents the traditional image of a southern white woman of purity and determination but frail health. Scarlett's love interests are Ashley, the man
she covets but who spurns her and marries Melanie, and Rhett, the rak-
ish gambler and businessman who becomes her partner. Mitchell wrote
most of the novel between 1926 and 1929, keeping it secret from all but
close friends until 1935, when she submitted it to editor Harold Latham
of Macmillan after meeting him over lunch in Atlanta. After hauling the
immense manuscript back to New York, he read it and expressed enthusiasm, as did Professor Charles Everett of Columbia University, who reviewed it for the press.[30]

Although Marsh destroyed most of the manuscript for *Gone with the
Wind* after his wife's death, apparently in accordance with her wishes,
Mitchell provided many clues about the way she conceived the story and
the sources she consulted. For at least a year after the novel's publication,
she faithfully answered readers' letters requesting information about the
novel. She told a fan in New York that she wanted to write a Civil War story
based in Georgia because Americans knew too much about the war in Virginia and too little about the war in her native state. To a fan in Chicago,

Mitchell admitted that she wanted to view the war "through the eyes of a woman" rather than from the standpoint of a neutral narrator. Raised in Atlanta, Mitchell understood that the civilian narrative was as important as the military one, and she made military events the backdrop to the central story of Scarlett and her struggles. While writing for the *Atlanta Journal*, Mitchell had interviewed the city's "oldest Inhabitants," asking them about how they lived under the blockade, what people ate, and how they coped during the siege. And in addition to her library reading, she had consulted numerous other sources, including newspapers and diaries.[31]

Mitchell's secrecy about her manuscript, especially her desire to destroy various drafts, was grounded in a desire to avoid accusations that her characters were based on real people. For example, she consulted with Franklin Garrett to determine that no one with the last name *Watling* lived in Atlanta during or after the Civil War before naming the prostitute/madam character Belle Watling. Although Mitchell admitted that the slave Prissy resembled a Mitchell family housemaid, Cammie, Mitchell denied that other characters were based on people she knew. But the author's family and friends also saw parallels between the young, feisty flapper Peggy Mitchell, who had a contested relationship with her fervently Catholic mother, and Scarlett O'Hara.[32]

At Macmillan's request, Mitchell shortened her hefty manuscript, a process that included deleting a lengthy chapter about Atlanta after the arrival of Sherman's army. Mitchell also did more fact-checking. In addition to her consultation with Kurtz, she verified her accounts of military events with further newspaper research and by taking car trips with Marsh after he received a promotion that enabled the couple to purchase a car. Following a 1931 trip to Dalton, Marsh wrote to his sister, "Peggy's book tells of the approach of the northern army down the railroad line to Atlanta and the first awakenings of fear that the Confederacy might eventually be defeated."[33]

*Gone with the Wind*, published in June 1936, differs from the traditional southern romances of Mitchell's youth. Dominated by the prolific Thomas Nelson Page, who published several dozen books between the 1880s and the 1920s, the plantation novel idealized rural life in the Old South. Often using Virginia or the South Carolina Low Country as a background, Page's novels revolved around gentlemen and ladies who lived in an alleged rural utopia preoccupied with noblesse oblige and tended by faithful servants. The Civil War upended their world, which was further

damaged by the combined efforts of Carpetbaggers, Scalawags, and feck-
less freedpeople. Mitchell rejected this formula. Like other writers of her
generation, among them historian W. J. Cash and novelist Erskine Cald-
well, she created a broad cast of characters, and although modern literary
critics view her depictions as somewhat one-dimensional, she nonetheless
included characters representing yeoman farmers, rednecks, merchants,
and immigrants. Her story of love and loss is not set in Tidewater Virginia
but in rural Clayton County, Georgia, with a plantation, Tara, that was a
modest, two-story building won in a poker game by Scarlett's Irish immi-
grant father, Gerald O'Hara. Far from representing a feminine ideal, the
central character, Scarlett, tosses aside suitors, dominates husbands, dis-
dains childbirth and children, and is utterly contemptuous of southern independence. Scarlett survives and thrives because she embraces the New
South, moves to the city of Atlanta, and does not care whom her desire for
prosperity and independence hurts. Rhett Butler, her on-again, off-again
love interest, questions whether the Confederacy can win the war in 1861
and does not join the effort until its final months, when military defeat
had become inevitable.[34]

As a love story and a work of popular literature, *Gone with the Wind*
has stood the test of time, selling millions of copies and never going out of
print. As a work of history, however, it has not, despite Mitchell's obses-
sion with detail and the effort she devoted to getting the facts straight. In
the words of historian Jim Cullen, Mitchell "took the facts and used them
to make myth."[35]

Mitchell believed that her novel presented a respectful image of African Americans, telling a New York reporter that "the negroes in this section . . . seem well pleased," but the novel's reception among African Americans in Atlanta in the 1930s is difficult to measure. A book and furniture
store located on the city's black commercial corridor, Auburn Avenue, advertised *Gone with the Wind* along with "Negro Dolls," luggage, and other
gift items for Christmas 1936. A black women's social club began calling
itself the Gone with the Wind Club. The city's major African American
newspaper, the *Atlanta Daily World*, did not review the book, although
it did print a 1939 editorial contrasting the state's problems with extreme
poverty and underfunded schools against the beautiful scenery that was
often depicted in works of art, poetry, and *Gone with the Wind*, "the greatest novel of all times."[36]

Despite Mitchell's beliefs about her black characters, *Gone with the Wind* does not veer very far from the representation of African Americans in works by Page and Dixon. After Dixon congratulated Mitchell on the novel's publication, she gushed, "I was practically raised on your books, and love them very much." As in Dixon's novels, Mitchell depicted the Ku Klux Klan as a force for good, and in Mitchell's novel as well as those of Page, slaves are childlike and need the guidance of white people. Scarlett's mother tells her that she is "responsible for the moral as well as the physical welfare of the darkies God has intrusted to your care"; slaves "are like children and must be guarded from themselves like children." None of the black characters in the novel are intelligent, and many are incompetent. In the movie version of *Gone with the Wind*, Prissy reveals that she knows nothing about birthing babies, prompting Scarlett to slap the slave, a scene that made young Malcolm Little, watching the film in Michigan years before he changed his name to Malcolm X, feel "like crawling under the rug." Mitchell employs a kind of reverse anthropomorphism in the novel, giving animal traits to humans, and although she uses this technique with both white and black characters, it is more prevalent with blacks. When Big Sam encounters Scarlett after the war, he embraces her with his "huge black paws," and he and his friends "caper . . . with delight." Even the character of Mammy, in many ways a respectful representation, shows "the uncomprehending sadness of a monkey's face" in one instance and at the end of the novel displays a facial expression like that of "an old ape."[37]

Sales of *Gone with the Wind* astounded Mitchell. Although its selection by Book of the Month Club for July 1936 guaranteed it would become a best seller, the book's length (1,037 pages) led to its pricing at three dollars, which might have been too much for many readers at the height of the Great Depression. Nonetheless, *Gone with the Wind* sold one million copies in the first six months after publication and remained popular thereafter, particularly when it won the National Book Award and the Pulitzer Prize.[38]

Atlanta newspapers offered effusive praise, lauding Mitchell for her research and recognizing that *Gone with the Wind* represented a break from sentimental novels of the past. The *Journal*'s reviewer, Samuel Tupper Jr., called the book "among the most powerful and original novels in American literature. . . . [I]t is a book to own and re-read and remember forever." The *Constitution* lauded *Gone with the Wind* as "a panorama of life in north Georgia, showing the effects of war on [social classes] high and low." Critic Yolande Gwin drew attention to the characters of Scarlett and Melanie, clearly identifying, as did so many Depression-era readers, particularly women, with Scarlett's shrewdness, strength, determination, and triumph over economic adversity more than with Melanie's sweetness. In spite of the novel's ambiguous ending, with Scarlett wanting to win back Rhett's love and Rhett's famous reply, "My dear, I don't give a damn," the *Constitution* saw it in a positive light: Atlantans were "finally united in picking up the broken bits and building a new civilization with the fragments of the old." It was a statement of local boosterism that might have been written by the Chamber of Commerce, and Mitchell's work, like that of Huff and Kurtz, resonated with Depression-era readers. But the fictional tale was far more compelling to readers than the grim tales of everyday survival told by Gay and Huff.[39]

Atlanta embraced Mitchell and the positive publicity generated by her novel. The book department of Davison's department store hosted a tea in her honor, both recognizing her celebrity and selling her books. Newspapers reported on Mitchell's background, her family, and her modest persona, conveniently overlooking her scandalous exploits as a young woman, her rejection by the Junior League, or her disastrous first marriage. On July 3, 1936, Medora Field Perkerson of the *Atlanta Journal*, a longtime friend of Mitchell's, interviewed her on WSB radio. The station's introduction credited the *Journal* staff with having "first recognized her talent," and Mitchell told listeners that she had relied on stories her brother researched and wrote for the *Atlanta Historical Bulletin* and the colorful recollections of both of her parents. She also related her childhood experiences riding her pony with Confederate veterans.[40]

Mitchell expressed shock that Americans had embraced Scarlett and not the gentle and ladylike Melanie. Melanie "is really my heroine," Mitchell insisted, one of the "true ladies" of the South who were "frail of body perhaps, but never of courage." After the novel's publication, Mitchell projected an image of Melanie-like femininity, even though friends recognized her Scarlett-like tendencies. Nonetheless, Mitchell affected a genteel pose for a photograph of her pouring tea that appeared in the *Constitution* captioned, "Mrs. John Marsh, of Atlanta, in private life." The caption also referred to "constant telephone calls" after the book's publication and her decision to escape the summer heat in Atlanta for a vacation in the mountains with her husband. She "hoped she'd never write another thing" because she "much preferred the duties of a housekeeper." But Mitchell did not keep house. She and John moved to a larger apartment in Ansley Park before the novel's publication, and they had domestic help to handle cooking, cleaning, and laundry.[41]

Mitchell garnered more headlines when she sold the movie rights to Selznick International Pictures for fifty-four thousand dollars, the most ever paid to an author for a first novel. As David Selznick (1902–65) began to cast the film, local and national interest spiked. In Atlanta, auditions for the principal roles—Scarlett, Rhett, Melanie, and Ashley—as well as Aunt Pittypat and the Tarleton twins took place at the Biltmore Hotel on Peachtree Street. Scores of actresses vied to play Scarlett, and among the rumored possibilities were Paulette Goddard, Norma Shearer, Jean Arthur, Joan Bennett, and Katharine Hepburn, though the role ultimately went to British actress Vivien Leigh. The selection of an Atlanta woman, Evelyn Keyes, to play Scarlett's sister Suellen, pleased residents of her hometown.[42]

Mitchell wanted nothing to do with Hollywood but did ask two of her friends—Kurtz and Susan Myrick (1893–1978), a reporter for the *Macon Telegraph*—to help Selznick ensure the authenticity of costumes, dialect, and historical narrative. Kurtz served as technical adviser and is officially credited as "historian." Both Myrick and Kurtz acted as Mitchell's advocates in attempting to re-create for the big screen what she had written in the novel, and both corresponded with her during the filming in 1939 to keep her abreast of developments.[43]

Kurtz later recalled that Mitchell told him, "Wilbur, don't you let them change any history in my book. I'm very proud of it." Kurtz embraced the project, even having his son, Henry, send him a box of Georgia red clay so that the soil in the movie might be the appropriate hue. Kurtz objected when Selznick wanted to shoot a scene in which Scarlett shoed a horse at Tara, reasoning that even in hard times a privileged woman would never have shoed a horse. Instead, to convey Scarlett's struggle with poverty, he suggested that she make soap. To ensure the authenticity of the film's railroads, Kurtz turned to Franklin Garrett. To address racial issues, Kurtz read *The Underground Railroad* by William Still, an African American historian, and provided the black actors with background information intended to help them represent slave life realistically. However, *Gone with the Wind* treats slavery as a benign institution. As historian Thomas Cripps has pointed out, neither Kurtz nor anyone else wrote memoranda conveying instruments of brutality, including shackles, chains, and whips.[44]

Annie Laurie Kurtz accompanied her husband during the year he spent in Hollywood, writing articles for the *Atlanta Constitution* about the filming of the movie and commenting on the Selznick organization's efforts—involving five hundred employees—to depict wartime Atlanta authentically. To reconstruct the city's iconic rail station, Selznick's assistants used both contemporary photographs and the actual architectural plans for the 1854 structure, "recently discovered in an old trunk full of papers" and now in possession of the Atlanta Historical Society. During the filming of the opening barbecue scene at Busch Gardens in Pasadena, California, Annie Laurie Kurtz "watched this panorama of action and color, and felt as though I were living in another age." In addition to hoopskirted women and dashing men, the scene was made realistic by the "delicious odor of the barbecued meat," evidently designed to inspire the actors and later their lunch. Kurtz provided readers of the *Constitution* with her mother's recipe for Georgia Brunswick stew, a staple at southern barbecues, and reported that Clark Gable, who played Rhett, asked her many questions about Atlanta and in doing so revealed "a familiarity with the book that is always pleasing to an Atlantan." Kurtz also shared the news that actor Jesse Clark, who had a small role as the O'Hara family's slave coachman, had grown up in Atlanta, where his father had once been headwaiter at Atlanta's premier hotel, the Kimball House. She enthused, "Watch for Jesse in the picture! You'll like him."[45]

For her part, Myrick had some success in her efforts to make the film an authentic representation of the novel. She did her best to coach the major actors about appropriate accents and dialect. When the Bette Davis film *Jezebel* had appeared before southern audiences in 1938, audience members thought the actors' phony accents demeaned southerners. Nonetheless, Mitchell was dismayed to learn that Leigh wore a bonnet during the scene where the widowed Scarlett dances with Rhett: "I cannot imagine even Scarlett showing such poor taste" as to wear a hat to an evening party. But Mitchell's greatest disappointment involved the appearance of Tara and the neighboring plantation, Twelve Oaks. In the book, Tara is an inelegant structure without columns. Indeed, Clayton County was notable for its lack of gracious homes with columns. To Myrick she wrote, "I grieve to hear that Tara has columns." In 1942, she confided to another friend, "Many of us were hard put not to burst into laughter at the sight of 'Twelve Oaks,'" which rivaled the size and grandeur of the Alabama State Capitol in Montgomery. Selznick's film failed to replicate Mitchell's effort to present a more realistic image of the plantation South than that presented in Thomas Nelson Page's novels.[46]

Screenwriters made many changes to the novel. Aside from the obvious challenges involved in turning a work of more than a thousand pages into a film (the movie went through several screenwriters and several directors before it was completed), the middle-class characters in the novel were largely eliminated from the script, and Selznick softened some of the racial references. He may have hoped to avoid the kind of public protests generated by *The Birth of a Nation* and may also have been motivated by the nation's apparent liberal shift, as seen in the recent reelection of Franklin Roosevelt. As Gary W. Gallagher has noted, "Selznick replaced Griffith's blatant racism with a paternalistic treatment of slavery that would have pleased the original Lost Cause warriors." Members of the O'Hara family and their faithful servants, Big Sam, Pork, and Mammy, demonstrate "reciprocal loyalty."[47]

The film version of *Gone with the Wind* moderates somewhat the novel's harsh depiction of Reconstruction as a time characterized by African American rule, political corruption, and discrimination against white people. The Ku Klux Klan is not identified by name, a decision Mitchell endorsed on the grounds that the Reconstruction Klan had been "a bitter necessity," whereas the 1920s Klan was "a despicable organization and one abhorrent to all decent Southerners." The 1920s Klan was an anti-Catholic as well as antiblack organization, making Mitchell's maternal relatives its potential victims. Where the novel has a black man attacking Scarlett, the film's perpetrators are a black man and a white man. A scene in which Prissy eats watermelon was edited out of the film, which also did not include the word *nigger*. Although Selznick wanted to use the word, he deferred to the wishes of the Production Code Administration (film censors), the NAACP, and members of the black press who lobbied forcefully for its exclusion. Mitchell knew about the debates and shared Selznick's view that the term had been used in antebellum days and would have been appropriate in the movie, but she avoided public comment on the matter. Conversely, Selznick held talks with NAACP leaders Walter White and Roy Wilkins about hiring an African American consultant but refused to do so. Nevertheless, some African American actors protested certain aspects of the production, including segregated bathrooms. In addition, Butterfly McQueen, who played Prissy, objected when Leigh slapped her too hard during one scene, leading Leigh to apologize.[48]

In the end, producers of *Gone with the Wind* were more concerned about whether Confederate heritage groups might catch them in a moment of historical inaccuracy than about racial dynamics during filming or in the final version of the movie. Although the *Chicago Defender* denounced the film, blacks in Atlanta and across the nation overlooked objectionable elements and offered praise for Hattie McDaniel's depiction of Mammy, which they found respectful. When McDaniel's portrayal made her the first African American Oscar nominee and winner (in the Best Supporting Actress category), the honor further neutralized African Americans' public protest against the film. The NAACP gave its implicit approval to *Gone with the Wind*, part of a trend toward political consensus in the New Deal era.[49]

The emphasis on consensus and compromise also prevailed at the film's Atlanta debut. In 1937, Atlanta's media-savvy mayor, William B. Hartsfield, had proposed to Selznick that the film premiere in the place where the novel had been written. It was an unorthodox suggestion, since the vast majority of movies debuted in either New York or Los Angeles. Selznick was evasive at first but eventually came around to the view that national publicity surrounding an Atlanta rollout would be worth the effort. In addition, he hoped to please Mitchell so that she would write a sequel that he could option. Because Atlanta, like other southern cities, was rigidly segregated, Selznick acceded to public pressure to keep the film's black stars away from the occasion. He also declined an invitation to appear with the Atlanta University Players, an African American thespian group, though he offered to send them copies of screenplays for several of his earlier films. Distributed by Metro-Goldwin-Mayer, *Gone with the Wind* debuted on December 15, 1939, at Loew's Grand Theatre, which seated more than one thousand people but did not allow African American patrons. They would have to wait to see the film at the Bailey's Royal Theatre in April 1940.[50]

Many of the film's actors, including Vivien Leigh, Clark Gable, and Olivia de Havilland (Melanie), attended the premiere, and they were amazed at the reception they received from Atlantans. After the actors arrived at the airport, motorcades brought them into the city. A reporter for the *New York Times* recorded that African Americans who lived along the route "stood on porches of blackened tumbledown shacks . . . in wide-eyed groups." Even the arrival of minor actors garnered publicity: Ann Rutherford, who portrayed Scarlett's sister Careen was the first actor to arrive on December 13, and her appearance at Terminal Station "had the effect of firing on Fort Sumter." The following day, Rutherford visited the *Atlanta Journal* to see the table and chair Mitchell had used when she was a young reporter before moving on to the Confederate Soldier's Home, where she hugged and kissed the remaining six residents. The *Atlanta Constitution* told fans exactly when every actor would arrive so that those seeking autographs might position themselves to their best advantage. The *Atlanta Journal* noted that two million copies of the novel were in print and compared Mitchell's experiences to Cinderella.[51]

*Gone with the Wind* festivities began on December 14 with a ceremony in the heart of the Civil War city. Members of the United Daughters of the Confederacy and the Old Guard Battalion of the Gate City Guard lit a gas lamp as the "Eternal Flame of the Confederacy." The featured speaker was Kurtz, whose arrival by train after a year in California received nearly as much press attention as did the arrival of some movie stars. Kurtz related the story of the lamppost, which had been struck by a federal artillery shell that left a hole in its base in 1864, and shared the little-known story that the shell had also killed Solomon Luckie. Knowing that local newspapers would cover his speech, Kurtz's decision to include Luckie's story was a small gesture that reflected his commitment to setting the historical record straight.[52]

Later that day, throngs of Atlantans took to the streets as crowds between fifteen and twenty people deep sought to watch the movie's stars as they rode by, confetti floating down. City employees and schoolchildren received a half day off so that they could see de Havilland, Gable (and his wife, Carole Lombard), Leigh (with her paramour and future husband, Laurence Olivier), and Selznick and his wife, Irene, on this historic occasion. Kurtz's son, Wilbur Jr., found the sight of so many people in downtown Atlanta "staggering" and believed that "the stars, Selznick and M-G-M officials have been swept off their collective feet."[53]

The Junior League ball at the Municipal Auditorium capped the day's activities. League members hoped that Mitchell would attend, making the event truly exceptional, and in November, reports circulated that there was "a remote possibility" that she would appear. But she did not, claiming the need to preserve her strength for the premiere. Nearly twenty years after the Junior League had rejected her for membership, Mitchell refused to forgive the slight. However, she hosted the Selznicks, Leigh and Olivier, de Havilland, Myrick, and Wilbur and Annie Laurie Kurtz for cocktails the night before the ball.[54]

Despite Mitchell's refusal to attend, the ball was a smashing success. When tickets went on sale in November, the line to purchase them was four blocks long, and more than fifteen hundred people went home without one after they sold out. Forty-two Junior League members entered a League-sponsored contest to see which local debutante most closely matched Leigh's measurements and therefore the prize of leading the grand march wearing Scarlett's costume from the barbecue scene. When one unhappy Atlantan complained to the *Atlanta Constitution* because the contest was open only to League members, editor Ralph McGill responded by declaring, "A city-wide contest would have been a second battle of Atlanta and an utterly impossible task." The lucky winner, Margaret Palmer, led a parade of fifty hoopskirted women at the beginning of the festivities, while many of the men present wore Confederate uniforms.[55]

Though African Americans attended the ball and the premiere, they did so only as singers or servants. Two hundred black waiters attended an estimated six thousand white guests at the ball. Dressed as slaves and performing in front of the facade of Twelve Oaks, members of the Ebenezer Baptist Church Choir, including ten-year-old Martin Luther King Jr., sang such Negro spirituals as "Plenty Good Room" and "Get on Board Little Children." The *Atlanta Journal* reported that "the swaying of their bodies was indeed a striking page from Margaret Mitchell's great book." Other members of Atlanta's African American community organized a *Gone with the Wind* dance at a local black club.[56]

The ball culminated with the introduction of the stars including Gable, Hollywood's biggest male star. "Deafening applause" greeted him when he stood to acknowledge the crowd, whose ovation lasted so long that he sat down and then stood again. Commentators noted Leigh's beauty as well as her velvet dress, diamond and ruby bracelet, and diamond ring. De Havilland created a stir by arriving late, forcing police to clear a path so that she could make her way through the crowd. After the stars had their moment, Kay Kyser and his dance band entertained the guests while NBC broadcast the affair over the radio.[57]

The movie premiere occurred on Friday night, December 15. Before the event, the stars toured the Cyclorama in Grant Park and posed for photographs against the backdrop of the enormous diorama. Leigh, understandably nervous about how she would be received as "Atlanta's Scarlett," called it "the most wonderful thing I have ever seen," while Gable allegedly said that he liked everything about the painting except that "I am not in it," prompting Kurtz to alter the figure of a dead soldier in the diorama to resemble the Hollywood star.[58]

That evening, the stars arrived one by one at Loew's Grand Theatre as searchlights lit the night. While black ushers led white moviegoers to their seats, the choir of Big Bethel African Methodist Episcopal Church sang outside the theater. By prior arrangement, Mitchell arrived last and sat with the stars. Also in attendance were four Confederate veterans, the youngest of whom was ninety-three. The audience loved the film, clapping and cheering when it ended. Invited by Mayor Hartsfield to give a short speech, Mitchell commended Selznick's "courage, and his obstinacy and his determination . . . until he had the exact cast he wanted. . . . [H]e had the absolutely perfect cast." During intermission, she told Medora Perkerson that she loved Leigh as Scarlett.[59]

The casting of Leigh had generated some controversy, and it was not clear whether local and national audiences would embrace an Englishwoman's portrayal of Scarlett. The premiere put their misgivings to rest. The *Atlanta Constitution* stationed ten reporters outside the theater to query moviegoers at the end of the film, and many respondents singled out Leigh for special commendation. Frank G. North said that "Vivien Leigh stole the show" and applauded her "correct southern accent." Mavis Garey told a reporter that the movie was as "good as the book" and that Leigh was "outstanding." Franklin Garrett was "so overcome with emotion I can hardly express an opinion. It was marvelously acted." Ralph McGill lauded the "tremendous, emotional" film and declared that "Vivien Leigh steals the picture." Golfer Bobby Jones called the film "wonderful" and "another 'Birth of the Nation.'"[60]

Gable and Lombard left Atlanta by plane immediately after the premiere, and other actors left by train a few hours later. The *Constitution* announced, "Rhett and Scarlett Gone with the Wind," and boasted that the event was "the greatest premiere ever given a motion picture." Adding a note of humor, the paper quoted a Cincinnati newspaper headline: "Atlanta's Gone 'Nuts.'" Mitchell's goal of focusing attention on the Atlanta Campaign and her native city had been achieved with a success she could not have imagined. In the words of film historian Matthew Bernstein, *Gone with the Wind* "proved to be a milestone in Atlanta's history, placing the city at the center of national and even international attention." In the imagination of many Americans, Atlanta had become the center of popular culture relating to the Civil War. *Time, Life, Newsweek,* and other national magazines highlighted the movie and the Georgia capital, with *Newsweek* featuring more photographs of the city than of the film. The *New York Times* ran stories about both the filming and the premiere, including a piece illustrated with a photograph of hoopskirted women at the Junior League ball and headlined "Atlanta Retaken by Glory of Past: 'Gone with the Wind' Flies into City and Thousands Relive Its Stirring War Days." Movie critic Frank S. Nugent criticized the novel as overly long but applauded the movie's cast and concluded that the film left him with a "warm and grateful remembrance of an interesting story beautifully told."[61]

Atlanta's African American press was less impressed. The *Atlanta Daily World* lauded black Atlantans' contributions to the festivities—the performances of the distinguished choirs from Ebenezer Baptist Church and Big Bethel African Methodist Episcopal Church, the thousands of African Americans who had watched the parade, and the hundreds of servants who had played supporting roles in city events. But it also printed a story about the use of dialect in the film. In February 1939, the paper had run an article defending the use of dialect, noting that "prior to the Civil War very few Negroes spoke anything else," but in December it suggested that the use of dialect in *Gone with the Wind* glorified illiteracy. The *Daily World* took the opportunity to draw attention to the disparities between Georgia's funding for black and white public schools. The Reverend John C. Wright of the First Congregational Church went further in a piece the paper printed on December 16: "At heart the South is still the Confederacy . . . Dixie is still their national anthem, and the black man is most acceptable when he approximates most nearly the role of the white man's chattel." Black people had been excluded from the premiere except as "props to make more authentic the scenes and the period being brought back to life." Listening to the church choirs, Wright heard "nothing but the hiss of the slave driver's whip and the clanking of the chains that held their forefathers in bondage."[62]

The premiere of *Gone with the Wind* offered a diversion from troubling international news. Three months earlier, Germany had invaded Poland, leading to the start of the Second World War. One day after running stories about the cost of the premiere ($100,000) and quoting studio officials as saying that the enormous expenditure had been worth it, the *Atlanta Journal* carried the headline "Nazis Claim 34 British Planes in Great Battle." Americans anxiously watched the developing situation.[63]

Leigh, now a beloved figure in Atlanta and recipient of the Best Actress Oscar for her portrayal of Scarlett, returned to the city in December 1940 for a "second premiere" of *Gone with the Wind* designed to renew enthusiasm for the film and raise money for the British War Relief Society. In addition to Leigh's award and that of McDaniel, *Gone with the Wind* picked up the Oscar for Best Picture and Best Director as well as for adapted screenplay, cinematography, production design, and film editing. It also sold a record number of tickets. Organizers of the second premiere invited McDaniel to attend and planned to have her and Leigh reenact the movie's corset-lacing scene, but McDaniel declined to attend, citing her busy schedule. Her decision may also have been grounded in distaste for Jim Crow—born and raised in the West, she had no desire to stay in a substandard hotel. Ultimately, the second premiere was a lackluster event. Bad weather delayed Leigh's arrival, and she was preoccupied by news of the war, which included the destruction of her London home in a recent bombing raid. And exactly one year later, the bombing of Pearl Harbor drew the United States into the Second World War and pushed memories of the Civil War into the background as Americans turned their attention toward the new conflict.[64]

# CHAPTER 6

# The Civil War Centennial

O N JULY 21, 1960, Peter Zack Geer (1928–97), chair of Georgia's Civil War Centennial Commission and the organization's public voice during the early 1960s, announced, "We in Georgia plan to commemorate the brave men and women and their noble deeds." This effort would include educating young people about the war in Georgia, locating and conserving manuscripts and photographs to document the war, and preserving monuments and military graves in the state. Reflecting a commonly held view among members of state centennial commissions around the country, Geer declared that Georgia's centennial would also highlight national unity. According to this view, a war that had divided the nation in 1861 ultimately made it stronger and more unified after 1865. In a post–World War II landscape dominated by two superpowers armed with nuclear weapons, public officials including Geer hoped that the Civil War centennial would become a demonstration of American nationalism in the face of threats posed by Soviet communism. But Geer and others encountered an unanticipated challenge to their carefully laid plans. By the early 1960s, the civil rights movement was gaining momentum in Georgia and elsewhere in the South. While members of the Georgia Civil War Centennial Commission (CWCC) tried to maintain a narrative of military valor and national unity, civil rights activists provided an alternate narrative based on the Civil War's message of freedom and human rights.[1] For a century, white and black Atlantans had commemorated the Civil War separately. During the centennial, their efforts collided.

By the time that crowds gathered in downtown Atlanta in 1945 to celebrate Japanese surrender and the end of World War II, the city was clearly ascendant. Crippled by the Great Depression during the 1930s, Atlanta benefited from a wartime economic boom fueled by military bases and war industries, including the Bell Bomber plant in suburban Marietta. Atlanta also benefited from the skillful leadership of Mayor William B. Hartsfield, who led the city for twenty-three years beginning in the late 1930s. When Atlanta staged the Cotton States Exposition in 1895, the city had fewer than seventy-five thousand residents. By 1950, its population had grown to more than three hundred thousand, and by 1960 it was approaching half a million.[2]

Automobile culture transformed the city, along with many other postwar urban areas. With assistance from President Dwight Eisenhower's introduction of the Interstate Highway System in 1956, Atlanta, once a railroad center, became an automotive hub. Tourism, including business conventions, became an economic driver for the city, and Atlanta continued to identify with its Civil War past and its image as the setting for *Gone with the Wind*.[3]

Margaret Mitchell's 1949 death produced an outpouring of grief from local citizens and tributes from around the world. Just forty-eight years old, Mitchell had been hit by a speeding driver while crossing Peachtree Street. Taken to Grady Hospital, she lingered for several days in a coma, while reporters stationed at the hospital waited for news and anxious Atlantans held a vigil outside. David O. Selznick sent a dozen orchids. Five days after the accident, Mitchell died. Both Vivien Leigh and Clark Gable issued statements of tribute, while the *Atlanta Constitution* eulogized Mitchell as the "South's First Lady." Editor Ralph McGill (1898–1969) shared his favorite passage in the novel (the moment when the cynical Rhett Butler decides to cast his lot with the Confederate army), and columnist Celestine Sibley (1917–99) lauded the "gallant little woman who gave the world its greatest story of Confederate courage." The *Atlanta Daily World*'s editor C. A. Scott (1902–2000), who represented the older generation of Atlanta's black leaders, wrote that Mitchell's "great contribution to the literary world brought hours of reading pleasure to people of all races, creeds, and colors."[4]

Although Mitchell's family chose a private funeral, details regarding the simple Episcopal service were shared with journalists, and the procession from the funeral home to Oakland Cemetery was photographed and published in the local press. Hartsfield ordered flags flown at half-staff at the Cyclorama and City Hall as Mitchell was laid to rest in the family plot next to her parents. Many newspaper accounts of her death and funeral praised her philanthropic efforts, which included raising money for war bonds, visiting with inmates at the federal prison, supporting the Atlanta Public Library, and providing financial contributions for local tuberculosis patients. The press did not report that Mitchell had given money to support students at the historically black Morehouse School of Medicine, an effort that did not become public for some years.[5]

With Mitchell's death, Atlanta lost an icon connecting the city to its public Civil War image. As the 1940s gave way to the 1950s, citizens of Atlanta and the nation began to ponder the forthcoming Civil War centennial. The death in 1956 of the last remaining Civil War veteran, Albert H. Woolson, a Union drummer from Minnesota, focused attention on the passing of the wartime generation and the need to frame the hundredth anniversary of the war so that it would be authentic and meaningful. In addition, the centennial would play out against a backdrop of the civil rights movement and the Cold War, both of which shaped it in significant ways.[6]

The civil rights movement gained momentum in the late 1940s when President Harry Truman ordered the desegregation of the armed forces and the Democratic Party began to move toward advocating desegregation in its 1948 presidential platform. In opposition, southern whites embraced the Confederate flag as a symbol of resistance, a trend that grew in the aftermath of the Supreme Court's school desegregation ruling in *Brown v. Board of Education* (1954). In 1956, the Georgia legislature showed its dedication to segregation by adopting a new state flag that included the Confederate symbol.[7]

The new Georgia flag featured a Confederate St. Andrew's cross as the dominant image, with the state seal to its left. It replaced one that had three stripes, reminiscent of the Confederate Stars and Bars, also featuring the state seal to its left. Democratic Party chair John Sammons Bell suggested the flag change via a politically influential group for which he acted as attorney and spokesman, the Association of County Commissioners, and claimed to be motivated by the desire to honor veterans of the war. According to a handbook of Georgia flags, the legislature wanted to "create a living memorial to the Confederacy and at the same time to give

Georgia a distinctive and historically significant flag." Bell's unstated but likely motive concerned desegregation of public schools. A member of the Georgia Commission on Education, he was a proponent of "traditional policies of segregation," as he put it.[8]

Historian John Coski has concluded that there is "no smoking gun to link the flag change with resistance to integration," but he points to compelling circumstantial evidence connecting the two. That evidence does not include a role played by the United Daughters of the Confederacy (UDC). The Georgia UDC opposed the new flag, stating that "the Battle Flag of the Confederacy is a Flag of history. . . . No one state can claim it for its own." The John B. Gordon Camp of the Sons of Confederate Veterans (SCV) took the same position. However, as Coski points out, South Georgia's Denmark Groover, a member of the legislature in 1956, claimed in the 1990s that the change had been proposed to pay homage to Confederate veterans but forty years earlier had stated that the flag "will show that we in Georgia intend to uphold what we stood for, will stand for and will fight for."[9]

Georgia's African American leaders contested the 1956 flag, linking the change with the *Brown* decision. On February 14, 1956, the *Atlanta Daily World* ran an editorial expressing outrage that the legislature expected African Americans to support a flag "that stood for the enslavement of its people." The newspaper argued that slavery "does not belong in the agenda of a proud Democracy" and reminded Georgians of the human toll of the Civil War. The new flag would honor "a rebellion" that "cost . . . thousands of lives on both sides." Despite the criticism, the 1956 flag remained in use until 2001.[10]

By the late 1950s, both black and white Georgians increased their conversations about how to commemorate the Civil War during the centennial. The Second World War and its aftermath inspired new interest in military history and helped lead to the creation of Civil War Roundtables, which met monthly and focused on military history. The first roundtable had been founded in Chicago before the war, but interest increased after the conflict ended. By 1960, close to one hundred roundtables existed across the United States, and they were especially popular in the Midwest. Atlanta's Civil War Roundtable began in 1949 when Richard Harwell, a Civil War scholar and manuscripts librarian at Emory University, held a private dinner party and invited local Civil War enthusiasts Wilbur Kurtz, Beverly DuBose, Franklin Garrett, and Carl Forrester. The dinner led to the formation of the Atlanta Civil War Roundtable (ACWRT), with its first formal meeting taking place in December at Atlanta's premier social venue, the Piedmont Driving Club.[11]

According to its initial constitution, the ACWRT was dedicated to the "serious discussion and study of the Civil War." Membership was "by invitation only," with applications requiring two active members to serve as sponsors. As a practical matter, the group's membership was restricted to white males. When Laura Perry applied for membership in 1960 and found the requisite two sponsors, she received an immediate response from ACWRT secretary W. G. Ryckman: "It has never been the policy of the Atlanta Round Table to accept women as members, but, of course, they are cordially invited and welcomed at meetings as guests of members." Social events for the ACWRT included its annual holiday meeting, known affectionately as the Christmas Truce. Its regular monthly meetings featured local speakers on such topics as "Longstreet: Bull-Headed Dutchman or Practical Patriot," with two members defending Longstreet and two assailing him. The ACWRT also hosted academic speakers, including Charles Roland of Tulane University and T. Harry Williams from Louisiana State. During the 1950s, membership in the roundtable grew to several hundred, among them faculty from area universities, most notably Civil War historian Bell Irvin Wiley (1906–80) of Emory University, and professional men from the ranks of law, accounting, and engineering, many of them veterans of the Second World War. These men had a natural interest in the study of military history.[12]

Members of Civil War Roundtables around the country were among the most enthusiastic supporters of the Civil War centennial. In 1957, the Washington, D.C., Roundtable advocated the creation of a national centennial commission. In testimony before Congress, roundtable member Karl Betts insisted that a commission would generate interest in the Civil War throughout the country. With the enthusiastic support of President Eisenhower, Congress passed a bill creating the U.S. Civil War Centennial Commission (CWCC) to be chaired by Ulysses S. Grant III (1881–1968), a retired major general with a distinguished record of service in both world wars. By selecting the grandson of the Civil War general, Eisenhower added a famous name to the commission and one whose reputation symbolized twentieth-century American military might, but Grant's tenure would be contentious. Seventy-eight years old and politically conservative, Grant, along with his assistant, Betts, hoped to focus the four-year remembrance on a series of events emphasizing military valor and American unity in the face of threats posed by communism. In 1958, they produced a pocket-sized booklet in which they expressed the desire that all Americans should participate in centennial activities so that they "may be influenced to adopt 'a truly American way of thinking' and pay tribute to the memories of forefathers 'who took part in the bitter conflict to determine the exact path our national government should follow.'" Neither man had any interest in dwelling on the war's causes or commemorating the role of African Americans in the war. In 1960, Betts told the *Nation* magazine that the CWCC did not intend to focus on the emancipation of slaves and insisted that many slaves remained loyal to their masters: "A lot of fine Negro people loved life as it was in the old South."[13]

Forty-four states established individual commissions, including Georgia, where Governor Ernest Vandiver (1918–2005) created it in 1959 and appointed Geer, his executive secretary, to run it. Vandiver, who had won the governorship the preceding year on a platform of opposition to school integration, undoubtedly hoped that interest in the Civil War centennial would draw attention away from public debate over the Supreme Court's school desegregation ruling. With offices in Atlanta, the state commission included Wiley and the president of the Atlanta Historical Society, Beverly DuBose Jr. (1918–86), along with state officials such as Supreme Court justice Carlton Mobley and state archivist Mary Givens Bryan—but no African Americans. Geer appointed committees to handle publicity and promotion; monuments, memorials, and commemorations; finance; official souvenirs; education; publications; and pageants and reenactments. His carefully crafted statements to the media emphasized that the commission's purpose was "commemoration" rather than "celebration" and those of Wiley stressed the need for a "dignified" remembrance of the war: "We all want the commemoration to call attention to the great nation that arose from the great tragedy of war. . . . The commemoration should enhance the harmony of a united nation."[14]

White people in Georgia and other southern states welcomed the centennial to a greater degree than the rest of the country, and all southern states created their own commissions to oversee activities between 1961 and 1965. Nonetheless, it was not a foregone conclusion that residents of the region would participate in the centennial. Some white southerners hoped to use the theme of Confederate memory as a bulwark in the fight against desegregation, but as historian Robert Cook has pointed out, "We

should resist the conclusion . . . that a racially motivated impulse to celebrate the Confederacy was the sole or even the paramount reason why
southern states opted to set up their own commissions." Nonetheless,
those termed "die-hards" by Cook criticized the U.S. CWCC for having too
few southern members and for using the term *civil war* rather than *War
between the States* in the commission's title. Others complained that any
federal effort led by someone descended from Ulysses S. Grant could not
possibly treat the region with respect and might focus attention on southern defeat instead of southern valor. Eisenhower helped to allay white
southern fears with a televised January 1961 address to the nation emphasizing the theme of sectional reconciliation and inviting Americans to participate in centennial festivities. To add solemnity to the occasion, the U.S.
CWCC asked clergy around the country to give sermons and arrange music suitable for the observance's opening in 1961.[15]

Vandiver's decision to create a centennial commission relegated Confederate heritage groups to the sidelines. Although Geer appointed the
heads of the state UDC and SCV as commission members, its most important work was handled by Geer, staff director Stanley Rowland Smith,
and committees chaired by state officials, leading businessmen, and professional and amateur historians. Carlon Carter, head of the Georgia Division of the SCV, probably spoke for most heritage group members when
he wrote to Smith in 1962, "For many, many years the Sons of Confederate Veterans, along with the United Daughters of the Confederacy and
the Children of the Confederacy, have been trying to do in their separate
capacities the things which the Centennial Commission is doing. There
comes a time when it behooves us all to coordinate our efforts to achieve
the common goal, and it is the belief of the Sons that now is that time."
Like many descendants of Confederates and students of the war, Carter
had high hopes for the centennial. He was especially interested in using
the centennial as a vehicle to impart lessons of history, as he understood
those lessons, to the younger generation, for "never in the history of this
great country of ours has an event such as these centennial years captured
the imagination of so many people." He offered his organization's help to
the commission.[16]

Centennial organizers in Georgia and elsewhere hoped that the celebration would provide marketing opportunities as well as a tourism bo-
nanza. Atlantans read about neighboring Alabama's February 1961 efforts
to re-create Jefferson Davis's inauguration in Montgomery, the Confedera-

cy's first capital. The event, attended by fifty thousand people, included costumed figures representing Davis and others reenacting the swearing-in, a parade, and a minstrel band.[17]

Not to be outdone, the Georgia CWCC planned yet another "premiere" of *Gone with the Wind*. David O. Selznick made the trip to Atlanta, as did two of the stars, Vivien Leigh and Olivia de Havilland, though others, including Leslie Howard, Hattie McDaniel, and Clark Gable, had died in the two decades since the film's release, as had Mitchell. To fill the void, Selznick's publicity machine commissioned portraits of Gable and Mitchell to be unveiled at the premiere and later donated them to the Margaret Mitchell Memorial Room of the Atlanta Public Library, which had been created in 1954. The Georgia Civil War Centennial Ball Committee planned a three-day extravaganza that included a costume ball at the Biltmore Hotel, chosen because of the "inability to serve [alcoholic] beverages" at City Auditorium, site of the 1939 ball. The city's leading corporations sponsored the event, including Coca-Cola, Rich's Department Store, and Southern Bell.[18]

As in 1939, Leigh stole the show. Recently divorced from Laurence Olivier, she arrived alone in Atlanta, where Hartsfield presented her with a bouquet of red roses and called her "our Scarlett." Leigh paid homage to the movie role that had launched her career as a major film star, telling reporters, "I loved the book and I love Scarlett." At the Biltmore, decorated with Confederate flags and white candles for the *Gone with the Wind* ball, Leigh appeared wearing a dress of white dimity sprigged with green that was intended to mimic the white and green organdy gown Scarlett wore in the film's opening scene. She was photographed shaking hands with Governor Vandiver and his wife, Betty, who wore period dress, as did others in attendance. At the premiere, seven thousand fans celebrated outside Loew's Grand Theatre, where the movie was shown for the first time since 1954, and for the remainder of its run, Loew's hosted four shows per day. The *Constitution's* fashion editor advised Atlanta women where to purchase antebellum-style clothing for the spring season, assuring them that "great-skirted dresses" could be achieved using tulle rather than hoops. The *Atlanta Daily World* ignored the *Gone with the Wind* event.[19]

Although its organizers considered the "re-premiere" a success, by early 1961 it had become clear that those who favored a centennial grounded in celebrating military valor, heritage tourism, and American unity were running squarely up against the emerging civil rights movement, whose activists saw opportunities to take the centennial in a different direction. In Atlanta, the unfolding drama played out when the city's leading department store, Rich's, unveiled a Civil War centennial exhibition on January 9, 1961. Four years earlier, Atlanta's civil rights leaders had successfully and nonviolently desegregated Atlanta's buses, following on the success of the 1955–56 Montgomery Bus Boycott. The boycott helped launch the public career of Atlanta native Martin Luther King Jr. (1929–68), at the time serving as pastor of Montgomery's Dexter Avenue Baptist Church. King moved back to Atlanta in 1960, and with his support, a group of young activists decided to stage a series of sit-ins to desegregate department store lunch counters and restaurants. On October 19, 1960, seventy-five students attempted to dine at several area establishments, including Rich's. King was among those arrested and jailed, drawing negative press attention to Atlanta and prompting concern from the publicity-conscious Hartsfield, who is credited with labeling Atlanta the "city too busy to hate." After calling together a group of sixty African American community leaders, Hartsfield negotiated a truce, promising to release those who had been jailed, including King, and to persuade store owners to desegregate their lunch counters. But Rich's dragged its feet, and the KKK staged counterprotests. After a disastrous Christmas shopping season, city officials brokered an end to the ordeal in March 1961: restaurants, restrooms, and changing rooms would be desegregated after local schools were integrated in the fall.[20]

Against this backdrop, Rich's opened its exhibition "commemorating the 100th Anniversary of the War between the States." That moniker no doubt appealed to white customers who objected to the term *civil war* and who sought reassurance that old times had not been forgotten in the city of Atlanta. Rich's exhibition brochure described how "a giant holocaust tore these United States," especially "the eleven states, including Georgia, which seceded from the Union." The brochure touted the fact that "more than life-size" statues of Generals Robert E. Lee (and his horse, Traveler, who were positioned in the lingerie department), Nathan Bedford Forrest, John B. Gordon, Joseph E. Johnston, and John Bell Hood could be found on the flagship store's ground floor. Noticeably missing from the lineup was James Longstreet, whose absence evidently failed to generate public comment, even from the *Atlanta Constitution*, which had defended his reputation under Henry Grady's editorship. The *Constitution* did, however, note that Lee's "sober countenance" did not reflect "a single bit of the embarrassment he must feel" about his location.[21]

Several Atlanta newspapers praised the exhibit, which also featured a grouping of Confederate flags, a set of Matthew Brady's photographs, and cases of weapons and artillery shells loaned by local collectors. For *Atlanta Constitution* columnist Harold Martin, the side-by-side display of a Confederate soldier's gray homespun uniform and the machine-made dress uniform of a Yankee soldier encapsulated the "tragic differences" between the industrial North and the agrarian South that prevented the Confederacy from winning the war. But a January 12, 1961, *Atlanta Journal* column on the exhibit shared space with coverage of a riot at the University of Georgia prompted by the enrollment of the first two African American students, Charlayne Hunter and Hamilton Holmes, under a court order. The newspaper included images of Hunter and of her dorm room window, which was broken by bricks thrown by white students, as well as of police using tear gas to disperse rioters. The Rich's exhibit made no reference to black soldiers or emancipation.[22]

Events involving the U.S. CWCC drew the attention of Atlantans in early 1961 when plans were made for a national assembly to take place in Charleston, South Carolina. In February, the director of New Jersey's state commission informed Betts, the executive director of the U.S. CWCC, that the Garden State's delegation included an African American woman, Madaline A. Williams, and that all of the delegation members wished to be housed together. Betts responded that the U.S. CWCC had no jurisdiction over hotel accommodations in Charleston, and the New Jersey delegation subsequently announced that it would not attend the assembly.[23]

Other state delegations threatened to join New Jersey in boycotting the meeting, creating a potentially explosive situation that garnered national media attention and became an issue for the newly inaugurated U.S. president, John F. Kennedy. Like his predecessor an avid student of U.S. history, Kennedy assigned several aides and his brother, Robert, the U.S. attorney general, to resolve the situation in a way that did not make the administration appear to condone segregation. The president wrote to Grant that the CWCC was a government agency that must honor "the Constitutional role of equal treatment of all Americans, regardless of race or color." Wiley, a member of the U.S. CWCC's executive committee, also worked behind the scenes, and meeting planners found a face-saving solution by relocating the meeting to a desegregated naval base outside Charleston. The *Atlanta Daily World* declared, "The Civil War Centennial Commission capitulated to President Kennedy's frontal assault."[24]

The Charleston meeting was nevertheless roiled by controversy. While the official sessions occurred at the naval base, a group representing southern state commissions, the Confederate States Centennial Conference, met concurrently in Charleston. Luncheon speaker Ashley Halsey Jr., a local journalist who published colorful articles about the Civil War in the *Saturday Evening Post*, gave an intemperate speech, which he softened slightly before repeating it later in the day at the official gathering. According to Halsey, the United States had fought a war in 1861 because it could not devise a political resolution to the issue of slavery, yet a century later, the U.S. Supreme Court was attempting to force racial integration on the South. Halsey asked, "Shall we have integration throughout our schools? Let the *people* vote on a Constitutional amendment to decide that." Halsey overlooked the fact that "the people" had voted Abraham Lincoln into office in 1860 and that Lincoln's moderate antislavery views had led to secession. Reacting to the evening speech and reports of the earlier one, New Jersey delegates held a press conference criticizing Halsey and calling for Grant's resignation. Donald Flamm, the chair of the New Jersey delegation, accused Halsey of making a "snide reference to [Lincoln's] paternity and origin," a statement certain to disturb northern delegates. The New Jersey representatives, including Williams, later left the base to attend a local NAACP gathering.[25]

The Charleston meeting ultimately brought negative publicity to the U.S. CWCC and may have contributed to Congress's decision to decrease the commission's budget. In addition, Betts was forced to resign after his heavy-handed style and clumsy handling of the situation in Charleston alienated Wiley and other members of the executive committee. Grant then resigned to protest Betts's departure. The Kennedy administration named historian Allan Nevins to replace Grant and young scholar James I. Robertson Jr. to replace Betts. President Kennedy also appointed Roy Davenport, a civilian employee in the secretary of the army's office and a Democratic Party activist, to serve as the commission's first African American member. The *Atlanta Daily World* characterized Davenport as "a top draw personnel specialist" and noted that Grant had "developed retirement 'jitters' when ordered by JFK to desegregate his meeting places." Betts, who continued to correspond with various state CWCC chairs after his resignation, wrote to Geer that he hoped that despite the Charleston debacle, "the original high objectives of the Centennial"—that is, a renewed focus on tourism and American exceptionalism rather than on civil rights—could still be attained.[26]

The *Atlanta Constitution* headlined its story on the Charleston events "Centennial Stirs Up Storm—Of Words," but editor Ralph McGill used the occasion to explore the centennial's purpose. The newspaper had a mixed record on race relations, having lauded the KKK's "impressive services" on Stone Mountain in 1915, but under McGill's leadership during the 1960s, it became a voice for progressivism. On April 8, 1961, McGill wrote, "There is sound reason to commemorate the conflict which brought an end to chattel-slavery and made us a union." He welcomed thoughtful discussion of the war and a commemoration that led to the publication of articles and books on the topic. But he condemned the "increasing numbers of persons wandering about the South wearing sleazy imitations of Confederate uniforms, growing beards, stirring up old hatreds." He reminded readers that "the Civil War was not an all-white affair" and specifically noted the presence of African American soldiers in the conflict.[27]

Atlanta's African Americans knew that the Civil War was not an "all-white affair." The centerpiece of the centennial for black residents of the city was January 1, 1963, the one hundredth anniversary of the Emancipation Proclamation. Since the war, the black community in Atlanta had celebrated January 1 as Emancipation or Jubilee Day. Although other forms of black history commemoration also gained favor, including Negro History Week, begun as a national occasion by Dr. Carter Woodson in the 1920s, Atlantans regarded Emancipation Day as the city's premier celebration of freedom and civic pride.[28]

Beginning in the early twentieth century, the local NAACP sponsored celebrations and used the occasions to recruit new members and raise money. The 1933 event, held at Sisters Chapel on the Spelman College campus, continued the long-standing tradition of having a young woman recite the proclamation and a minister give the keynote speech. That year, Mae Thomas Alexander read Lincoln's famous words, and Dr. Willis King (1886–1976) of Gammon Theological Seminary gave an address, "Seventy Years of Freedom," which the *Campus Mirror* described as "a real source of inspiration for Negro youths." In 1938, the newly appointed Reverend William Holmes Borders (1905–93) of Wheat Street Baptist Church held an audience "spellbound" with an Emancipation Day address emphasizing "Racial Solidarity." Occasionally, national NAACP leaders served as key-

note speakers: in 1934, Walter White (1893–1955), secretary of the organization, spoke about efforts to curb lynching. During the Second World
War, Emancipation Day parades drew large crowds. In 1944, companies
of black soldiers from Camp Sibert, Alabama, "marched upright and with
dignity," according to the *Atlanta Daily World*, followed by representatives
of the Red Cross and a war bond club, members of fraternal organizations,
church groups, college students, and marching bands.[29]

When the war ended, Emancipation Day celebrations shifted to civil
rights. In 1952, the *Daily World* editorialized, "Emancipation Day programs should be utilized as rallies for full freedom." In 1955, Thur-
good Marshall (1908–93), who had recently argued the *Brown v. Board*
school desegregation case before the U.S. Supreme Court on behalf of
the NAACP, served as featured speaker at Wheat Street Baptist Church.
Marshall told an audience of fifteen hundred that the landmark decision
was merely "a starting point" and that much work remained to be done
to fight segregation in public transportation, public housing, and public
bathrooms. The popular Dr. Benjamin E. Mays (1894–1984), president of
Morehouse College, spoke on another January 1 occasion to a "jam-packed
audience" at Big Bethel African Methodist Episcopal Church and told Atlantans to prepare for an "integrated world." Mays's appearance netted five
thousand dollars in contributions to the NAACP. In 1960, attorney Austin
T. Walden (1885–1965) gave a "penetrating" address at Wheat Street Baptist in which he praised the business success of Atlanta's black entrepreneurs and urged the city's African Americans to register to vote, pointing
out that only 31,163 of roughly 80,000 eligible blacks were registered.[30]

For the centennial of the Emancipation Proclamation, the celebration was held at Union Baptist Church and featured music by the choirs
of Wheat Street and Big Bethel, a reading of the proclamation by Quen-
natta Williamson, and a speech by civil rights attorney Donald L. Hollowell (1917–2004). Originally from Wichita, Kansas, Hollowell had moved
to Atlanta after serving in World War II and earning a law degree from
Loyola University in Chicago. Hollowell defended student protesters in
Atlanta's sit-ins and represented Hunter and Holmes in their effort to win
admission to the University of Georgia. After being introduced by Hunter,
Hollowell gave a speech that emphasized the work left to do, particularly
in the area of education, more than achievements already realized. He also
highlighted the importance of economic empowerment and of voting before concluding, that "Atlanta and Georgia will never be what they ought

to be until every last citizen is capable of taking advantage of all that this city and state has to offer."[31]

The Fulton County Republican Party also marked the Emancipation Proclamation centenary with a ten-dollar-per-plate fundraiser at which prominent African American journalist William O. Walker served as the featured speaker. A "crusader for social justice," Walker was publisher of the *Call and Post* newspaper, a former member of the Cleveland City Council, and had recently been appointed as Ohio's industrial relations director by incoming governor James A. Rhodes. Walker's speech combined praise for Abraham Lincoln with criticism of Democrats, whom he described as "the greatest obstacle to human rights and civil rights."[32]

On the national level, commemoration of the Emancipation Proclamation intersected with political dynamics that threatened another potential firestorm. The new leaders of the U.S. CWCC, Nevins and Robertson, recognized that African Americans could no longer be shut out of the commission's plans, both because of the centrality of slavery, emancipation, and black soldiers to the war narrative and because of the current political importance of the civil rights movement. Focused on producing a meaningful, dignified set of events to remember the Civil War, Nevins and Robertson made plans that included a meeting at the Lincoln Memorial on September 22, 1962, one hundred years to the day after Lincoln announced the forthcoming Emancipation Proclamation. Robertson, a southerner, an academic, and a journal editor, tried to assure representatives of southern state Civil War commissions that they need not worry that the event would be overly political. For their part, members of the southern commissions, concerned that obstructionism might lead to bad publicity that could jeopardize tourism, came around to endorse the U.S. CWCC.[33]

Although he personally supported the civil rights movement, Nevins hoped to keep the September ceremony focused on the general theme of freedom rather than on the specific theme of civil rights. His efforts suggest an overall emphasis on showing America's greatness in comparison with the lack of personal freedom in the Soviet Union at the height of the Cold War. Commission member Roy Davenport emphasized this theme when he said, "The true significance of the Proclamation today lies in its spirit of freedom for all men everywhere. . . . [T]his means freedom from the restraining effects of ignorance, fear, hunger, and disease . . . freedom of the human mind and spirit in all fields of creative endeavor." By emphasizing general notions of freedom and by failing to include a single African American speaker (though Mahalia Jackson was invited to sing the national anthem), CWCC organizers earned criticism from local black leaders, who, with support from Martin Luther King Jr., threatened to boycott the event. According to the *Atlanta Daily World*, the president of the Washington, D.C., NAACP declared that the absence of African American speakers "perpetuates the old stereotype of Negroes as musicians and entertainers while ignoring other important contributions made by them."[34]

In response to the criticism, the U.S. CWCC added Marshall, whom President Kennedy had appointed to serve as a U.S. Court of Appeals judge, to the program; he spoke briefly, as did attorney general Robert Kennedy and New York governor Nelson Rockefeller. Marshall's words offered a call to action: "We must . . . rededicate ourselves to the determination to recognize every American on his merit without regard to race, color or previous condition of servitude." However, the keynote speaker, U.S. ambassador to the United Nations Adlai Stevenson, returned to the theme of American superiority over the Soviet Union, describing the proclamation as having freed blacks from slavery and southern whites from "an outworn and crippling institution." He also emphasized the notion that "Western democracies and the unaligned peoples of the world have the shield against aggression that they need, and the aid necessary to uphold it." Kennedy did not appear in person, claiming a scheduling conflict, but sent a prerecorded film clip applauding African Americans for their "quiet and proud determination" in the fight for equality. The crowd was disappointingly small—just three thousand people, five hundred of them black—a low turnout that the *Atlanta Daily World* blamed on the controversy over the speakers.[35]

At an Emancipation Proclamation commemoration in New York City earlier in the month, Martin Luther King Jr. took center stage. The son of the pastor at Ebenezer Baptist Church and the church organist and choir director, King graduated from Morehouse College before earning divinity degrees from Crozer Theological Seminary in Chester, Pennsylvania, and Boston University. His involvement in the Montgomery Bus Boycott led him to become the civil rights movement's most powerful voice and most effective organizer, and in 1957 he founded the Southern Christian Leadership Conference as a vehicle for nonviolent social change. King grasped the potential to use the war's centennial and Lincoln's words about freedom and egalitarianism in the current struggle for racial equality.[36]

In 1944, while attending Atlanta's all-black Booker T. Washington High School, the fifteen-year-old King won a statewide public speaking award sponsored by the Negro Elks Club. In "The Negro and the Constitution," he contrasted the Civil War's great achievement in ending slavery with the continued discrimination against African Americans. America needed to translate the Thirteenth, Fourteenth, and Fifteenth Amendments into reality, King declared: "We may conquer southern armies by the sword, but it is another thing to conquer southern hate." He ended by invoking the spirit of Lincoln and his dream of a "new birth of freedom." The young orator hoped that a new generation would realize Lincoln's unfinished hopes.[37]

Nearly twenty years later, King invoked Lincoln's spirit when he spoke at an Emancipation Proclamation dinner hosted by the New York CWCC on September 12, 1962, at the Park Sheraton Hotel. Attended by two hundred guests, the event played out against a backdrop of racial tension in the South. Several southern Georgia churches used for voter registration had been burned to the ground, apparently by arsonists, in the weeks preceding King's speech, and James Meredith was in the midst of attempting to integrate the University of Mississippi, an effort that would produce rioting in Oxford less than three weeks later. Sharing the platform with Governor Rockefeller and historian Bruce Catton, King spoke of the Emancipation Proclamation and the Declaration of Independence as foundational documents that revealed to the world the nation's potential greatness. Yet in 1962, the country was plagued by widespread racial inequality—in law, in income, and in access to remunerative professions. King remarked on the recent violence and declared that the states of the former Confederacy were "in ceaseless rebellion" against the United States with their resistance to integration. His words also suggested criticism of the Kennedy administration for failing to take a principled stand against segregation: "No president can be great, or even fit for office, if he attempts to accommodate injustice to maintain his political balance." President Kennedy subsequently used the U.S. Army to protect Meredith when he enrolled at the University of Mississippi, and Robert Kennedy provided FBI assistance to investigate Georgia's church burnings.[38]

In October 1961, King had met with Kennedy at the White House, and according to King, when the president showed him the marker designating the exact spot where Lincoln had signed the Emancipation Proclamation, King responded, "I want you to come right back here, sir and sign the second Emancipation Proclamation." He told Kennedy that only 7 percent of schools in the South had desegregated following the *Brown* decision nearly a decade earlier, and immense disparities marked the incomes and living conditions of blacks and whites. King believed that a decree by Kennedy, like the one that Lincoln had issued, could affect change: the president could end segregation in housing, restaurants, and public transportation. When King related the story to a black crowd at Atlanta's Butler Street YMCA, those in attendance responded with a standing ovation, but Kennedy showed less enthusiasm. Fearing a backlash from white southerners in Congress, he refused to issue a second Emancipation Proclamation, and his death in November 1963 put an end to King's hopes.[39]

King's speech at the August 1963 March on Washington gave him another opportunity to use America's Civil War past to explore its civil rights present. By that summer, King had earned a national reputation as a civil rights leader. He had orchestrated a campaign against segregation in Albany, Georgia, in 1961–62 and had helped to organize nonviolent protests in Alabama the following year. Arrested for his activism, he wrote his "Letter from a Birmingham Jail" to counter the arguments of white clergy who advocated incremental change based on the passage of legislation. In the letter, smuggled out of jail and reprinted in a variety of news outlets, King defended the use of nonviolent protest against unjust laws and criticized white moderates for sitting on the sidelines in the face of racial injustice. In the summer of 1963, marchers flocked to the Nation's Capital to demonstrate for civil rights and demand job opportunities and an end to racial discrimination. King was the last of the many speakers who addressed the crowd of more than two hundred thousand, most of them black, from the steps of the Lincoln Memorial. It was the largest political demonstration Washington, D.C., had seen to that time. Although naysayers predicted violence, the crowd remained orderly.[40]

King began his remarks by paying homage to Lincoln, speaking of the president's "symbolic shadow [in which] we stand today." He called the Emancipation Proclamation a "momentous decree" that offered "a great beacon light of hope to millions of Negro slaves who had been seared in the flames of withering injustice." Most of the speech centered on America's failure to live up to Lincoln's words by falling short in efforts to affect meaningful change in the ensuing century: in King's words, "The Negro still is not free" but remains "crippled by the manacles of segregation and the chains of discrimination." But when King spoke of his dream for a

United States "free at last" from racial prejudice, he stopped his audience "in their tracks" with "an oratorical hymn to America, and its promise for the Negro," as the *Atlanta Constitution*'s Eugene Patterson reported. Veering away from his prepared text, King declared, "I have a dream that one day on the red hills of Georgia sons of former slaves and the sons of former slave-owners will be able to sit down together at the table of brotherhood." And he again mentioned his home state when he proclaimed, "Let freedom ring from Stone Mountain of Georgia." Millions of listeners heard King's words over national television and radio. The following year, he received the Nobel Peace Prize, and members of Atlanta's white business community, cajoled by Mayor Ivan Allen Jr. (1911–2003), who succeeded Hartsfield in 1962, and Coca-Cola president Robert Woodruff, held a banquet in King's honor.[41]

King's magisterial speech in Washington dwarfed anything that happened in Georgia during the centennial, but the state's CWCC continued to churn out press releases, appoint committees, and organize events. One of the most popular events commemorated the centenary of the Andrews Raid, the unsuccessful 1862 Union effort to destroy the railroad that had captivated Wilbur Kurtz.[42]

The story of the Andrews Raid was tailor-made for the kind of centennial that many Georgians envisioned, an episode that revealed the heroism of both the alert Confederates and the brave Unionists, with several raiders posthumously receiving the nation's first Medals of Honor. The Georgia CWCC organized a three-car excursion train, including the reconditioned locomotive *General*, and it was pursued by the locomotive *Texas* for a reenactment of the "Great Locomotive Chase," already the subject of a 1950s film by Walt Disney for which Kurtz served as technical adviser. Geer billed the event as "a family activity, with emphasis on authenticity, accuracy and good taste." After participating, members of the ACWRT were treated to a lecture by Kurtz, the foremost authority on the topic, who declared that the episode gave all Americans something to applaud. The raid had been "a loss for the Union," but "in a larger sense, we can but be grateful that one century later we Southerners, Northerners and Westerners—as united Americans—can meet to discuss in admiring harmony the surpassing bravery, daring and imagination exhibited by raiders and pursuers alike." In addition to roundtable members, Kurtz's audience included guests from thirty-two states, Canada, and West Germany. Local sculptor Julian H. Harris designed a commemorative medal for the Andrews Raid centennial with William Fuller's image on one side and the *General* on the other, and the Georgia CWCC sold the medals in bronze or silver.[43]

Other efforts to commemorate the Andrews Raid fizzled, however. Georgia's two senators hoped that the U.S. Postal Service would issue a commemorative stamp but were disappointed. The Georgia CWCC attempted to have a Congressional Medal of Honor granted to Private Charles P. Shadrach, an Ohio soldier executed for his part in the raid but overlooked (along with Private George Wilson) when the others received their medals. Stanley Rowland Smith reminded Betts that "one of the basic aims of the National Civil War Centennial and the Georgia Civil War Centennial is to show the development of brotherhood in peace and unity that has taken place in the past century. We can hardly find a better example of this unity than we have right here: a southern state trying to correct an omission of honor and recognition."[44]

The Georgia CWCC also had success in adding markers to supplement those commissioned by the UDC and the Old Guard of the Gate City Guard in the early twentieth century and those produced by Kurtz in the 1950s, when he researched and wrote text for a series of historical signs regarding the Atlanta Campaign. In an article noting Kurtz's eightieth birthday on February 28, 1962, the *Atlanta Journal* praised his "flair for accuracy" and noted that he had been responsible for uncovering information that led to the relocation of a monument marking the spot where General William H. T. Walker was shot.[45]

The Georgia CWCC focused on three new Civil War "marker centers" to remember the 1864 Battles of Peachtree Creek, Atlanta, and Ezra Church. In 1963, Beverly M. DuBose Jr. replaced Geer as chair of the Georgia commission when Geer was elected lieutenant governor. As a teenager in the 1930s, DuBose had toured the Atlanta battlefields with his father, Kurtz, and Garrett. Because the Georgia CWCC lacked a state-allotted budget, it had to appeal for government help to fund every project it undertook. DuBose decided to start with Peachtree Creek and obtained two thousand dollars from the City of Atlanta to establish a parking area and a paved walkway leading to a monument that had been erected by the Old Guard in 1935 and that bore an inscription honoring the valor of men both blue and gray. A women's group, the Neighborhood Garden Club, added landscaping, stone benches, and an underground sprinkler system. To further encourage public interest in military history, the Georgia Historical Commission printed a booklet identifying the state's eighteen hundred Civil War markers.[46]

In 1964, national attention focused on the centenary of the Atlanta Campaign. In February, members of the Old Guard of the Gate City Guard traveled to New York to attend a gathering hosted by the Old Guard of New York. As Atlanta's honorary militia, the Old Guard had made its first trip to New York as part of an 1879 "peace tour." This time, the Atlanta men represented one of the original thirteen colonies. According to their leader, Colonel Ben M. Butler, the Atlantans "stole the show" by parading in their distinctive white, blue, and gold uniforms while the band played "Dixie." As in 1879, the visitors stayed at the Old Guard Armory and socialized with the other twelve units.[47]

The U.S. CWCC met in Atlanta on June 10–12, 1964, drawing two hundred attendees and breaking new ground for inclusiveness. Because the national organization was now racially integrated, local planners chose the Americana Motor Hotel on Williams Street, the city's first hotel to welcome African American as well as white guests. Commission chair Allan Nevins repeated his emphasis on the need for a "dignified" centennial free of "tawdry exhibitionism and cheap theatricals." But Nevins also discussed the civil rights movement indirectly when he mentioned that "the great battle for a better America still rages." The *Atlanta Constitution*'s McGill spoke about the South's current struggles, especially its efforts to provide adequate funding for public education.[48]

Scholarly sessions covered a diverse range of topics. Historians Allen Julian and Franklin Garrett spoke to the group about the Atlanta Campaign and the role of railroads, respectively. Bell Wiley, whose scholarship focused on the lives of common soldiers, women, and slaves, chaired a session about the Confederate home front that included an emphasis on women and a presentation by the noted historian Mary Elizabeth Massey of Winthrop College. At a session on "Problems of the Civil War," Roy Davenport spoke on "Personnel Problems, Then and Now" and Tulane University's Charles P. Roland discussed "Confederate Military Leadership." Two members of the Illinois Commission, Clyde Walton of the Illinois State Historical Library and Ralph G. Newman of Chicago's Abraham Lincoln Book Shop, talked about scholarship for the future in "After the Centennial—What?" Mayor Allen spoke at the final luncheon, returning to a traditional theme, the shared valor of all Civil War soldiers, with an examination of the deaths of Confederate General William H. T. Walker and Union General James B. McPherson during the Atlanta Campaign.[49]

For the gathering's banquet, Wiley and DuBose hosted a barbecue on Stone Mountain, a choice that allowed the organizers to avoid the public debate over integration of restaurants. Interest in the Stone Mountain Confederate carving was rekindled in the run-up to the centennial, and at a 1959 meeting of the U.S. CWCC in Richmond, Virginia, members heard presentations from two Georgians: Wiley, who emphasized the need for scholarships and fellowships to fund future study of the war, and Doris Lyle, president of the Georgia UDC, who dubbed the Confederate carving a "capsule of history." With only the head of Robert E. Lee completed, the project might be perceived as a white elephant, but she insisted that the rest of the carving could be completed and paid for with admission fees. For their part, state officials, professional historians, and Confederate heritage groups hoped that a finished Stone Mountain would promote tourism.[50]

The UDC retained a proprietary interest in Stone Mountain that dated from Helen Plane's initiation of the idea. In 1945, the Georgia Division joined Hartsfield in calling for a new effort to finish the work, because, in his words, "the South owes a debt of honor to the living and revered dead" of the Confederacy and because the Children's Founders Roll campaign of the 1920s had led thousands of young people to donate pennies. The mayor insisted that tourism would generate revenue to sustain the project. In 1958, the Georgia Legislature finally acquired twenty-five hundred acres encompassing Stone Mountain, purchasing the largest parcel from the Venable family for $1.125 million. The governor created the seven-member Stone Mountain Memorial Association that included several state officials as well as Doris Lyle. The association sought to complete the carving in time for the start of the centennial.[51]

The state hoped to attract tourists by adding a recreational lake and moving antebellum buildings to the site, but first it needed to rid the mountain of the Ku Klux Klan. By 1960, most Georgia political leaders regarded the Klan as a liability in the effort to attract tourists and business investment. In 1946, the state attorney general took action in court to revoke the Klan's charter, and the legislature enacted a law banning the wearing of masks on public property. At the same time, however, the civil rights movement's successes caused the Klan to step up its activism. In July 1962, the group organized a rally on Stone Mountain after the NAACP held its national convention in Atlanta, the city's lunch counters were integrated, and African Americans began to press for an end to segregation in restaurants and hotels.[52]

On Saturday night, July 7, a group of Klansmen led by Georgia Klan Dragon Calvin Craig and Imperial Wizard Robert M. Shelton of Alabama, met in a pasture on the southwestern edge of the mountain, a parcel owned by James R. Venable. In addition to burning a cross, those in attendance heard speeches attacking the U.S. Supreme Court, the NAACP, Jews, Negroes, the police, John and Robert Kennedy, Allen, and Vandiver, who had forbidden the Klan from holding meetings on the state-owned mountain. According to one observer, all of these individuals and groups were accused of being "either Communists or communistically influenced." The estimated seven hundred people in attendance, including women and children, then began to climb the state-owned side of the mountain, singing the national anthem and "Dixie" and raising an American flag. When a contingent of state troopers, DeKalb County police, and park security officers attempted to stop the Klan's advance, a melee ensued, and several Klansmen were clubbed and one was taken to a hospital. Not only outnumbered ten to one but also fearing further violence, especially given the presence of children, the officers ultimately agreed to allow twenty Klansmen to climb the mountain for a "religious ceremony." But as officers moved aside to let the delegation pass, the entire crowd surged up the mountain. According to some accounts, Klan leaders placed women and children in the front to ensure that police would not stop the onrushing crowd. Vandiver subsequently ridiculed the Klan for hiding behind women and children and promised that any future KKK efforts to rally on the mountain would be met with adequate force, including National Guard if necessary.[53]

Two years later, when the mountain hosted the barbecue, a severe electrical storm nearly derailed the event by preventing the skyride from operating, but those able to climb to the top ate a meal of southern fried chicken while listening to local author Maggie Davis talk about *The Far Side of Home*, her novel that follows a non-slave-owning Confederate soldier from Georgia through the Atlanta Campaign. Northern delegates admired the mountain and carving, expressing the hope that it would be completed. The following month, new Georgia governor Carl Sanders (1925–2014) waved a Confederate flag when the carving effort officially resumed after a lapse of thirty-six years.[54]

With its scholarly presentations and allusions to current events, the CWCC meeting represented one side of the Atlanta centennial; another side was represented by a series of less serious events, including a sham battle held at Stone Mountain in July 1964. DuBose planned a reenactment at the base of Stone Mountain to commemorate the Battles of Peachtree Creek, Atlanta, and Ezra Church.[55]

In what became known as the Battle of Stone Mountain, three thousand spectators watched as more than four hundred "authentically uniformed" participants, many with vintage weapons from the 1860s, reenacted the fighting. Supplementing the cast of several hundred infantry, additional men on horseback acted as mounted cavalry, and women pretending to be nurses cared for the mock wounded. Before the battle began, Allen Julian provided some historical background, and at the end the Confederates declared victory, though the actual events of a hundred years earlier had a far different outcome. The Georgia CWCC also staged other mock battles. In 1963, DuBose had helped to organize a reenactment of the Battle of Chickamauga in Northwest Georgia, and earlier in the summer of 1964, a reenactment at Kennesaw Mountain entertained crowds in Cobb County. In addition, the Battle of Jonesboro was reenacted south of Atlanta in August.[56]

Atlantans marked the centenary of the city's surrender to General Sherman on September 2, 1964, and its partial burning and destruction by the Union army the following November with fireworks. The pet project of Hartsfield, the mock burning of Atlanta was held nightly between October 1 and October 10 as part of the annual Southeastern Fair. Workmen constructed a 350-foot-long reproduction of the Five Points neighborhood, complete with rail station, hotels, banks, churches, and stores. At precisely 10:30 each night, a three-minute pyrotechnical display set to music (including "Dixie" played as a dirge) signaled the close of the fair for the day. Hartsfield brought William Tecumseh Sherman Fitch, the general's great-great-grandson, to Atlanta to view the exhibit, and the *Atlanta Constitution* printed a photograph of him holding a pack of matches. The former mayor seemed delighted with the results of his effort, telling a reporter, "It's all in a light vein. . . . We want to show people what Atlanta has done in the last 100 years."[57]

According to historian John Bodnar, "The Civil War Centennial Commission did a great deal to promote local celebrations of the war and its era." The Georgia CWCC sponsored many events during the four-year centennial, including an essay contest for high school students that was won by Ann Gregory of Eatonton for "Industries of Georgia, 1861." Speakers from the Georgia CWCC fanned out across the city and state during the centennial, providing informational talks to civic groups, while the Atlanta Public Library distributed a list of recommended war-related titles, among them Mary Gay's "little-known" *Life in Dixie during the War*. The Georgia CWCC's goal of publishing a series of scholarly books did not come to fruition, although the U.S. CWCC's Robertson helped obtain copies of microfilmed Atlanta Civil War newspapers from Ohio so that local scholars might have access to these resources.[58]

The Georgia CWCC sent narrative material to newspapers in the state, which then ran stories about what happened during the war. The *Atlanta Journal* reprinted entire pages of 1864 newspaper stories in a 1961 series on "The Atlanta Century" that earned an award from the U.S. CWCC. Ulysses S. Grant III presented the award to the *Journal's* editors in Atlanta and praised the series for "promoting, both at home and abroad, better understanding of the great American conflict of a hundred years ago." The *Atlanta Constitution* regularly printed "War Diary" entries that recounted specific historical events. Beginning on January 1, 1964, the state commission sponsored a year's worth of two-minute radio programs that aired daily on eighty stations across Georgia, relating the news one hundred years ago on that day. "Confederate Diary" spots aired on WSB-TV three times a week from April to September 1964. For its part, the *Atlanta Daily World* printed an occasional series, "Centennial Scrapbook: The War for the Union, 1861–1865," that was distributed by King Features Syndicate. Although the series was not specifically framed for an African American audience, it included topics often left out of traditional southern narratives, including Native Americans who served in the Union army and challenges Lincoln faced in his 1864 reelection effort. And the use of the phrase *The War for the Union* indicated a very different viewpoint from that espoused by those promoting a "Confederate Diary."[59]

The centennial provided a boost to tourism and advertising, just as the Georgia CWCC had hoped. The State of Georgia promoted automobile tourism with a booklet, *7 Georgia Centennial Tours*, that featured maps and reprinted photographs from the 1860s. At Stone Mountain, shops reported brisk sales of items such as minié balls, Confederate money, and small bales of cotton, some of it purchased by visitors from the North who had never seen these items before. In 1961, the U.S. CWCC published *Aids for Advertisers*, distributed to companies in Atlanta by Coca-Cola executive Wilbur Kurtz Jr. The booklet suggested ways to incorporate the Civil War into ad campaigns, with specific advice for drug companies, clothing companies, banks and financial institutions, tobacco companies, railroads, and airlines. As it always did, the CWCC reminded businesses that the centennial was a commemoration, not a celebration. Atlanta companies supported the centennial in a variety of ways. Citizens and Southern National Bank ran an ad campaign, while the Trust Company of Georgia sponsored a pamphlet about the Battle of Peachtree Creek. Coca-Cola offered "A Tribute to American Valor," dedicated "To the lasting memory of all the men who fought in the Great Brothers' War—those who fought and lived, those who fought and died, those who gave much, and those who gave all." With this ad, Coke got to the heart of the matter. No longer viewed as a War between the States, the conflict was now cast as a disagreement among brothers.[60]

In May 1964, DuBose issued a report. By way of background, he asserted that the U.S. Civil War "retained the glamour of the age of chivalry," adding that it also constituted the first modern war because it involved advanced weapons, including automatic rifles and surveillance balloons. DuBose noted the shared sacrifice of men on both sides of the conflict and a death toll that represented more than the combined mortality figures of all the other U.S. wars to date, including Korea. He concluded, "The Civil War was our War, wholly American, fought on American soil by Americans for American ideals and beliefs. This War touched almost everyone."[61]

African Americans were among those touched most profoundly by the Civil War. Nationally, 189,000 black men fought for the Union, and nearly four million African Americans were freed from slavery. In this light, the *Atlanta Daily World* printed "Our History and the Civil War Centennial" in February 1963. Noting that Jews, Irish, Swedes, Hungarians, Poles, and many others groups were partnering with the U.S. CWCC to ensure that their stories were told, the newspaper asked a simple question: "What about the Negro?"[62] With the exception of the inclusion of African American delegates and at least one speaker at the Atlanta meeting of the U.S. CWCC, Georgia's CWCC largely ignored African Americans and their history of the Civil War. Donald Hollowell, Charlayne Hunter, and Martin Luther King Jr. did not, however. Their efforts reminded all Georgians that the Civil War's legacy of freedom applied to black Americans above all. With the civil rights movement now tied to the war's ideals and gaining momentum and national recognition, white people in Atlanta and elsewhere had increasing difficulty turning the other way.

## CHAPTER 7

# Shades of Gray

IN 2016, former member of the U.S. Congress and mayor Andrew Young said that in Atlanta, Civil War commemoration is not "just black and white; there's always been shades of gray." Young's comment was in reference to a controversial plan by a wealthy Atlantan, Rodney Mims Cook Jr., who offered millions of dollars to construct a park in a poor black neighborhood and erect statues of civil rights leaders as well as a statue of his forebear Livingston Mims. But Atlanta NAACP president Richard Rose objected because Livingston Mims, another former mayor of the city and donor of the land used to create an earlier park in the area, had been an officer in the Confederate army. Although Cook dropped the plan to erect a statue, Rose insisted that Mims's name could not be used for the park; Cook, for his part, insisted: the name was a "deal breaker." Young ultimately helped find a compromise. The park would be named for Rodney Mims Cook Sr., the benefactor's father and a civil rights supporter. The two sides agreed, and the incident came to represent a classic example of what is often called the "Atlanta Way," in which leaders engage in intense negotiations with stakeholders to broker compromise.[1] By the 1970s, Atlanta had become a majority-black city with African American political leadership ascendant at City Hall, and black mayors beginning with Maynard Jackson in 1974 grappled with the complicated issue of Civil War memory. The period since the Civil War centennial of 1961–65 has witnessed ongoing debate over the Stone Mountain Confederate carving, efforts to preserve the Atlanta Cyclorama and the Margaret Mitchell House, conflict over the state flag, and the thorny issue of how to interpret the Civil War for an international audience at the 1996 Olympic Games. Atlanta's long-standing commitment to business development and compromise—the "Atlanta Way"—was tested as never before.

With the purchase of Stone Mountain from the Venable family in 1958, the State of Georgia created the Stone Mountain Memorial Association (SMMA) to complete the Confederate carving and develop the surrounding parkland as a tourist destination. Although the effort to finish the task in time for the Civil War centennial failed, work had begun in earnest by that point. To attract tourists anxious for an "authentic" Old South experience, the SMMA purchased a plantation house and outbuildings and moved them to Stone Mountain from sites around the state, and the complex opened in 1963. On weekends, guests might be greeted by the actress Butterfly McQueen, who played the role of the slave Prissy in *Gone with the Wind* and who worked as a guide, signed autographs, and posed for snapshots with visitors.[2]

The United Daughters of the Confederacy (UDC) wanted recognition for the organization's historical role in the Confederate carving and asked for a chapel to be named in the UDC's honor; instead, the association proposed a flag terrace. To raise money, the UDC sold bricks from the Confederate Soldier's Home, which the state razed in 1967 following the deaths of its final residents. In October 1964, the UDC dedicated a terrace in front of Stone Mountain's Confederate Hall. The terrace featured an American flag flying above four Confederate flags. The *Atlanta Constitution* noted that the presence of the Daughters signaled their first official act on the mountain since Gutzon Borglum's dismissal. Gertrude Kibler of Atlanta, honorary president of the Georgia Division, attended the terrace dedication as part of the organization's state convention. Forty years earlier, she had watched Helen Plane pull the cord to reveal Gutzon Borglum's head of Robert E. Lee.[3]

The SMMA generated negative publicity when newspapers reported cost overruns in the development of a skyride, an artificial lake and marina, and the plantation, but the Stone Mountain Inn caused the most negative press. In May 1964, the *Atlanta Constitution* charged that although the entire Stone Mountain complex had already cost the state $11.2 million, the motel sat empty and six of seven members of the SMMA board did not even know about its construction until well into the project. Editor Eugene Patterson was especially angry that the state had spent money to install bidets, which he defined for readers as "a form of sitz bath" common in European hotels but not in American motels. Public outrage over the bidets led the state to spend even more money to remove them.[4]

The Confederate carving was the SMMA's top priority, but the choice of a sculptor generated controversy. Among those considered was Lincoln Borglum, Gutzon Borglum's son and an accomplished sculptor in his own right, who was backed by those who still preferred the elder Borglum's vision for the mountain. Another possibility was Julian Harris, who had been employed as an interim carver in the 1940s, but Lamar Dodd, chair of the University of Georgia's Art Department, argued against Harris's hiring, leading to suggestions that Dodd did not want to privilege someone who had ties to his university's rival, Georgia Tech. The SMMA ultimately selected Walker Hancock (1901–98), who proved to be a wise choice. His previous commissions had included the St. Louis Soldiers' Memorial (1937–39) and the widely acclaimed Pennsylvania Railroad War Memorial (1949–52). Hancock's distinguished career also included four years of service in the U.S. Army as one of the "Monuments Men" who protected works of art during the Second World War. Some of Hancock's colleagues had helped to recover works of art stolen by the Nazis.[5]

When he accepted a contract from the board, Hancock believed that he was being hired to sculpt a new memorial at the base of the mountain and that Augustus Lukeman's carving would remain in its unfinished state. Hancock proposed adding an abstract figure holding aloft a broken sword to symbolize the fractured Union. However, Hancock was soon confronted with a series of what he called "surprises." At a meeting with Atlanta politicians and newspaper reporters, he was astonished when reporters questioned his personal dedication to the cause because he hailed from Missouri, which was not a Confederate state. The sculptor assured his critics that both of his grandfathers had been Confederate soldiers and that his father had been an official with the Sons of Confederate Veterans. He was even more astounded to learn from politicians that "the people of Georgia" insisted on the completion of Lukeman's equestrian figures of Jefferson Davis, Robert E. Lee, and Stonewall Jackson before Hancock could add his own creative touches. In his memoir, Hancock recalled that such "difficulties" would "plague me for the next fifteen years. Perhaps I should have withdrawn politely."[6]

Like Gutzon Borglum, Hancock spent years visiting Stone Mountain to oversee the project. The use of thermo-jet torches (replacing Borglum's pneumatic drills) made the work proceed far more efficiently. Hancock modified Lukeman's design by carving only the upper bodies of the horses and allowing the lower portions to fade into the granite mountain. With the help of designer Ralph Griswold, Hancock developed a plan to frame the carving with bronze towers on either side. After spending years working on the towers and completing sixty-five-foot plaster models, Hancock encountered another surprise as he prepared to have the bronzework completed in England: the SMMA had run out of money. Hancock must again have wondered whether he should have "withdrawn politely" from the project. In the end, he was forced to abandon the towers partly because of finances and partly because the base of the mountain, previously believed to be vertical, instead had a large protrusion of metamorphic rock that was revealed when workmen removed rubble left by earlier crews.[7]

With much fanfare, the Stone Mountain Memorial Dedication Committee planned the unveiling. Chaired by Georgia senator Herman Talmadge, committee members included Governor Lester Maddox; Atlanta mayor Ivan Allen; UDC Georgia president Jewell Renfroe and national president Alice Whitley Jones; philanthropists, including Coca-Cola president Robert W. Woodruff; representatives of the news media, including C. A. Scott of the *Atlanta Daily World*; and Professor Bell Irvin Wiley of Emory University. The committee formally invited President Richard Nixon to be the keynote speaker at what was billed as a "forum for another historically timely appeal for American unity."[8]

National unity did not characterize the United States in 1970. A few weeks before the Stone Mountain event, in an effort to crush the Viet Cong and end the war in Vietnam, Nixon sent troops to invade Cambodia, a move that led to nationwide protest over a war that was becoming unpopular even in the conservative South. Preoccupied with the military situation, Nixon announced at the last minute that he would not attend the unveiling in Stone Mountain and instead sent Vice President Spiro Agnew. A divisive figure, Agnew had recently generated controversy with his comments labeling students, radicals, and other dissenters "an effete corps of impudent snobs who characterize themselves as intellectuals" and suggesting that "we can afford to separate them from our society with no more regret than we should feel over discarding rotten apples from a barrel."[9]

Wiley and several other committee members objected to having Agnew in attendance at the ceremony, with Wiley declaring that "as a Southerner, I am deeply disturbed that the address is to be made by Agnew." Agnew's presence constituted "an affront" to Robert E. Lee, who believed in the right of dissent, resigning his commission in the U.S. Army to join the Confederacy. As a college president after the Civil War, "Lee believed in higher education. He didn't believe college students and professors were bums. He believed in youth and reconciliation." Newspapers across the country reprinted Wiley's words to the committee, and the history professor received a variety of letters from friends and foes. One Memphis woman insisted that if Lee were alive, he would side with the vice president rather than the "violent left wing radical college students and professors that seem hell bent on destroying America."[10]

In addition to the publicity caused by Wiley's protest, the Ku Klux Klan generated headlines when Imperial Wizard James R. Venable, whose family had previously owned the mountain, protested the choice of William Holmes Borders to give the benediction. Borders, "a member of the negro race," as Venable put it, was pastor of Atlanta's Wheat Street Baptist Church, a speaker at Emancipation Day celebrations beginning in the 1930s, and a leader in civil rights efforts, including the successful integration of Atlanta's public transportation in the 1950s. Members of the dedication committee hoped that the choice of the Reverend Billy Graham to give the opening invocation might please white conservative evangelicals and offset criticism of Borders, but Graham's last-minute decision to skip the event left attendees wondering since his name appeared in the program. Given the tension generated by Vietnam, Agnew, and racial dynamics, the event's theme of "Unity through Sacrifice" seemed like a stretch. According to the *Atlanta Constitution*, after "a long week of political flack over Agnew's appearance, officials were ready . . . to let bygones be bygones."[11]

The actual event on Saturday, May 9, 1970 was peaceful but "subdued," as the *Atlanta Constitution* put it. The newspaper also noted that the event drew just ten thousand people, far from the seventy thousand to one hundred thousand the dedication committee had hoped would attend. Among the audience were descendants of Stonewall Jackson and Augustus Lukeman as well as Hancock himself, who was not on the program and received little attention. Agnew made a dramatic entrance in a helicopter that flew across the mountain carving before landing in a parking lot nearby. His twelve-minute speech praised Jackson's "loyalty," Davis's "dignity," and Lee's "honor," and the audience applauded when Agnew quoted Lee: "Abandon all these local animosities and make your sons Americans." Agnew then turned his attention to the Vietnam War, saying that men of the North and the South were fighting side by side in Indochina. He referred to the Cambodian situation indirectly by saying that President Nixon believed in the need to eliminate "close sanctuary from which [American soldiers] can be attacked," a comment that received "mild applause," according to one account. He ended with a clarion call for unity and invoked the memory of the Civil War. "Let no one here or abroad mistake disagreement with disunity. We are reminded here today that we have paid too great a price for being one nation to let ourselves now come apart at the seams." Borders ended the program with a benediction that included not only Confederate leaders but also Agnew, Nixon, and, in a spirit of inclusiveness not seen previously at public ceremonies on Stone Mountain, Abraham Lincoln.[12]

While Agnew spoke about unity at Stone Mountain, protesters filled the streets of American cities and college campuses to voice their opposition to the Cambodian invasion and their sympathy for four unarmed student protesters killed at Kent State University by National Guardsmen five days earlier. Governor Maddox dismissed classes on all state university campuses in Georgia on Friday after hundreds of college students held protests at Emory, Georgia Tech, Georgia State, and Oglethorpe Universities. While the Confederate carving was unveiled at Stone Mountain, five thousand protesters—most of them young white high school and college students—staged an antiwar demonstration fifteen miles away in Atlanta. Some students waved flags representing the Viet Cong or red and anarchist flags to show their opposition to Nixon's war policies while shouting "1, 2, 3, 4, Tricky Dicky, End the War." One protester, apparently unnoticed by police, added a red flag to the statue of John B. Gordon at the capitol.[13]

Historian Cynthia Mills has written that "the meaning of public sculpture is not fixed but changes as audiences' experiences and beliefs grow increasingly distant from original understandings." In the aftermath of the Stone Mountain unveiling, a war of words continued, as local people attempted to appropriate Lee's legacy. At the 1924 unveiling of Borglum's version of Lee's head, the general had been hailed as representing the best of the Confederacy. At the 1928 unveiling of Lukeman's version, Lee was applauded as representing the best of America. In 1970, contentious debate concerned how he would have handled the Vietnam protests. The *At-*

*lanta Constitution* weighed in after taking aim at Agnew. On the day before the ceremony, the newspaper called for a southern welcome out of respect for the vice president's office but also called the choice of Agnew as speaker "a shame and a disgrace." Echoing Wiley, the paper opined that Agnew dishonored the legacy of Lee, a man of "patience" and "self-control" who would never have criticized dissenters as "effete snobs." In response, Frank O'Neill of Atlanta wrote to the paper's editor to call Agnew "an ignorant and opportunistic man" who did not deserve to be vice president or to "dedicate a memorial to genuinely talented and worthy, if misguided, men." In a November 1969 speech, Nixon had coined the phrase *silent majority* to refer to the portion of the American public that quietly supported his policies, and the paper printed another letter in which a "Member, Silent Majority," wrote, "I have great respect for the memory and the ideal of General Lee, and I think if he were alive today he would be just as against all this rioting as Mr. Agnew is." At a fundraising dinner in Texas a few weeks later, Agnew lambasted the liberal press and its "daily torrent, assailing our ears so incessantly [that] we no longer register shock at the irresponsibility and thoughtlessness behind the statements."[14]

As the story of Stone Mountain began to wind down, the story of the Atlanta Cyclorama generated increased public interest. The painting became newsworthy again when preservationists warned that it was disintegrating. Not only was the physical structure that supported it unsound, but it had been coated with rat poison during the 1930s restoration, and red clay added to the diorama for authenticity kicked up dust every time the air-conditioning system cycled on.[15]

Discussions of the Cyclorama's future elicited strong emotions. *Atlanta Constitution* columnist Jack Spalding called the painting "a civic treasure but a neglected one" and identified a further complicating factor. The Grant Park neighborhood where it resided had once been a genteel enclave of big trees and Victorian homes, a tourist destination that included the city zoo as well as the Cyclorama, but now attracted African American homeowners. Three issues needed to be addressed: Would the city spend the money to restore an icon representing its Civil War history? If so, how would the city's growing black population react to the expenditure of a significant amount of tax money for the painting's renovation? Finally, would white tourists visit the neighborhood? In Spalding's words, neither "the Civil War nor the Grant Park neighborhood are high fashion at this time."[16]

In 1973, Atlanta had elected Maynard Jackson (1938–2003) as its first African American mayor. Grandson of civil rights leader John Wesley Dobbs and son of a pastor and a college professor, Jackson graduated from Morehouse College before earning a law degree from North Carolina Central University. He took the mayor's office at the age of thirty-five by winning the votes of African Americans and white liberals. Committed to serving all of the city's constituents, Jackson left no doubt about his support for the restoration effort. On the steps of the Cyclorama building during July 1975 and flanked by members of a citizens' group, Save the Cyclorama, he declared "Cyclorama Day." He also displayed personal items belonging to a Confederate soldier who had died in the Atlanta Campaign that had been discovered in the Cyclorama museum.[17]

Although Jackson committed his administration to the painting's preservation, debate arose over whether it should be moved to a location where it might draw a greater number of tourists—perhaps someplace closer to downtown Atlanta's convention hotels. One suggestion was a triangular piece of land at the intersection of Peachtree and West Peachtree Streets, near the place where Henry Grady's carefully orchestrated tribute to Ben Hill had occurred in 1886. Another possibility was the site of Loew's Grand Theatre, the location of *Gone with the Wind*'s 1939 premiere, which was for sale. On March 25, 1977, the *Atlanta Constitution* reported that "smart money says the City Council and Mayor Maynard Jackson will reluctantly decide to move the Cyclorama downtown." The *Constitution* backed this move on the grounds that it would generate revenue for the city. Nonetheless, in April 1977, the Atlanta City Council voted to fund the painting's restoration but keep it in Grant Park, where, proponents argued, it was much closer to the site of the battle it depicted. In addition, they believed that the painting was too fragile to be moved.[18]

The question of funding the restoration, estimated to cost $7.8 million, now moved to the fore. Jackson promised that the city would find the money but also insisted that companies contracted to do the work must hire members of minority groups, including African Americans, Hispanics, and Asians. When several members of the Georgia Legislature subsequently proposed moving the painting to Stone Mountain, the mayor reacted angrily, alleging that the proposal was racially motivated: "I resent implications from certain quarters that because the mayor is black, the city will let the Cyclorama rot." The Jackson administration cobbled together the funding, receiving $1.5 million from the state, $1.8 million in local bond funds, $2.5 million in revenue bonds to be sold later, and $2 million from an anonymous donor. A lightning strike that damaged the painting in July 1979 accelerated the plan, and work began in earnest on October 31.[19]

To handle the fragile painting, the city hired New York–based conservator Gustav Berger, whose team of sixteen repaired 874 holes in the painting's fabric ranging in size from half an inch to several feet and added a new backing to reinforce the painting. In the diorama, the Georgia clay floor was replaced by fiberglass. Workers removed lead, chlorine, and arsenic that had been applied to the painting in the 1930s to prevent fungus and mildew and to kill rats. Another team restored the locomotive *Texas*, which was housed in the Cyclorama's "musty concrete basement." Contractors created a new 184-seat auditorium where visitors could view a twelve-minute film contextualizing the Atlanta Campaign.[20]

On June 1, 1982, the refurbished Cyclorama opened with a big celebration. Mayor Jackson spoke, as did Berger. The 3rd Army Band, folk dancers, and rock groups performed. One Atlantan who attended, E. Gordon Robinson, praised the military band but expressed disappointment at what he regarded as a serious omission. "They never did play 'Dixie,'" he told columnist and humorist Lewis Grizzard. "How could they leave out 'Dixie'?" Reflecting the political change that had come to the city, officials at City Hall had quietly but firmly nixed "Dixie" and decreed that there would be no Confederate uniforms or flags and no flag of Georgia with its Confederate symbol. It appeared that times had indeed changed in Atlanta.[21]

The headaches that the Cyclorama caused for Atlanta's first black mayor were duplicated by the headaches that the Margaret Mitchell House restoration caused for his successor, Young (1932–). A native New Orleanian and Congregational minister, Young had moved to Atlanta in the early 1960s and became one of Martin Luther King Jr.'s closest lieutenants. Young won election to Congress in 1972, making him the first African American from the South to serve in that body since Reconstruction. President Jimmy Carter, a fellow Georgian, subsequently appointed Young to serve as the U.S. ambassador to the United Nations, and then in 1981 he won the first of his two terms in the Atlanta mayor's office. Like Jackson a consensus builder, Young understood the importance of Mitchell and her novel, noting in his memoir that she promoted "myths and legends of the Old South . . . on a grand scale." But he also acknowledged that "even before Coca-Cola became the world's most well-known brand and CNN was piped into every home with a cable connection," *Gone with the Wind* "defined the city of Atlanta to the world."[22]

As mayor, Young had to consider whether to support a local effort begun in the 1980s to preserve Mitchell's apartment at Tenth and Peachtree Streets, the tiny unit where she began her married life with John Marsh in 1925 and lived until 1932, writing most of *Gone with the Wind* seated at a typewriter in the living room. Although opponents of preservation pointed out that Mitchell disparaged the apartment as "the Dump" and moved out when her finances improved, she was fond of applying humorous monikers to many buildings, including the *Atlanta Journal* office where she once worked (the Black Hole of Calcutta) and the newspaper cafeteria (the Roachery).[23]

On the one hand, Mayor Young knew that the property was decrepit and that developers wanted to tear it down and put up a new structure, but he also listened to preservationists who wanted to save the apartment as well as people who believed that the apartment would draw tourists. Although many locals supported the preservation effort, Celestine Sibley, a friend of Mitchell's and an *Atlanta Constitution* columnist, questioned it, recalling that the author had wanted no shrine to her memory and believed that *Gone with the Wind* served as her legacy. In addition, objections to the novel's Lost Cause–influenced depiction of the antebellum South further complicated the issue of whether to preserve Mitchell's apartment.[24]

The City of Atlanta had done very little to commemorate its most famous author, partly because Mitchell was known to be an intensely private person who avoided publicity and had no interest in being officially recognized. The Special Collections Department of the Atlanta Public Library sponsored the only significant memorial to her memory, which consisted of items donated by her family. In accordance with Mitchell's wishes, Marsh had bequeathed hundreds of his wife's personal items to the library, and they form the centerpiece of the Margaret Mitchell Collection. They include the typewriter on which she wrote *Gone with the Wind*, a collection of books that she used in researching the novel, her Pulitzer Prize and National Book Award, foreign-language editions of *Gone with the Wind*, photographs, and memorabilia relating to her work as a Red Cross volunteer in the Second World War. The collection opened to the public in 1954, two years after Marsh's death, in the Margaret Mitchell Memorial Room, but when the library moved to a new building close by in 1980, the Mitchell Collection no longer had a separate space. Nonetheless, the library's Special Collections Department displays items from the Mitchell Collection, and they attract visitors from around the world. In 1967, the City of Atlanta designated Margaret Mitchell Square near the library at the intersection of Peachtree Street, Forsyth Street, and Carnegie Way. Twenty years later, the city added a fountain featuring metal columns intended to evoke southern antebellum architecture. No other sites were dedicated to Mitchell or her novel.[25]

In late 1987, a developer's application to demolish Mitchell's apartment building brought the matter to a head. Mayor Young sided with preservationists after learning that Atlantans had pledged a considerable amount of money to renovate the structure. Moreover, preservationists who helped to save the historic Fox Theatre in the 1970s inspired the formation of the Atlanta Urban Design Commission, which worked to save other historic properties from the wrecking ball. During nearly a year of negotiations, the commission created a preservation plan for the city that included a landmark-designation system.[26]

The next step was to find a leader savvy enough to handle the fundraising, renovation issues, and political dynamics of what became known as the Margaret Mitchell House. A local philanthropist, Mary Rose Taylor, who had seen the film but had never read the book, stepped forward to steward the project, demonstrating the sort of resolve and tenacity that Scarlett O'Hara and her creator would have admired.[27]

Born in Denver and raised in Greensboro, North Carolina, Mary Rose attended the University of North Carolina in the early 1960s and was a supporter of the civil rights movement. After working as a journalist in New York, she moved to Atlanta as a reporter for the local NBC news affiliate. Several years later, she married C. McKenzie "Mack" Taylor, a wealthy local developer. With her husband's support, Taylor quit her job and became a full-time philanthropist, focusing her efforts on saving the Mitchell House. Taylor, who had read about efforts in the late 1980s to save the Dump, formed a nonprofit, Margaret Mitchell House Inc., in November 1990. Despite the many pledges of support in preceding years, the Dump had barely ten thousand dollars in the bank when she took on the project, and that money was quickly spent on repairing the structure's roof.[28]

Taylor's effort faced continued opposition despite the mayor's support. In 1991, the *Atlanta Journal* printed a story, "Margaret Mitchell's 'Dump':

Trash or Treasure?," in which state representative Mable "Able Mable" Thomas of Fulton County stated, "The house may have some historic associations, but African-Americans shouldn't help restore and glorify it." She added, "We don't need another symbol of past injustices." Undeterred, Taylor developed a $2 million plan to restore the house and build a museum. She held a fundraiser at the Fox Theatre with a *Gone with the Wind* screening, preceded by a short film that featured Young (by now the former mayor) and the current mayor, Jackson, who had returned to the office for a third term in 1990.[29]

Atlanta would be hosting the 1996 Summer Olympics, bringing the attention of the world to the city, and Taylor and her team hoped that the house and museum would open for local and international visitors by that time. With the goal of increasing the restoration's visibility, she allowed the Mitchell House to be used for a September 1994 art installation staged in conjunction with an arts festival in Piedmont Park, the site of the Cotton States Exposition ninety-nine years earlier. For the installation, *Multi-Cultural Diplomats*, by Massachusetts Institute of Technology artist Ritsuko Taho, the grounds of the Mitchell House were covered with thousands of inflated rubber gloves, each containing a piece of colored paper on which an Atlantan had written a wish. Taylor's hopes for positive publicity and a smooth construction/completion effort ended in the early morning hours of September 17, when arsonists set fire to the Mitchell House.[30]

Within hours after the flames were extinguished, Taylor planted herself in front of the house and began fending off looters. Within weeks, she signed a contract with German automaker Daimler-Benz to pay for the building's $4.5 million restoration, prompting a flattering local newspaper story featuring a photograph of Taylor in a scarlet jumpsuit captioned "She gives a damn." Restoration efforts proceeded, and the house was scheduled to open on June 30, 1996, less than three weeks before the start of the Olympics. On May 12, however, the Mitchell House was torched a second time, destroying nearly the entire building, though Mitchell's ground-floor apartment was spared.[31]

The double arsons drew international media coverage, and Taylor mounted an exhibit about Mitchell and the house at a visitor center next door. During the Olympics, many people drove past the ruins and stopped at the visitor center, including French racewalker Nathalie Fortain, who described *Gone with the Wind* as "the most famous American novel we know in Europe. We're very sorry about what happened." She continued, "It's a revelation to see where Margaret Mitchell was inspired to write this large novel, in this small space."[32]

When the Mitchell House finally opened in 1997, Taylor had triumphed not only over bricks and mortar but also over the city's racial divisions. Taylor made several decisions that helped her effort. First, she created a business plan for the house that included two goals: preserving it as a city landmark and using it as a venue to promote a broader discussion of the South's literary tradition. Toward this end, she created the Center for Southern Literature, which met at the house, and recruited her literary friends Pat Conroy and Tom Wolfe to serve on its advisory board and speak at fundraising events. Second, Taylor worked to make sure that the Mitchell House reflected and incorporated African Americans and their history as well as that of the white southern past. She insisted that African Americans hold a significant number of seats on the Mitchell House board of directors. Among the directors was Dr. Otis Smith, one of more than twenty African Americans who had earned medical degrees at Morehouse School of Medicine in the 1940s with the help of a secret financial backer who they later learned was Margaret Mitchell. To ensure the city's continued support of her effort, Taylor became active in city politics and co-chaired Bill Campbell's successful 1993 campaign for the mayor's office.[33]

Historian Jennifer Dickey has noted that "a defining moment" for the Mitchell House came in 2001, when Taylor invited author Alice Randall to give a lecture for the Center for Southern Literature. Earlier in the year, Randall had published *The Wind Done Gone*, a parody of *Gone with the Wind*. The Mitchell estate had attempted to prevent Randall from releasing her novel, and it generated mixed reviews and a great deal of controversy. Randall's appearance at the Mitchell House before a crowd of several hundred led to protests, with one individual wearing a Confederate uniform standing outside the house. Randall engaged in heated exchanges with audience members, claiming that "my own mother was damaged by" the racism in *Gone with the Wind* "and has all kinds of problems with racial identity," calling one employee of the house "my example of another generation of black women damaged by" the novel, and sniping at Taylor herself. Nevertheless, Taylor declared the evening was a success because it had brought important issues before the public.[34]

Pearl Cleage's appearance at the Mitchell House in 2006 was another literary milestone. Two years earlier, Taylor had stepped down after fourteen years as executive director of the museum, and the Mitchell House merged with the Atlanta History Center, though Taylor maintained her ties to the enterprise through the Center for Southern Literature. Cleage's appearance was certain to be controversial. A resident of Atlanta since 1969, when she enrolled at Spelman College, Cleage (1948–) had published plays, novels, and works of nonfiction emphasizing themes of feminism and African American identity and had joined the college's faculty as writer in residence. When the Mitchell House burned in 1996, Cleage wrote a piece in the *Atlanta Tribune* headlined "Going, Going, Gone," in which she made clear that although she did not advocate arson and did not know who set the Mitchell House fire, she was nonetheless "delighted" at the building's destruction. Mitchell's Dump was "an insult of monumental proportions" toward black people, and "we should rejoice in the destruction of such a blatant monument to white supremacy." Although she did not publicly comment on Cleage's piece, Taylor was thrilled by the editorial, believing that it would generate the kind of debate that could inspire public interest in racial dialogue.[35]

Cleage gave a dynamic lecture to a packed house. Raised in a "black nationalist household" on the west side of Detroit, she had begun reading *Gone with the Wind* at the age of eleven but stopped when her mother told her that Scarlett was a slave owner and "unworthy of the emotional investment one must make in the main character of any novel." Cleage ultimately decided to finish it and stunned members of the audience by admitting that she "loved the book, from first page to last," as a compelling love story and because of "the power of the word." The novel would have been better, in Cleage's opinion, if Mitchell had recognized that "Mammy and Prissy and Uncle Peter and Big Sam *each had their own spark of divine fire.* . . . But Margaret Mitchell didn't live long enough to write that book, so I'm left to take comfort in the fact that the fictional Miss Scarlett, and her slave-owning real-life counterparts, lost the war." Cleage noted that the war had freed her forebears and allowed her to pursue her own career as a writer.[36]

If the Margaret Mitchell House drama ended in a compromise that pleased many, the debate over the Georgia state flag caused divisions that dominated headlines for several decades and proved to be one of the most intractable issues on which to achieve compromise. In 1956, the state had adopted a new flag featuring the Confederate St. Andrew's cross. Although a white member of the state legislature from South Georgia raised the issue of changing the state flag in 1969, this effort did not gain traction with colleagues. However, a racial incident in Forsyth County brought the issue back before the public in January 1987. When civil rights marchers, among them Coretta Scott King (1927–2006) and Andrew Young, met in Cumming to remember the 1912 lynching of a black man that had led the county's one thousand black residents to flee, Klan members staged a counterprotest, shouting racist slogans at the marchers. The Klan's activity led to a second civil rights march that drew an estimated twenty thousand participants, and Georgia governor Joe Frank Harris (1936–) ordered an investigative committee to examine the episode. The committee concluded that the Confederate symbol on the state flag was a factor inciting racism and violence and recommended its removal.[37]

Advocates of a new flag won a powerful ally when Zell Miller (1932–2018) became governor in 1991. A rural Georgian with Confederate ancestors, Miller tried to use his family history and political popularity to win support for a flag change, eliciting support from many Atlantans, including African Americans, progressive whites, and businessmen, some of whom expressed concern about the state's reputation in the run-up to the Olympic Games. Veronica Fields, a student at historically black Clark Atlanta University, got to the heart of the matter later that year, writing, "When Martin Luther King, Jr. and other leaders of the Civil Rights movement started demonstrating during the 1950s, the Rebel logo gained more popularity than it had during the Civil War." She added, "America's so called 'Melting Pot' is boiling over. Who do you think is getting scorched?" Miller made the issue the centerpiece of his January 1993 State of the State address. Reminding colleagues of his family's ties to the Confederacy, including a great-grandfather wounded at the Battle of Chancellorsville, Miller noted that the 1956 flag had been chosen during a period of resistance to racial integration and that "we have long since repudiated every element of those shameful 1956 days of defiance—except for the flag they created." The governor concluded, "If you're truly proud of this state, and all its 260 years, if you look forward and want to play a significant part in what Georgia can become, then help me now to give bigotry no sanction and persecution no assistance."[38]

Although Miller's popularity remained high and both the *Atlanta Journal* and the *Atlanta Constitution* supported the effort, the legislature refused to go along. The Speaker of the Georgia House, South Georgia's Tom Murphy, announced that "95 percent of my people do not want the flag changed." In an attempt to forge a compromise, the governor asked his supporters in the legislature to introduce a bill to restore the pre-1956 flag as the state's official flag but retain the current flag for ceremonial and memorial occasions. This idea, however, provoked opposition from civil rights leaders, with the Southern Christian Leadership Conference's Joseph Lowery declaring, "The state ought to have one flag and it ought not to be the rebel flag." Miller's bill passed the Senate but was withdrawn for lack of support in the lower chamber. Even the Olympics failed to generate momentum toward changing the flag. In fact, some critics castigated local Olympic organizers for rejecting Atlanta's Old South and Civil War heritage by selecting a goofy mascot, Izzy, that symbolized nothing. Nevertheless, the City of Atlanta and its suburban counties ignored the state's inertia and began flying the pre-1956 flag.[39]

The Olympic Games presented civic leaders with an important challenge: how to present a city with a Confederate past to an international audience. Local planners, including Andrew Young and businessman Billy Payne, hoped to use the Games to showcase Atlanta as a place characterized by tolerance, hospitality, and business opportunity. Like organizers of the Cotton States Exposition a century earlier, Olympic planners wanted to downplay the Old South and the Civil War. As the *Atlanta Journal*'s Jim Auchmutey put it, "Rebel flags, hoop skirts and other Old South vestiges give Atlanta's Olympic planners indigestion." He might have added *Gone with the Wind* to that list. Olympic organizers could not entirely ignore Atlanta's wartime legacy, but they could downplay it and focus instead on the civil rights movement. As a starting point, symbols pertaining to the Civil War, including the state flag, were absent from official venues. Concerned that Atlanta might be associated in the public's mind with the Ku Klux Klan (Stone Mountain was an Olympic venue), the *Journal* quoted Young: Stone Mountain is part of "our past. It's who we are," but also noted that the mountain that had been the site of the Klan's twentieth-century rebirth was now home to a middle-class black neighborhood.[40]

Olympic planners commissioned an opening ceremony on July 19, 1996, that engaged the South's contested past in a way that was designed to offend no one and culminated in a tribute to the civil rights movement. An "artistic segment," "Atlanta," featured chrome pickup trucks circling the Olympic stadium, cheerleaders performing acrobatic routines, African American step dancers, and European American clog dancers. A "pageant opera," "American South," presented dancers in butterfly-like costumes with broad wingspans in the middle of the stadium representing the pre–Civil War "American Southern Spirit," with additional actors manipulating twenty-eight-foot puppets in white dresses and tuxedos. The Atlanta Symphony Orchestra played "Ol' Man River" in the background. An enormous mechanical thunderbird then entered the stadium, shrouding the dancers with a gray cover reflecting the devastation of the Civil War and the history of slavery and discrimination. To symbolize Atlanta's phoenix-like emergence from war, dancers appeared in multicolored wings. Flashing lights added drama, as did music from the symphony and the choirs of Morehouse and Spelman Colleges. The opening ceremony also paid tribute to Martin Luther King Jr. and the civil rights movement before ending with Muhammed Ali lighting the Olympic cauldron. Although the second week of the Atlanta Olympics was marred by a pipe bomb that exploded in Centennial Olympic Park, killing two and wounding dozens, the Games brought several million visitors, helping the city rebrand itself as an international city where everyone got along and where the past was safely in the past.[41]

The reemergence of the flag issue served as a reminder that the past was not safely in the past, and it fell to Georgia's post-Olympics governor, Roy Barnes (1948–), to replace the state's controversial banner. Barnes wanted to avoid the divisions that characterized Miller's effort as well as to avoid South Carolina's travails. South Carolina had raised a Confederate battle flag at its capitol in 1962 during the Civil War centennial but did not take it down when the centennial ended. Organized efforts to remove the battle flag included a threatened boycott by the NAACP, which jeopardized the economic viability of the state's tourist beaches and historic sites. Barnes worked behind the scenes and marshaled his considerable political skill and resources. He received support from an array of allies, including the Chamber of Commerce and the University of Georgia's beloved former football coach, Vince Dooley. After Barnes was sure that he had enough votes, his surrogates in the legislature introduced a bill that changed the state flag, and the bill passed in a startlingly short period of time, thereby avoiding another lengthy public debate. The new flag featured the state seal on a blue background above three historical Georgia flags flanked by U.S. flags under the heading "Georgia's History." By including the 1956 flag as part of "Georgia's History," the governor and his supporters could refute those who claimed that the new flag erased the state's Confederate heritage. In a gesture to Confederate heritage supporters, Barnes also brought back to the Georgia Capitol a seven-foot portrait of Robert E. Lee that the UDC had donated to the state in 1963 and that had been transferred to storage in the 1980s.[42]

Although Barnes made history, he did so at a personal cost. Proponents of the 1956 flag—dubbed "flaggers" by the media—labeled the governor "King Roy" and protested the lack of public input into the change. One vocal Barnes opponent, Elijah Coleman, raised money to plant 1956 flags on private land throughout the state, especially along what he called "Scalawag Alley" highways between Atlanta and the Alabama state line. Barnes also made politically controversial decisions when he ended tenure for the state's new public schoolteachers and supported the construction of the Northern Arc, a highway along Atlanta's outer perimeter. His growing unpopularity and the national political trend toward conservatism resulted in Barnes's defeat and the election of Sonny Perdue (1946–), the state's first Republican governor since Reconstruction. After his 2003 inauguration, Perdue wasted no time in securing passage of a bill that created yet another state flag. Reminiscent of the pre-1956 banner, the 2003 flag included the state seal on a blue background in the upper left-hand corner and red and white stripes. Perdue submitted the new flag to voters in a nonbinding 2004 referendum, and it received overwhelming approval, in part because of the Georgia Chamber of Commerce's endorsement, which included a mailing that touted Andrew Young's support for the new flag. The referendum quieted those who had complained about a lack of public input into the 2001 flag change, and despite occasional protests by flaggers, Georgians appear to have made peace with their flag.[43]

With the debate over flags still fresh in the public mind, Atlantans demonstrated little enthusiasm for mounting a significant commemoration of the Civil War's sesquicentennial, 2011–15. In a minimal gesture toward promoting tourism, the state appropriated $380,000 to create a website promoting Civil War sites. The Georgia Historical Society added a few historical markers around the state to highlight the role of African Americans, women, and Unionists, whose stories had largely disappeared from public memory. In April 2011, the society unveiled a marker regarding "The Burning and Destruction of Atlanta" that emphasizes General William T. Sherman's destruction of "railroads, factories, and commercial buildings of possible use to the Confederacy" and states that Sherman destroyed just 40 percent of Atlanta's buildings, "contrary to [the] popular myth" that he leveled the entire city. Despite its benign language, the sign generated controversy because of its placement next to the Georgia Railroad Depot, at Martin Luther King Jr. Drive and Central Avenue. Although the sign is placed at the spot where Sherman's firing of the city is believed to have started, the Reverend R. L. White, a local NAACP official, argued that the sign's proximity to Martin Luther King Jr. Drive "strikes us as a kind of in-the-face thing." For his part, Edward DuBose of the Georgia NAACP opined, "We don't think the Civil War should be celebrated or commemorated. It should be a time [when] the nation should repent." Other black leaders felt differently, however. Michael Julian Bond, a member of the Atlanta City Council and the son of civil rights leader Julian Bond, insisted that "the basic roots of freedom for African Americans effectively began in this spot." National news outlets picked up the controversy, emphasizing the sesquicentennial's potential to create racial division.[44]

The Atlanta History Center mounted two sesquicentennial exhibits, *War in Our Backyards*, examining the Civil War in its local context, and *Confederate Odyssey*, displaying firearms, uniforms, and flags from local collector George W. Wray Jr. In 2013, the Atlanta History Center began to hold annual celebrations of Juneteenth, the date in 1865 when enslaved people in Texas learned of their freedom. The two-day event includes storytelling, crafts, and uniformed interpreters acting as soldiers in the U.S. Colored Troops. During the sesquicentennial, the *Atlanta Journal-Constitution* printed a few stories about how white and black Atlantans currently perceive what happened during the war, and a local group, B*ATL, offers walking tours, wreath-laying ceremonies, and lectures to commemorate the Atlanta Campaign every July.[45]

Since the sesquicentennial ended, some issues regarding Civil War remembrance have been resolved with minimal controversy. In 2012, declining visitor numbers and the need for further restoration work prompted Mayor Kasim Reed (1969–) to announce that the Cyclorama would move to the campus of the Atlanta History Center. More than twenty-five million dollars in donations (including ten million dollars from Lloyd and Mary Ann Whitaker) enabled not only the conservation of the painting but the construction of a new facility that also houses the *Texas*, one of the locomotives involved in the Andrews Raid. The History Center's president, Sheffield Hale, emphasized that the painting would not be interpreted as either Union propaganda (its original purpose) or Confederate propaganda (the function it served during the heyday of the Lost Cause).

Instead, the painting provides a record of Atlanta in 1864 and the battle that helped to end the Civil War and shape the modern city. The new exhibit opened to the public in February 2019. The Atlanta Cyclorama and its counterpart at Gettysburg are the only remaining circular paintings in the United States.[46]

The June 2015 massacre of nine black church members in Charleston, South Carolina, by a white supremacist brought new focus to the issue of Confederate symbols. Before committing the crime, the perpetrator had been photographed draped in a Confederate flag, and the murders led South Carolina to remove the Confederate flag from its capitol as well as to broader national discussion about Confederate symbols. One month after the tragedy, the Atlanta NAACP called for the destruction of the Stone Mountain carving, while New Orleans mayor Mitch Landrieu launched an effort to have the city council declare four Civil War–era statues a "public nuisance." Landrieu succeeded, and the statues were removed in the spring of 2017. Landrieu's decision to move the statues in the middle of the night generated national headlines. Baltimore's mayor took similar action a few months later.[47]

Richmond, Virginia, capital of the Confederacy, took a different approach. The modern city government has always understood the economic importance of Civil War tourism, so rather than taking down statues, Richmond added new ones to a city known previously for its enormous equestrian bronzes of Lee, Jackson, and Davis. Public sculptures in Richmond now include a tribute to African American tennis star Arthur Ashe, a native of the city, and the Virginia Civil Rights Memorial. The Shockoe Bottom neighborhood, which once housed a slave market, now includes a statue of Maggie Walker, the first African American woman to charter a bank. In 2018, after a lengthy effort that included multiple meetings with a variety of interest groups, a commission appointed by Richmond's mayor recommended removing the Davis statue, "the most unabashedly Lost Cause in its design and sentiment," leaving Lee and Jackson in place.[48]

In Atlanta, stakeholders have taken varying approaches to Civil War commemoration in the twenty-first century. One approach is to avoid controversy by treating the subject lightly. Stone Mountain Park, the state's most visited tourist attraction, projects a "Lasershow Spectacular" onto the mountain every night from April through October, attracting a diverse crowd of spectators, including many family groups, motivated in part by the modest cost of admission. The Lasershow attempts to offer something for everyone. Most of the show is projected against the mountain but not against the Confederate carving. Beginning with the American flag, the show then honors individual branches of the military, Atlanta sports teams, and area colleges and universities. The music includes Chuck Berry's "Bye Johnny" and Jerry Lee Lewis's "Great Balls of Fire" (illustrated by fireworks). Only about five minutes of the fifty-minute presentation concerns the Civil War, introduced by an image of a cannon. As "Dixie" is played as a dirge, spectators see the figures of Jefferson Davis, Robert E. Lee, and Stonewall Jackson on horseback, outlined in colored lights, appear to ride away. Images of the Confederate states outlined in colored lights separate from the North and then return as the music shifts to "Battle Hymn of the Republic" to symbolize the united nation. The show then quickly moves on to offer tributes to Martin Luther King Jr., John F. Kennedy, Hank Aaron, Rosa Parks, the American family, first responders, the space shuttle, and soldiers from the American Revolution and the Second World War. The extravaganza closes with images of an American eagle, Mount Rushmore, the White House, the U.S. Capitol, and Uncle Sam before the letters USA appear over the Confederate carving while more fireworks explode.

As kitsch, the Lasershow succeeds admirably, a kind of NASCAR version of the 1996 Olympic Games opening ceremony with its gliding butterflies representing "American Southern Spirit." Both tableaux offer Atlantans anxious to avoid the messy topic of Civil War commemoration an escape from serious reflection. Tony Horwitz, the Pulitzer Prize–winning author who traveled the South to chart "dispatches from the unfinished Civil War," viewed the show during the 1990s and called it "a puddle of political correctness. The message seemed to be that there was no message."[49]

Another approach to Civil War commemoration focuses on the addition to public spaces of new monuments and portraits. This process began in the 1970s when Governor Jimmy Carter, understanding that the State Capitol was surrounded by statues representing leaders of Georgia's Confederate and Jim Crow eras, commissioned new portraits for the building's interior. They honor Martin Luther King Jr., Reconstruction-era legislator Bishop Henry McNeal Turner, and educator Lucy Craft Laney. In 1978, members of the Georgia Legislative Black Caucus unveiled a sculpture for the Capitol's exterior commemorating the Reconstruction-era expulsion of all African American members of the State Senate and House of Representatives. *Expelled Because of Their Color* by Spelman College sculptor John Riddle Jr. examines the history of African Americans from slavery to freedom and political empowerment. The circular bronze features a series of small abstract figures climbing upward topped by figures holding aloft a crown in the shape of the state of Georgia to symbolize the achievement of black political power. On August 28, 2017, after years of negotiations and delays caused by the death of the first sculptor, an eight-foot bronze statue of King was unveiled at the Georgia Capitol. Completed by Martin Dawe, the statue faces the city's iconic Martin Luther King Jr. Drive and commemorates King's August 28, 1963, address at the March on Washington. In 2018, the High Museum of Art added a fifty-eight-foot cut-paper installation, *The Jubilant Martyrs of Obsolescence and Ruin*, by Kara Walker. Mounted on a curved wall intended to evoke the Cyclorama, *Jubilant Martyrs* consists of a series of large silhouettes that represent scenes of racialized violence in the Old South. According to the High Museum's description, the artist "casts her critical gaze on the Confederate figures carved into the Stone Mountain monument in direct challenge of the bigoted history it commemorates."[50]

Sheffield Hale, CEO of the Atlanta History Center, and Michael Thurmond, CEO of suburban DeKalb County (home to Stone Mountain), have worked to find consensus on the future of Georgia's Confederate monuments. Hale, an Atlanta native, wrote an opinion piece for the *Atlanta Journal-Constitution* in 2013, nearly two years before the Charleston murders drew national attention to the issue. He described the Civil War centennial as a "missed opportunity to deal truthfully" with the war's legacy and complained about the "apathy" that had become apparent during the sesquicentennial. Hale insisted that "the Atlanta History Center does not seek to celebrate the Civil War" but reminded fellow citizens that "the outcomes of the Civil War are relevant to all, just as the promise of the civil rights movement is integral to all Americans." After New Orleans and Baltimore removed Confederate statues, Hale and his staff created the Confederate Monument Interpretation Guide. The History Center believes that decisions regarding the retention or removal of monuments "should be made locally in a way that respects all community members" but that monuments "must be contextualized and transformed into educational tools." To facilitate this process, the History Center's website provides a template that includes background material about statues, information on current historical scholarship, and recommended language to help communities add context to their monuments.[51]

Thurmond (1953–) has made consensus building a centerpiece of his public career, which began in the 1980s when he became the first African American since Reconstruction to represent Athens, Georgia, in the state legislature. Thurmond later won election to the post of Georgia's labor commissioner, ran unsuccessfully for the U.S. Senate, and served as superintendent of DeKalb's school system before becoming the county's CEO in 2017. Author of *Freedom: Georgia's Antislavery Heritage, 1773–1865* and a frequent public speaker and local television and radio interviewee, Thurmond argues for a broader interpretation of Stone Mountain that places the Lost Cause interpretation of the war in historical context and includes narratives of women, slaves, and Unionists. Speaking in front of the Confederate carving at Stone Mountain on the fiftieth anniversary of Martin Luther King Jr.'s April 4, 1968, assassination, Thurman declared, "If you want this day to be special, you will rededicate yourself to fulfilling the unfinished work that Dr. King left behind." Another speaker, State Senator Emanuel Jones, endorsed the idea of a bell tower atop the mountain to honor the "I Have a Dream" speech and King's legacy of activism, an idea first proposed by Bill Stephens, CEO of the SMMA. Admiring Thurmond's commitment to a consensus-based path forward on the topic of the mountain, Republican governor Nathan Deal (1942–) appointed him in August 2017 to serve as the first African American member of the SMMA board.[52]

The issue of what to do with Confederate monuments is complicated by several factors, beginning with a state law passed in 2001 as part of Governor Barnes's ill-fated flag bill, that prevents any effort to "deface, defile, abuse contemptuously, relocate, remove, conceal or obscure" a Confederate monument. The popular Deal made incremental changes during his two terms in office (2011–19) while trying to avoid stoking public controversy over the issue of Confederate commemoration. In the aftermath of the Charleston murders, Deal withdrew the state's Sons of Confederate Veterans specialty license plate because it displayed a large Confederate flag. The action led eight hundred flag supporters to rally on Stone Mountain, where their face-off against counterprotesters generated national news. The governor's negotiations with the Sons of Confederate Veterans led to a new license plate with a smaller Confederate flag. Deal also changed the name of state holidays honoring Robert E. Lee's birthday and Confederate Memorial Day so that they are known simply as "state holidays" that "those so inclined" may celebrate as they choose. However, Deal has been quoted as saying that discussions of removing the Confederate carving from Stone Mountain are "not useful," a view shared by Georgia

House Speaker David Ralston, who opposes recent legislation that would give local communities control over statues. According to Ralston, "The history of Georgia applies wherever you live in Georgia. . . . [T]o let different communities pick and choose the history of the state and what we're going to memorialize, to me, seems to be divisive."[53]

Although Atlanta mayors and politicians statewide have sought consensus on the issue of Confederate symbols since debate over the flag ended in the early 2000s, Stacey Abrams, who in 2018 became the first African American woman to run as the Democratic candidate for governor, endorsed the position that the Stone Mountain Confederate carving should be removed. Abrams narrowly lost to Brian Kemp, with both candidates avoiding the topic of Stone Mountain during the campaign. Other African American politicians have not followed Abrams's lead on Stone Mountain, although Congressman John Lewis, an esteemed veteran of the civil rights movement, has supported the removal of Alexander Stephens's statue from the National Statuary Hall in the U.S. Capitol. Andrew Young has not directly addressed the issue of Stone Mountain but has maintained a centrist position on the issue of monuments, telling a reporter that those who want to erase history are "like the Taliban trying to destroy the ancient cultures of people they no longer support." Young added that "For a city to thrive and survive we need to overcome and forgive. . . . The civil rights movement thrived because of reconciliation."[54]

Efforts to remove monuments in Atlanta have encountered legal and logistical roadblocks. In 2017, a group of activists in affluent, politically liberal, majority-white Decatur rallied against an obelisk erected in 1908, objecting to its language that Confederate soldiers "were a covenant-keeping race." Although the group secured the approval of DeKalb's county commission and a legal opinion from the county's attorney allowing for the relocation of the monument as long as it is visible, the city failed to find a new location suitable to stakeholders.[55]

In late 2017, Kasim Reed, term limited and in the final weeks of his tenure as Atlanta's mayor, appointed a committee to consider whether to remove monuments within city limits and change street names with Confederate connections. Reed said that his decision to convene the committee on short notice and to insist that it issue an immediate report was based on the murder of Heather Heyer during a white supremacist rally in Charlottesville, Virginia, the previous August. At an Atlanta rally to protest Heyer's death, the 1911 Peace Monument in Piedmont Park, which features an angel standing over a Confederate soldier surrendering his gun, became the target of a crowd of black-clad "antifa" protesters. While a lone African American policeman guarded the statue, Black Lives Matter marchers attempted to shield him from the antifa rowdies. No one was hurt, but the antifa protesters defaced the Peace Monument with red paint and broke off its olive branch. After quick deliberations, the mayor's committee of eleven recommended the renaming of Confederate Avenue, East Confederate Avenue, and streets named for Confederate generals as well as the removal of two monuments on city property that represented Lost Cause ideology—the Peace Monument and the Peachtree Battle monument (1935), both of which had been erected by the Old Guard.[56]

Reed's successor, Keisha Lance Bottoms (1970–), convened her own committee consisting of three members of the city council. Advised that Georgia law prevented the removal of the two statues and in light of a new state law increasing the legal penalties against those who vandalize monuments, the committee voted to leave the monuments where they are and to add signage contextualizing them. The Peace Monument is now flanked by two large signs that note the monument's focus on white veterans while ignoring black veterans and "the acceptance of segregation and white supremacy by both Southern and Northern populations" at the time of the monument's placement. Additional language identifies the monument as "an artifact" that "should no longer stand as a memorial to white brotherhood." According to Hale, Atlanta is the first U.S. city with a no-removal state law to add such markers. Similar markers have been added to Confederate monuments at Oakland Cemetery. Although the NAACP's Atlanta branch president, Richard Rose, accused the city council of being "complicit on compromising on racism," the contextual markers represent another effort to achieve success through the "Atlanta Way." DeKalb County has also added a plaque providing context to its Confederate obelisk.[57]

As debate continues over Confederate monuments, traditions that link Atlanta to past forms of Civil War commemoration endure. The NAACP continues to sponsor annual commemorations of Emancipation Day at African American churches. The Jubilee Day services acknowledge the Emancipation Proclamation but are more likely to emphasize "slaves who . . . acted to secure their liberty" than the role of Abraham Lincoln, as Rose put it in 2018. Before an audience of several hundred African Americans and a few whites, Rose spoke of the need to register voters and raise money and to avoid glorifying the Confederacy, noting that Adolf Hitler is part of German history but is not honored on the side of a mountain. In Rose's words, the Civil War "was not an honorable dispute" but a "failed insurrection against the United States." Although the war "has never ended," he urged his audience, "Let's put it to rest."[58]

The UDC continues to draw crowds numbering in the dozens to its annual observances of Confederate Memorial Day. Organized by the Alfred Holt Colquitt Chapter, the services at Oakland Cemetery evoke the traditions begun by the Atlanta Ladies Memorial Association—the laying of wreaths, the playing of music, and the ritual of mourning the dead. But there are key differences between the original Confederate Memorial Day celebrations and the modern ones. Although the occasions still feature white women wearing pastel dresses and hats, the role of keynote speaker is not reserved exclusively for men. In 2018, Ava Cheryl Manley, a retired nurse, suggested that Confederate soldiers enlisted because they wanted to fight for their states, with slavery as a "secondary issue." She also insisted that twenty-first-century standards should not apply to men who lived 150 years ago. She argued, "We can love [our] ancestors without loving what the war was about" and "honor the warrior but hate the war." Concluded Manley, "All history, both good and bad, has something to teach us."[59]

In the twenty-first century, Atlantans continue to grapple with the question of how to remember a war that shaped their city and region. Can Atlantans achieve a broad consensus about the war, one that acknowledges its causes rooted in slavery, its loss of life and physical destruction, its legacy of racism, and the actions and motives of men and women who lived a century and a half ago and commemorated the war in a time very different from our own?

Perhaps the best indication of Atlantans' changing attitudes is represented by the city's Martin Luther King Jr. Day celebrations, which have largely replaced Confederate Memorial Day as annual civic occasions. Robert E. Lee's birthday in January is no longer a state holiday, but Martin Luther King Jr. Day is a federal one. Throughout the metropolitan area, Atlantans honor King's legacy with parades, lectures, church services, theatricals, free admission to local sites and museums, and days devoted to service projects, and significant numbers of both black and white Atlantans attend these events. Again, in Andrew Young's memorable words, "In Atlanta, it's not just black and white; there's always been shades of gray."[60]

# NOTES

| | |
|---|---|
| *AC* | *Atlanta Constitution* |
| *ADW* | *Atlanta Daily World* |
| AHC | Atlanta History Center, Kenan Research Center |
| *AJ* | *Atlanta Journal* |
| *AJC* | *Atlanta Journal–Constitution* |
| APWS Collection | Atlanta Pioneer Women's Society Collection, Atlanta History Center, Kenan Research Center |
| AUC | Atlanta University Center, Robert W. Woodruff Library |
| BIW Papers | Bell Irvin Wiley Papers, Emory University, Stuart A. Rose Manuscript, Archives, and Rare Book Library |
| DFC | DuBose Family Collection, Atlanta History Center, Kenan Research Center |
| GB Papers | Gutzon Borglum Papers, Library of Congress |
| GCWCC Collection | Georgia Civil War Centennial Commission Collection, Georgia State Archives |
| HWG | Henry Woodfin Grady |
| HWG Papers | Henry Woodfin Grady Papers, Emory University, Stuart A. Rose Manuscript, Archives, and Rare Book Library |
| JBGF Papers | John Brown Gordon Family Papers, University of Georgia, Hargrett Rare Book and Manuscript Library |

MM                   Margaret Mitchell

*NYT*                *New York Times*

SMC                  Stone Mountain Collection, Emory University, Stuart A.
                     Rose Manuscript, Archives, and Rare Book Library

SMCMA Records        Stone Mountain Confederate Monumental Association
                     Records, Stone Mountain Collection, Emory University,
                     Stuart A. Rose Manuscript, Archives, and Rare Book
                     Library

UGA                  University of Georgia, Hargrett Rare Book and
                     Manuscript Library

WGKS Papers          Wilbur G. Kurtz Sr. Papers, Atlanta History Center,
                     Kenan Research Center

Winter diary         Rogers Winter diary, Stone Mountain Confederate
                     Monumental Association Records, Stone Mountain
                     Collection, Emory University, Stuart A. Rose Manuscript,
                     Archives, and Rare Book Library

## PREFACE. SOLOMON LUCKIE AND THE LAMPPOST

1. *AC*, December 14, 1939; *AJ*, December 14, 1939; WABE radio, June 6, 2017. The *AC* (founded 1868) and *AJ* (founded 1883) were Atlanta's leading newspapers. They merged to become the *Atlanta Journal-Constitution* in 2001. Atlanta Gas Light Company's *Blue Flame News*, February 1956, notes the lamps' placement in 1855 and the destruction of Atlanta's gas plant in November 1864.

2. Brundage, *Where These Memories Grow*, 5.

3. For an overview of scholarship about Civil War memory, see Cook, "Quarrel Forgotten."

## CHAPTER 1. THE LOST CAUSE

1. *AC*, April 28, 1875.

2. *Gate City Guardian*, February 16, 1861; *Atlanta Daily Intelligencer*, February 18, 1861; Wilson, *Baptized in Blood*, 10–11, 19–21; Alan T. Nolan, "The Anatomy of the Myth," in Gallagher and Nolan, *Myth of the Lost Cause*, 11–34.

3. Faust, *This Republic of Suffering*, xiv, 236–37. In an article in the Boston-based *Atlantic Monthly* after the war, John Townsend Trowbridge wrote about his experience visiting the site of intense fighting at the Wilderness in Virginia. By 1865, American soldiers had been reinterred at two national cemeteries nearby, but a pair of unburied bodies—identified by Trowbridge's guide as North Carolinians by the distinctive buttons on their jackets—were left behind. Trowbridge called the treatment of these unburied bodies "shameful" (Trowbridge, "Wilderness," 45–46). In 1866, Congress passed legislation creating a system of national cemeteries. The Army Quartermaster's Department was charged with their upkeep. See Piehler, *Re-*

*membering War the American Way*, 3, 51; Guelzo, *Reconstruction*, 1; Janney, *Remembering the Civil War*, 229.

4. Blight, *Race and Reunion*, 1–3.

5. Venet, *Changing Wind*, 25–35.

6. Ibid., 64–67, 83–90, 102–4, 141–42, 146–47.

7. Ibid., 156–79; Richards, *Sam Richards's Civil War Diary*, 228–33.

8. Venet, *Changing Wind*, 169–73; Sidney Root, "Memorandum of My Life," 4, 16, Sidney Root Papers, AHC; Carrie Berry diary, September 7, 1864, Carrie Berry Papers, AHC.

9. *Atlanta Daily Intelligencer*, September 18, 1864; Henry Hitchcock diary, November 15, 1864, Library of Congress. Sarah Huff, a child during the war, remembered Atlanta's "profound stillness" in *Atlanta Journal Magazine*, July 15, 1934. The Library of Congress's Miscellaneous Manuscript Collection is an excellent source for the burning and destruction. For an overview, see Stephen Davis, *What the Yankees Did to Us*, 370–71, 392–99, 427.

10. *Atlanta Daily Intelligencer*, February 11, 1866; Venet, *Changing Wind*, 184–89, 193–95; Garrett, *Atlanta and Environs*, 1:669–70; Russell, *Atlanta*, 116–265.

11. *AC*, November 27, 1875.

12. Ibid., February 10, 1874 (Dunning), November 27, 1875 (Calhoun), February 4, 1882 (Angier); see also January 7, 1879 (Angier as mayor); Venet, *Changing Wind*, 195–96. For a discussion of Angier, see Dyer, *Secret Yankees*, 139–44.

13. *AC*, October 15, 1876 (Congress), October 14, 1888 (Sherman), November 29, 1888 (mayor), November 10, 11, 1890 (obituaries). The *Chicago Inter Ocean*, October 5, 1888, reported that "Philadelphia papers" had printed the allegations between Markham and Sherman.

14. Dyer, *Secret Yankees*, 144–46; Faust, *This Republic of Suffering*, xi–xiii; Hacker, "Census-Based Count"; typescript of Mary Williams's letter to the *Columbus Times*, March 12, 1866, Atlanta Ladies Memorial Association Records, AHC; Janney, *Burying the Dead*, 39. The term "republic of suffering" paraphrases Frederick Law Olmstead.

15. *Atlanta Daily Intelligencer*, June 14, 1866. The bodies of all but sixteen of the Union soldiers were eventually moved to Chattanooga's National Cemetery or elsewhere. See Davis and Davis, *Atlanta's Oakland Cemetery*, 114.

16. *Atlanta Daily Intelligencer*, June 15, 1866; Venet, *Changing Wind*, 217–19; Brown, *Civil War Canon*, 101. According to William A. Blair, *Cities of the Dead*, 50, "For more than a decade, and possibly for more than two, the dominant motivation behind Confederate commemorations was to maintain a sectional identity that defied complete assimilation within the Union."

17. Neff, *Honoring the Civil War Dead*, 144–45; Blight, *Race and Reunion*, 51, 78–81.

18. Gallagher, *Jubal A. Early*, 24. See also Gallagher, *Confederate War*; Gary W. Gallagher, "Shaping Public Memory of the Civil War: Robert E. Lee, Jubal Early, and Douglas Southall Freeman," in Fahs and Waugh, *Memory of the Civil War*, 39–63.

19. Foster, *Ghosts of the Confederacy*, 40–41; Neff, *Honoring the Civil War Dead*, 159–60.

20. "History of the Atlanta Ladies Memorial Association," 27–34, Atlanta Ladies Memorial Association Records, AHC; *AC*, June 30, October 18, 1870.

21. *AC*, April 28, 1874; "History of the Atlanta Ladies Memorial Association," 33–34, Atlanta Ladies Memorial Association Records, AHC.

22. *AC*, December 9, 1868 (money sent to Virginia), July 27, 1870; Venet, *Changing Wind*, 219. For a list of ALMA officers in the nineteenth century, see ALMA subject file, AHC.

23. "History of the Atlanta Ladies Memorial Association," 27–28, Atlanta Ladies Memorial Association Records, AHC; Faust, *This Republic of Suffering*, 236.

24. *AC*, July 29, 1869 ("holy duties"), June 24, 1871 ("in her defense"), May 14, 1872 (hotel discount), April 25, 1875 (Mayor C. C. Hammock's proclamation), March 21, 1879 (Kimball House), April 24, 1895 (holiday); see also May 6, 1895.

25. Ibid., September 25, 1868 ("one day's pay"), August 31, 1871, June 16, 1874 (Madame Jarley), October 18, 1884 (city appropriations), May 2 and June 6, 1871 (parties), April 30, 1891 (collection box that raised $108.66), March 11, 1874 (general discussion of ALMA fundraising), April 22, 1886 (annual two-hundred-dollar contribution).

26. Ibid., April 22, 1886, April 21, 1888, May 3, 1889 (headstones), April 22, June 7, 1891 (shafts).

27. Ibid., April 27, 1894; Venet, *Changing Wind*, 220.

28. John Milledge had been advocating for a veterans' organization for nearly a decade before the group formed. See *AC*, May 1, 1881, April 3, 1889, April 26, 1890, April 8, 1895 (vets). ALMA's declining influence corresponded with the death of Fannie Milledge.

29. Rodgers, *History*, 25, 117, 133–34 (Calhoun speech). Lieutenant W. L. Calhoun served in the siege of Vicksburg and was later wounded at Resaca during the Atlanta Campaign. For a typescript account of his wartime role, see Calhoun Family Papers, AHC.

30. Rodgers, *History*, 4, 24, 152; Marten, *Sing Not War*, 4, 19–20, 78; Miller, *Empty Sleeves*, 8–9. According to Russell, *Atlanta*, 94, 2,660 of Fulton County's 3,110 men between the ages of fifteen and fifty served.

31. *Atlanta Daily Intelligencer*, July 6, 1867; Samuel P. Richards diary, July 4, 1867, Richards Family Papers, AHC; Matthews, "Negro Republicans," 146–47; Drago, *Black Politicians and Reconstruction*, 28–34, 160–63; Venet, *Changing Wind*, 193–201.

32. Brundage, *Southern Past*, 59; Clark, *Defining Moments*, 51, 218; William A. Blair, *Cities of the Dead*, 137–38. For Turner's speech, see *Milledgeville Union and Recorder*, January 15, 1884. For celebrations of Emancipation Day, see *AC*, January 2, 1889, January 2, 1890.

33. *AC*, December 26, 27, 28, 30, 31, 1889 (riot and lynchings), January 2 (Emancipation Day), February 18 ("colored desperado"), March 13 (Martha Hopps), 1890; Kytle and Roberts, *Denmark Vesey's Garden*, 77–78. The Jesup episode attracted

national media attention. The *NYT* reported on December 26, 1889, that Georgia's governor called out troops to quell violence. The *Los Angeles Herald*, December 27, 1889, identified turpentine and sawmills as Jesup's employer and reported blacks moving out. The *Chicago Tribune*, December 30, 1889, reported Brewer in the swamps. The Georgia Lynching Project circa 1875–1930, a project of Emory University, identified the victims of the Jesup lynching. See Scholarblogs.emory.edu/ga-lynchings.

34. *AC*, January 2, 1897, January 2, 1903. For the changing meaning of January 1, including "Heartbreak Day," see William A. Blair, *Cities of the Dead*, 15–16.

35. Jennifer Lund Smith, "The Ties That Bind: Educated African-American Women in Post-Emancipation Atlanta," in Inscoe, *Georgia in Black and White*, 91 (quotation), 101. Childs found employment at Tuskegee Institute the year after giving this speech (Clark, *Defining Moments*, 172).

36. "Souvenir Booklet, Sixtieth Anniversary Celebration of the Pastorate of Dr. Edward Randolph Carter, April 19, 1942," copy in Edward Randolph Carter and Andrew Jackson Lewis Collection, Auburn Avenue Research Library. See also "Funeral Service of Edward Randolph Carter," June 11, 1944, in Carter and Lewis Collection.

37. Link, *Atlanta, Cradle*, 158–59; Carter, *Black Side*, ix. Throughout his life, Carter cultivated relationships with prominent whites, including fellow Athens native and Prohibitionist Henry Grady. Five thousand white and black admirers attended the sixtieth anniversary celebration of his pastorate on April 19, 1942, at which George Truett, the white pastor of First Baptist Church of Dallas, Texas, preached the sermon. Shortly before Carter's death on June 8, 1944, he wrote a prayer that was broadcast on WGST radio as part of a D-Day observance (*AC*, June 9, 1944).

38. Carter, *Black Side*, xiii, 11, 16–17.

39. Ibid., 17–20, 169.

40. Gay, *Life in Dixie*, 15, 272–73; *AC*, July 20, 1898. In 1980, the Gay home was moved from its original location to another in Decatur after the Junior League of DeKalb County purchased it. Today it is a popular venue for parties and weddings.

41. Gay, *Life in Dixie*, 10–11, 68, 127, 144–45, 169.

42. Ibid., 42, 108–15.

43. Ibid., 131–37, 168.

44. Ibid., 181, 207, 256.

45. *AC*, August 29, 1891 (Gay identifies as Confederate veteran), December 4, 1892 (publication of *Diary*), May 2, 1893 ("flattering reception," "dark days"), November 28, 1894 (self-publishes), October 13, 1895 (review of *Diary*), July 20, 1989 (third edition published). Additional references to *Diary* appear in *AC*, July 21, October 9, 1892, April 1, 1895, January 5, 1896. For Gay's activism in support of Stephens's memory, see *AC*, April 4, 1884, August 11, 1887, May 20, 1891, October 15, 1892, May 23, 1893. For Gay's obituary, see *AC*, November 7, 1918. For Gay's success in achieving economic independence through her writing, see Michele Gillespie, "Mary Gay: Sin, Self, and Survival in the Post–Civil War South," in Chirhart and Wood, *Georgia Women*, 1:210, 215.

46. APWS Collection; Venet, *Changing Wind*, 87–89, 102–4, 145–46. See also Dyer, *Secret Yankees*.

47. Bylaws of the Atlanta Pioneer Women's Society, APWS Collection; *AJ*, February 6, 1910; Pioneer Citizens' Society of Atlanta, *Pioneer Citizens' Story of Atlanta*. The cover page says "One Dollar a Copy."

48. APWS Collection; *AJ*, February 14 (Morgan), June 2 (Sisson), 6 (Rice), 1909, May 8, (Torbett), 1910.

49. APWS Collection; *AJ*, May 30, 1907 (Winship), March 28 (Peters), December 5 (Massey), 1909, n.d. (Cozart).

50. APWS Collection; *AJ*, June 13, 1901 (Kicklighter), August 1, 1909 (Venable).

51. APWS Collection; *AJ*, August 1, 1901 (Venable), June 13 (Kicklighter), March 7 (Haralson), 1909, May 8, 1910 (Torbett), n.d. (Blackburn).

52. APWS Collection; *AJ*, March 14, 1909 (Maggie Wilson), May 30 (Winship), July 4 (Moore), December 5 (Massey), 1909, June 8, 1913 (Wilson).

53. *AC*, April 27, 1879.

54. Ibid., July 7, 1875.

55. Ibid.

56. Ibid., April 20, 1881.

57. *AC*, July 4, 1876; William A. Blair, *Cities of the Dead*, 125–26.

58. Eckert, *John Brown Gordon*, 7–17. Gordon's daughter wrote a memoir of her parents that provides valuable biographical information. See Caroline Lewis Gordon, "De Gin'ral an' Miss Fanny," JBGF Papers. The Raccoon Roughs took their name from their coonskin hats.

59. Eckert, *John Brown Gordon*, 23–27, 36–39. Gordon did not play a pivotal role at the Battle of Gettysburg.

60. Ibid., 105–7, 117, 122.

61. Varon, *Appomattox*, 2–3.

62. Marten, *Sing Not War*, 19–20, points out that Confederate veterans held a higher place in postwar southern society than did their northern counterparts.

63. Eckert, *John Brown Gordon*, 128–40.

64. Ibid., 141–57, 177–86, quotation on 148; Varon, *Appomattox*, 250.

65. *AC*, April 28, 30, May 3, 7, 1878; *NYT*, April 30, May 1, 4, 1878; *Boston Advertiser*, April 29, 1878. The *Bangor Daily Whig and Courier*, May 2, 1878, complained about Gordon's "magnanimous condescension" in rebelling against the government and about his involvement in the KKK. An advocate for Henry Grady's "New South" (see chapter 2), Gordon toured textile mills in Lynn and Lawrence. See Eckert, *John Brown Gordon*, 191–93.

66. *AC*, November 8, 1874, November 9, 1876, November 16, 22, 1878. Rebecca Latimer Felton continued to dog Gordon throughout his career. She had a nearly pathological hatred for him and devoted sixty-eight pages of her memoir to smearing him. See Felton, *My Memoirs of Georgia Politics*, 478–546.

67. *AC*, September 4, 1889 (Gordon accepts presidency), April 28, 1895 (Moorman).

68. "A Noble Georgia Woman," *Confederate Veteran*, March 1919 (Gay); Foster, *Ghosts of the Confederacy*, 104–7; Marten, *Sing not War*, 12.

69. *AC*, December 23, 1894 (Lee's birthday), November 24, 25, 1894 (encyclopedia), March 31, 1895 (Chicago), April 28, 1895, July 12, 1895 (Richmond monument), May 19, 1895 ("long live the memories"; circulation among veterans).

## CHAPTER 2. THE NEW SOUTH

1. Harold E. Davis, *Henry Grady's New South*, 29–30; Jones, *25th North Carolina Troops*, 28–29. Many of the men in the 25th were from Athens, Georgia.

2. William Grady to Ann Grady, February 14, April 10, 1862, HWG Papers. Ann Grady's letters do not survive.

3. William Grady to Ann Grady, July 27, 1864, telegram to Mrs. W. Grady, August 12, 1864, HWG to Ann Grady, October 23, [1864], HWG Papers; Jones, *25th North Carolina*, 125–27, 213.

4. Harold E. Davis, *Henry Grady's New South*, 30.

5. HWG to mother, October 21, 1872, HWG Papers. Bryan, *Henry Grady or Tom Watson*, 40; Harold E. Davis, *Henry Grady's New South*, 30–32; Joel Chandler Harris, *Life of Henry W. Grady*, 10–11.

6. HWG to mother, October 21, 1872 (purchased newspaper), n.d. [1873 or 1874] (borrowed money), HWG Papers. In a December 1, 1878, diary entry, HWG berated himself for spending twenty-five cents "foolishly," an indication of how broke he was (HWG Papers). On Brown, see *Atlanta Herald*, May 20, 1873; Harold E. Davis, *Henry Grady's New South*, 33–36.

7. *Atlanta Herald*, March 14, 1874. For a discussion of Grady and other New South newspapermen, see Woodward, *Origins of the New South*, 145–47; Prince, *Stories of the South*, 99.

8. HWG obituary, *AC*, December 23, 1889; Harold E. Davis, *Henry Grady's New South*, 37–38. The three politicians were also known as the Bourbon Triumvirate. See Wynne, "Bourbon Triumvirate." Hain, *Murder in the State Capitol*, 183–200, alleges that Edward Cox murdered Alston, a prominent Atlantan, because of his efforts to uncover the inhumane practice of convict lease. She hints at involvement by the Atlanta Ring though not by Grady, who was a friend of Alston.

9. Lee article in HWG scrapbook 1, 1869–73, HWG Papers. Grady originally published the Toombs article in the *Philadelphia Times*, and it was reprinted in the *AC*, July 6, 1879. Toombs was a close friend of Alexander Stephens, a critic of Davis's wartime policies. See Cobb, *Away Down South*, 7, 74; McPherson, *Embattled Rebel*, 5.

10. Like the Toombs article, this piece appeared first in the *Philadelphia Times* before the *AC* ran it on April 20, 1877. HWG preserved Jackson's letter in his scrapbook. See M. A. Jackson to HWG, May 3, 1877, scrapbook 4, 1877–79, HWG Papers.

11. *AC*, February 12, 1881.

12. See James M. McPherson's foreword to Jefferson Davis, *Rise and Fall*, 2:iii–iv; Blight, *Race and Reunion*, 259. For HWG's review, see *AC*, June 5, 1881.

13. *AC*, June 5, 1881. See Grady scrapbook 4, 1877–79, HWG Papers, in which his penciled marking indicates that Grady ghostwrote Longstreet's article based on their conversations.

14. *AC*, July 27, 1879. Davis criticized Longstreet in *AC*, April 23, 1873, saying that "his late political antecedents are sufficient to destroy any and all former good opinion formed of him." Longstreet recalled that Davis never truly forgave him for criticizing the performance of Davis's favorite general, A. S. Johnston, after the fall of Fort Donelson in 1862 (*AC*, October 10, 1883). Johnston died at the Battle of Shiloh a few months later. See Wert, *General James Longstreet*, 410–11, 422–23. For a discussion of Longstreet as Lost Cause target, see Connelly and Bellows, *God and General Longstreet*, 32–38.

15. *AC*, January 31, 1879; Link, *Atlanta, Cradle*, 142–45. Anne Sarah Rubin has pointed out that Sherman was not a despised figure in the postwar South (*Through the Heart of Dixie*, 129–30).

16. *AC*, January 1 (Grady's article), November 16 (Sherman speech), 19, 1881. Regarding Freedman's Day, K. Stephen Prince has written that "the fair was as white as the cotton that dotted the fields" ("Rebel Yell for Yankee Doodle," 345).

17. Pierce, *Benjamin H. Hill*, 51–85, 204–15; Hill, speech to the University of Georgia Alumni Association, quoted in Gaston, *New South Creed*, 34; Ruth Blair, "Atlanta's Monuments," 273; Kytle and Roberts, *Denmark Vesey's Garden*, 100–107, 116–20.

18. Eckert, "General and the Editor," 5–7; Harold E. Davis, *Henry Grady's New South*, 79–81.

19. *AJ*, May 1, 1886; *AC*, May 1, 1886; *NYT*, May 1, 1886.

20. *AC*, May 1, 1886; Keith S. Bohannon, "'These Few Gray-Haired Battle-Scarred Veterans': Confederate Army Reunions in Georgia, 1885–1895," in Gallagher and Nolan, *Myth of the Lost Cause*, 90–91. The *AC* revisited the story of Longstreet's participation in the 1886 event in a January 15, 1888, article.

21. *AC*, May 1, 1886, May 30, 1893; Cita Cook, "Winnie Davis: The Challenges of Daughterhood," in Swain, Payne, and Spruill, *Mississippi Women*, 21–38.

22. *NYT*, May 5, 1886; *Los Angeles Times*, May 9, 1886; *New York Tribune*, May 2 ("desolation"), May 9 ("arch-traitor"), 1886; Nixon, *Henry W. Grady*, 230 (other newspaper quotations); Janney, *Remembering the Civil War*, 5, 159; Foster, *Ghosts of the Confederacy*, 104–44; Cook, *Civil War Memories*, 53–60. For additional articles on Davis, see *New York Tribune*, May 3, 4, 10, 1886.

23. *AC*, January 15, 1888 (reduced circumstances), January 3, 1904 (Helen Longstreet's article; her husband had died the previous day). In 1905, Helen D. Longstreet published *Lee and Longstreet at High Tide: Gettysburg in the Light of the Official Records*.

24. *AC*, March 16, April 16 (quotation), 1885; Foster, *Ghosts of the Confederacy*, 89.

25. *AC*, June 9 (Grady's father), 18 (vice presidents), July 5,wh1885 (Arp). Arp was a nom de plume for Charles Henry Smith (1826–1903).

26. *AC*, July 29, 1886 (ten thousand dollars). Beginning in the 1890s, the United Daughters of the Confederacy took charge of Confederate Memorial Day festivities at this site, while the ALMA continued to honor Confederates on April 26 at Oakland Cemetery (*AC*, April 26, 1890; see also November 5, 1889, April 25, 1968). Kirk Savage discusses the shift from "great-man" to "standing-soldier" monuments in *Standing Soldiers, Kneeling Slaves*, 176, 182–83. See also Neff, *Honoring the Civil War Dead*, 205.

27. *NYT*, November 6, 1896 (Inman obituary); HWG, "The New South," in Joel Chandler Harris, *Life of Henry W. Grady*, 83; Harold E. Davis, *Henry Grady's New South*, 175–78.

28. HWG, "The New South," 83–93; Harold E. Davis, *Henry Grady's New South*, 176–77.

29. HWG, "The New South," 83–93.

30. Ibid.

31. Ibid.; *AC*, December 23, 1886; *NYT*, December 23, 1886.

32. *NYT*, December 23, 1886; *Harper's Weekly*, January 1, 8, 1887; *New York Evening Post* reprinted in *AC*, December 25, 1886; *Frank Leslie's Illustrated Newspaper*, January 15, 1887. For the ovation in the hotel lobby, see *Chicago Inter Ocean*, December 24, 1886.

33. *New Orleans Times-Picayune*, January 2, 1887; *Milwaukee Daily Journal*, December 30, 1886; Woodward, *Mind of the South*, 147. *Frank Leslie's Illustrated Newspaper* included HWG's likeness on January 15, 1887. See also *Atchison Daily Globe*, January 12, 1887; *St. Louis Globe-Democrat*, December 12, 1886; *Milwaukee Sentinel*, January 2, 1887; *Raleigh News and Observer*, December 12, 1886; *San Francisco Daily Evening Bulletin*, January 7, 1887. For HWG as a possible vice president, see *NYT*, December 28, 1886.

34. *AC*, December 24, 1886 (two stories).

35. *St. Louis Globe-Democrat*, January 12, 1887 (convict lease), December 31, 1886 (voter suppression); *New York Freeman*, January 1, 8, 1887 (juries, convict lease). See also *Boston Daily Advertiser*, December 25, 1886; *Milwaukee Sentinel*, December 29, 1887.

36. *AC*, October 21, 1883; Prince, *Stories of the South*, 123; Venet, *Changing Wind*, 199–201, 205–10. Grady wrote about the practice of convict labor in an article in the *Philadelphia Times*, December 4, [1877–79]. He claimed that Georgia had 1,278 convicts and that "the Governor has been forced to break one or two leases because of cruel treatment" (Grady scrapbook 4 [1877–79], HWG Papers).

37. Grady, speech "At the Boston Banquet," in Joel Chandler Harris, *Life of Henry W. Grady*, 180–98; *AC*, December 23 (quotation), December 24 (Cleveland), December 26 (funeral), 1889; *NYT*, December 15, 1889. Harold E. Davis, *Henry Grady's New South*, 2–7, discusses details of the death and funeral. After temporary burial in a friend's family vault at Oakland Cemetery, Grady's remains were re-

interred in a plot at Westview Cemetery, where he had tried unsuccessfully to promote Union and Confederate burials from the Atlanta Campaign. For Davis's death, see Cobb, *Away Down South*, 74–75.

38. *AC*, December 26, 1889 (casket viewings); *Boston Congregationalist*, December 19, 1889; *Chicago Daily Inter Ocean*, December 17, 1889; *San Francisco Daily Evening Bulletin*, December 13, 1889; *Bangor Daily Whig and Courier*, December 18, 1889; *Indianapolis Journal* quoted in *Chicago Daily Inter Ocean*, December 18, 1889; *Bulletin of Atlanta University* 15 (January 1890): 3, quoted in Link, *Atlanta, Cradle*, 155.

39. Buck, *Road to Reunion*, 193; Woodward, *Origins of the New South*, 195; Gaston, *New South Creed*, 137, 189.

40. *AC*, December 29, 1889 (Arp), September 15, 1895 ("stirring sentiment"), September 21, 1895 ("lamented Grady"), October 22, 1895 (Bowen); Prince, "Rebel Yell for Yankee Doodle," 340–71.

41. Harvey, *World's Fairs*, 54–56; Perdue, *Race*, 11.

42. Cooper, *Cotton States and International Exposition*, 5–17, 29; Harvey, *World's Fairs*, 147, 238; Harvey and Watson-Powers, "Eyes of the World," 6–7; Garrett, *Atlanta and Environs*, 2:313, 319.

43. *AC*, September 19 (opening parade), 22, 1895; Perdue, *Race*, 15–22; Cardon, *Dream of the Future*, 2, 15–16.

44. *AC*, September 19, 1895; Garrett, *Atlanta and Environs*, 2:325–26; Perdue, *Race*, 7–9.

45. Review of Washington's speech, *AC*, September 20, 1895; other newspapers quoted in *AC*, September 24, 1895. For a discussion of Du Bois and other critics, see Perdue, *Race*, 28–30.

46. *AC*, October 22 (opening day), September 18 (restaurant), September 22 (lodging), 1895. During the opening festivities, blacks and whites sat in separate sections.

47. Ibid., September 22, 1895; Cardon, *Dream of the Future*, 46–50.

48. Millie J. McCreary diary, October 9, 25, December 21, 27, 1895, AHC; *AC*, December 19, 1895 (Herndon). Perdue, *Race*, 31–32, 37–42, concludes that "the response to the Negro Building was overwhelmingly positive." Born in slavery, Herndon moved to Atlanta in 1882 and earned a living as a barber. He eventually became owner of multiple barbershops and in the early twentieth century founded the Atlanta Life Insurance Company. See Rabinowitz, *Race Relations*, 86.

49. *AC*, September 22, 1895. The governors of Vermont, Nebraska, New Jersey, and Colorado also attended, as did General John Schofield. See Cooper, *Cotton States and International Exposition*, 111–12. President McKinley gave Longstreet a patronage job. See Wert, *General James Longstreet*, 425. According to Bohannon, "These Few Gray-Haired Battle-Scarred Veterans," 101, "The great expansion of the federal pension system in the late 1880s and early 1890s undoubtedly rankled many ex-Confederates." For "sectional discord" at the Chickamauga park, see Janney, "I Yield to No Man," 394.

50. *AC*, November 12, 1895; see also November 10, 1895.

51. *AJ*, November 3, 1895. The Davis cradle is featured in *Photo-Gravures of the Cotton States Exposition*. For a discussion of fairs and efforts to "speed the process of reunification," see Bodnar, *Remaking America*, 30–31.

52. *AC*, September 22, 1895. For Cleveland's visit, see Perdue, *Race*, 48–49, 83; Cardon, *Dream of the Future*, 54–55, 83–84; Rydell, *All the World's a Fair*, 87–88. The plantation is depicted in *Photo-Gravures of the Cotton States Exposition*.

53. *AC*, January 1, 2, 1896; Garrett, *Atlanta and Environs*, 2:313. According to Rydell, *All the World's a Fair*, 102, Atlanta's fair, coupled with those of New Orleans and Nashville, introduced four million people to "a vision of the New South." See also Harvey, *World's Fair*, 285.

## CHAPTER 3. SECTIONAL RECONCILIATION IN A TIME OF RADICAL TENSION

1. Russell, *Atlanta*, 125, 241–44.

2. Ibid., 215, 222, 227, 230; Rabinowitz, *Race Relations*, 122–24.

3. *AC*, July 18 (Atlanta Relief Association, "Stars and Stripes Forever"), July 19 (decorate homes), July 25, 1898 (paintings); *AJ*, July 18, 1898 (decorate homes; re-purposed Hall of Agriculture). On July 20, 1898, the *AC* reported that in addition to the Confederate Tabernacle, veterans had access to a sleeping hall and a mess hall.

4. *AC*, July 21, 22, 23, 1898.

5. Ibid., July 21, 1898 (three stories). For a discussion of "collective vindication," see M. Keith Harris, *Across the Bloody Chasm*, 66–67. On other occasions, speakers gave more temperate interpretations of the war: local Methodist minister Walker Lewis, for example, preached a sermon on the importance of North-South military reunions (*AC*, July 25, 1898). Evans, originally from Stewart County, Georgia, was a county judge at the time of the Civil War, joined a local company, was promoted several times, and commanded a division in Robert E. Lee's army by the end of the war. He subsequently moved to Kentucky and then to Atlanta in 1881. See *AC*, July 20, 1898; *AJ*, July 20, 1898.

6. *AC*, July 21 (Cyclorama), July 21–22, 1898 (specific group reunions). The UCV's Georgia headquarters was located at the corner of Decatur and Pryor Streets.

7. Ibid., July 12 ("one of the funniest"), 18, 19, 21 ("ignorant negro"), 1898; *AJ*, July 12, 1898.

8. *AC*, July 7, 22 (proposal to change the name), 20 (creation of the SCV), 1898; *AJ*, July 22, 1898 (SCV proposed name change).

9. *AC*, July 14, 1898; Karen L. Cox, *Dixie's Daughters*, 1–3; Foster, *Ghosts of the Confederacy*, 137; Emert, *Georgia Division of the Children*, 1–3. On July 20, 1898, the *AC* identified an organization called the Order of Robert E. Lee, Daughters of Veterans, formed in 1897. Eligibility was based on descent from a Confederate officer. *AJ*, July 18, 1898, discussed Helen Plane and included her image with the story.

10. *AC*, July 22 (widows of generals), 23 (Hallie Rounsaville), 1898. James Longstreet and his second wife also appeared at least once, as did Winnie Davis, Daughter of the Confederacy. For coverage of generals' wives and Winnie Davis, see *AJ*, July 18, 21, 23, 1898.

11. *AC*, July 21 (comparison to Nashville), 23, 24 (attendees), 1898.

12. Ibid., July 13 (smokeless powder), 20 (Wheeler), 22 (resolution), 23 (prisoners), 1898. Wheeler was joined in Cuba by another prominent Confederate, Fitzhugh Lee. See *AJ*, July 3, 8, 13, 21, 1898.

13. Cook, *Civil War Memories*, 110–13.

14. *AC*, December 14 (McKinley's tour), 15 (two stories, including McKinley speech), 16 (several stories including Wallace Reed, parade), 1898; Reed, *History of Atlanta, Georgia*; Neff, *Honoring the Civil War Dead*, 222–226; Crimmins and Farrisee, *Democracy Restored*, 81. See also *AJ*, December 14, 1898. McKinley also hoped that his tour would build national support for America's new empire, including the president's goal of keeping the Philippines under U.S. control. See William A. Blair, *Cities of the Dead*, 181–83. In 1900, Congress voted to reinter 128 Confederate soldiers from a variety of locations at Arlington National Cemetery, near Washington, D.C. See McElya, *Politics of Mourning*, 144–45; Foster, *Ghosts of the Confederacy*, 153.

15. UCV, Roll of the Dead, October 19, 1930, copy in UDC Collection, AHC.

16. Mrs. Trox W. Bankston, Georgia Division president from Covington, served as trustee of the Soldier's Home. See "Report of the President of the United Daughters of the Confederacy, Georgia Division," 1922, 45, copy in United Daughters of the Confederacy Collection, AHC. For a discussion of the 1910 resolution, see Karen L. Cox, *Dixie's Daughters*, 80–81.

17. For the Atlanta home, see Rosenburg, *Living Monuments*, 5, 46–72. He notes that by the time Georgia's facility was completed, South Carolina, Alabama, and Mississippi were the only original Confederate states that had failed to construct homes.

18. Ibid. According to Marten, *Sing Not War*, 14, the South's economic woes between the 1870s and 1890s made the need for soldiers' homes acute. For the UDC's role, see "Open Letter to the Sons of Confederate Veterans and Mr. Hollins Randolph," n.d., GB Papers. For a list of residents at the home, 1901–30, see Confederate Soldier's Home of Georgia Register of Inmates, AHC.

19. John B. Gordon, "Last Days of the Confederacy," speech delivered in Brooklyn, New York, February 7, 1901, JBGF Papers. He copyrighted the speech in 1901.

20. Selwyn N. Owen to Calvin S. Brice, July 6, 1894, JBGF Papers; press release by Emmett Jay Scott, Tuskegee, Alabama, November 29, 1902, in Washington, *Booker T. Washington Papers*, 6:598–99; Silber, *Romance of Reunion*, 95; Blight, *Race and Reunion*, 361–62. The JBGF Papers contain additional manifestos of support for the speech. On the Spanish-American War, see also Silber, *Romance of Reunion*, 178–86.

21. *AC*, July 20 (McPherson event), 21 (barbecue and speeches), 22 ("throngs"), 1900. According to Kammen, *Mystic Chords of Memory*, 110, "Bitterness, vindictiveness, and resentment lay just beneath the surface."

22. John B. Gordon, *Reminiscences of the Civil War*, xii–xiii, 12–25; Gallagher, *Lee and His Generals*, 269–70; Eckert, *John Brown Gordon*, 331–35.

23. *AJ*, January 10 (death), 13 (lying in state), 1904; *AC*, January 12, 13, 14, 15, 1904 (death and burial).

24. *AC*, January 3 (Longstreet's death), 7 (*Athens Banner* quoted), 1904; *AJ*, January 9, 1904 (Capers interview). Wheeler, a native Georgian, made his home elsewhere after the war. Helen Longstreet often spoke about the Civil War and her husband's role in it to school groups around Georgia. See correspondence in Helen Dortch Longstreet Papers, AHC. By the time she died at age ninety-nine, her storied life included service as Georgia's assistant state librarian. During World War II, she worked as a riveter at Marietta's Bell Bomber plant. For her obituary, see *AC*, May 4, 1962.

25. Ely Burkwell to W. M. Crumley, June 27, 1904, and H. J. Weller to W. M. Crumley, July 12, 1904, are two of many letters received by the Gordon Monument Commission in the JBGF Papers. For the unveiling and photograph, see *AC*, May 26, 1907. A statue of Civil War governor Joseph E. Brown and his wife, Elizabeth, was unveiled at the Capitol in 1928. Their son, who served as governor from 1909 to 1913, donated the money. See Crimmins and Farrisee, *Democracy Restored*, 103.

26. See Allen Tankersley to Hugh Gordon Jr., October 16, 1944, April 18, 1954, Gordon to Tankersley, February 3, 1947, March 26, 1947, JBGF Papers. The JBGF Papers contain many additional letters pertaining to this topic.

27. Tankersley, *John B. Gordon*, vii–x, 247–74. Tankersley had trouble finishing the work. He traveled widely to visit archival repositories seeking Gordon manuscripts and interviewed family members. He hoped that family members would share Gordon's letters but was told that most of his personal papers had burned in the 1899 fire that destroyed his home. Louisiana State University Press at one time indicated an interest in publishing the biography but evidently backed out when Tankersley failed to complete the volume in a timely fashion. Tankersley died at age fifty-one two years after the book's publication. For his obituary, see *AC*, July 27, 1957. For additional articles about his graduation from Emory, high school teaching career, and military service, see *AC*, March 22, 1927, October 2, 1942, November 25, 1948. Hugh Gordon Jr.'s June 1, 1955, congratulatory letter to Tankersley is in JBGF Papers. John B. Gordon remained celebrated in many venues. In April 1944, his image appeared on the cover of the *American Bar Association Journal*, which also included a biographical sketch.

28. Autobiographical writing in Myrta Lockett Avary Papers, AHC; *AC*, September 18, 1884 (marriage), June 26, 1886 (death of son); February 11, 1890 (James Avary as coroner), August 19, 1911 (divorce). For James Avary's funeral notice, see *AC*, October 21, 1942.

29. Autobiographical material in Myrta Lockett Avary Papers, AHC. According to Censer, *Reconstruction of White Southern Womanhood*, 236, "Novelists dropped from view because of the contemporary southern opinion of women's writings; for various reasons, they were often dismissed as unimportant."

30. Avary, *Virginia Girl*, 150–71; *AC*, May 10, 1903. In 1938, Avary wrote that she had "used my position on Northern journals to publicise the South" (Myrta Lockett

Avary to Ruth Blair, April 15, 1938, Myrta Lockett Avary Papers, AHC). On August 28, 1937, the *AJ* declared that Avary "helped ease [the] breach between North and South."

31. Avary and Martin, *Diary from Dixie*, xix; Gardner, *Blood and Irony*, 170–73.

32. Avary, *Dixie after the War*, 269–70, 409–19. Avary also edited Stephens, *Recollections*.

33. Michele Gillespie, "Mary Gay: Sin, Self, and Survival in the Post–Civil War South" in Chirhart and Wood, *Georgia Women*, 1:214–15.

34. *New York Tribune*, January 18, 1904; *AC*, May 12, 1924 (Rucker obituary). See also *AC*, August 17, September 18, 1897, December 22, 1901. Rucker is buried at Oakland Cemetery. For more on Rucker, see Rabinowitz, *Race Relations*, 280–81.

35. Du Bois, *Autobiography*, 61, 74; Lewis, *W. E. B. Du Bois*, 11–12, 22–29, 56–67, 79–116, 174, 211.

36. *NYT*, April 24, 25, 1899; *AC*, April 19, 25, November 2, 1899 (Philippines); Lewis, *W. E. B. Du Bois*, 226. Lynching statistics from the Legacy Museum, Montgomery, Alabama; Brundage, *Lynching in the New South*, 8, 82–107.

37. "The Problem of Negro Crime," January 1, 1899 [1900], W. E. B. Du Bois Collection, University of Massachusetts, Amherst; *AC*, December 31, 1899. Du Bois also suffered a deep personal tragedy when his only child died of diphtheria at the age of two. Du Bois had been unable to locate a black physician to treat the child. See Du Bois, *Autobiography*, 215, 222; Lewis, *W. E. B. Du Bois*, 226–28.

38. "The Problem of Negro Crime," W. E. B. Du Bois Collection, University of Massachusetts, Amherst. Kathleen Clark (*Defining Moments*, 202) interprets Du Bois's speech as part of black leaders' "growing wariness" about white men's efforts at disfranchisement. The Georgia Legislature disfranchised African Americans by amendment in 1908.

39. Lewis, *W. E. B. Du Bois*, 260–62.

40. Ibid., 277–91; Du Bois, *Souls of Black Folk*, xli, 15–42; Aiello, *Battle for the Souls*, 157–200.

41. *AC*, May 10, 1903; Lewis, *W. E. B. Du Bois*, 316. Du Bois's essay on Reconstruction foreshadowed his 1935 book, *Black Reconstruction in America*.

42. Litwack, *Trouble in Mind*, 315; Dorsey, *To Build Our Lives Together*, 3 (quotation).

43. Dixon, *Clansman*; Barber, "Atlanta Tragedy," 474; *AC*, January 29, 1905. Barber moved his publication to Chicago after the riot and renamed it *The Voice*.

44. *AC*, October 29, 1905; Slide, *American Racist*, 19–28.

45. *AJ*, October 29, 1905; *AC*, January 29, 1905 ("race war"), October 29, 1905 (Broadway).

46. *AC*, January 14 (Doubleday ad), February 5 (Dixon publications), 1905; Kreyling, *Late Encounter*, 23–27. Abraham Lincoln advocated colonization of former slaves, as did Dixon. The original name for *The Birth of a Nation* was *The Clansman*.

47. *AC*, October 16 (Columbia), October 29 (two stories, including Dixon in Atlanta), October 31 (Dixon cheered), 1905; *AJ*, October 30, 31, November 1, 1905.

48. *AC*, November 6, 1905. According to this story, twenty-five hundred people were turned away because of lack of seats. Broughton went on to found Georgia Baptist Hospital. See also *AJ*, November 2, 1905.

49. Godshalk, *Veiled Visions*, 30–32, 61–62. Mixon, *Atlanta Riot*, 16, 29, analyzes white leaders' efforts to disfranchise African Americans by eliminating ward voting and color-coded ballots that helped the less literate identify political parties.

50. Godshalk, *Veiled Visions*, 37; Barber, "Atlanta Tragedy," 475.

51. *AJ*, September 23, 1906; Godshalk, *Veiled Visions*, 38, 88–90, 96; Mixon, *Atlanta Riot*, 77–80. For alleged attacks, see *AJ*, September 20, 21, 22, 1906.

52. *AC*, September 23, 1906; *AJ*, September 23, 1906; Lucy Rucker quoted in Litwack, *Trouble in Mind*, 316; Godshalk, *Veiled Visions*, 93.

53. Dorsey, *To Build Our Lives Together*, 160–61.

54. Du Bois, *Autobiography*, 286; Godshalk, *Veiled Visions*, 105–6, 122; Lewis, *W. E. B. Du Bois*, 335–36, 344, 383–85, 406–7.

55. "Where Are Our Friends?," *Voice of the Negro* 3 (October 1906): 437–39, 473; Godshalk, *Veiled Visions*, 3; Dorsey, *To Build Our Lives Together*, 166. On racial uplift, see Higginbotham, *Righteous Discontent*, 14–18.

56. *AC*, September 24 (preachers), 26 (comments from around the South), 27 (protecting women), 1906; Link, *Atlanta, Cradle*, 189. For the Committee of Safety, see Godshalk, *Veiled Visions*, 139–40.

57. Godshalk, *Veiled Visions*, 152–61. Only forty white men were arrested during the riot. Many were treated with leniency. See Godshalk, *Veiled Visions*, 98, 149–50. In one of the last letters written before his death in November 1915, Washington told Rucker that a coalition of white and black leaders should unite to stop "mob rule" in Atlanta (Washington to Henry Rucker, October 7, 1915, in Washington, *Booker T. Washington Papers*, 13:380–81). Washington's letter to Rucker was prompted by the lynching of Leo Frank, discussed in chapter 4.

58. *AC*, March 28, 1907. On August 10, 1907, the *Constitution* reported that Dixon and Broughton had resumed their friendship after their disagreement regarding the play.

59. For the Guard's wartime role, see Venet, *Changing Wind*, 48–49. *AC*, November 9, 1910, reported that the Guard was the "first to depart from Atlanta to join the Confederate forces to uphold the sovereignty of the state."

60. *AC*, September 24, 1879, November 9, 1910; Fairman, *Chronicles of the Old Guard*, 1:84–98.

61. *AC*, October 8 ("broad Americanism"), 9 (photograph of statue), 11 (unveiling, speeches), 15 (photograph of Old Guard), 1911.

62. Ibid., April 27, 28, 1907.

## CHAPTER 4. THE UDC AND THE STRUGGLE OVER STONE MOUNTAIN

1. Lamar, *When All Is Said*, 111, 135. Cook, *Civil War Memories*, 125, notes that more than 85 percent of Civil War veterans had died by 1920.

2. Wilson, *Baptized in Blood*, 162–64, 173–76; Lumpkin, *Making of a Southerner*,

113. As an adult, Lumpkin rejected the tenets of her childhood and embraced civil rights. See Cobb, *Away Down South*, 193.

3. *AC*, June 10, 1908 (Evans elected), July 3, 1911 (death), July 27 (2 articles), September 28 (Van Zandt), 1919.

4. Ibid., October 10, 11, 1919; *AJ*, October 10, 1919.

5. *AC*, October 7, 11, 1919; *AJ*, October 10, 1919; Karen L. Cox, *Dixie's Daughters*, 50.

6. *Atlanta Chapter United Daughters*; UDC, *Minutes*, 20; Georgia Division, UDC, Constitution, Article II, UDC Collection, AHC; membership discussed in UDC, Georgia Division, *Minutes of the Thirty-Fourth Convention, Atlanta, Georgia, October 23, 24, 25, 1928* (n.p., n.d.), 63, UDC Collection, AHC; Roth, *Matronage*, 55; Foster, *Ghosts of the Confederacy*, 172; Karen L. Cox, *Dixie's Daughters*, 5, 20, 23–25, 39, 50, 84–85; W. Fitzhugh Brundage, "'Woman's Hand and Heart and Deathless Love': White Women and the Commemorative Impulse in the New South," in Mills and Simpson, *Monuments to the Lost Cause*, 67–68; Brown, *Civil War Canon*, 108. Foster, *Ghosts of the Confederacy*, 172, estimates that the Daughters had two to three times the membership of the Sons.

7. *AC*, May 27, 1925; McElya, *Clinging to Mammy*, 4–13. Bosworth was related to furniture magnate J. J. Haverty. The UDC gave five dollars in gold for the best essay on "Mammy in the Old Plantation Days." See UDC Collection, AHC.

8. *AC*, August 12, 1906, July 28, 1907. The Francis Bartow Cottage, one of four constructed with funds from the UDC, was proposed in 1905 and completed in 1938. See Foster, *Ghosts of the Confederacy*, 172–73.

9. LaCavera, *History of the Georgia Division*, 1:187–88.

10. *AC*, May 24, 1920. For casualties and hearsay about casualties, see Stephen Davis, *What the Yankees Did to Us*, 138, 165, 209, 215, 243–48; see also Davis's discussion of Atlanta's destruction on 370–71, 392–99, 427. The tablet "The Battle of Atlanta" incorrectly identifies Atlanta rather than Milledgeville as Georgia's capital during the Civil War.

11. LaCavera, *History of the Georgia Division*, 1:82–83; Mary Borglum quoted in Casey and Borglum, *Give the Man Room*, 173. For biographical details about Plane, see her obituary, *AC*, April 25, 1925; 1860 federal census showing W. F. Plane owning five thousand dollars in real estate and six slaves; C. Helen Plane Scrapbook, AHC; William Plane's last words quoted in Helen Plane exhibit, Memorial Hall, Stone Mountain Park.

12. Gutzon Borglum to Helen Plane, August 17, 20, 1917, Caroline Helen Plane Papers, SMC; Sam Venable to Helen Plane, August 8, 1914 (the project "appeals very strongly to me"), Gutzon Borglum to Sam Venable, August 24, 1915, Samuel Hoyt Venable Papers, SMC; Gutzon Borglum, speech to Atlanta Chapter, UDC, March 8, 1917, GB Papers. According to LaCavera, *History of the Georgia Division*, 2:617–18, Plane read articles by William H. Terrell and John Temple Graves advocating Confederate carvings. For an overview of the carving's history, see David B. Freeman, *Carved in Stone*, 5, 28, 47–48, 60–61.

13. W. Fitzhugh Brundage, "White Women and the Politics of Historical Mem-

ory in the New South, 1880–1920," in Dailey, Gilmore, and Simon, *Jumpin' Jim Crow*, 115–39; Gannon, *Americans Remember Their Civil War*, 3; Jacob, *Testament to Union*, 134–38. According to Jacob, a few years earlier, Borglum had submitted an unsuccessful proposal to sculpt Grant. Borglum complained that too many Civil War sculptures in Washington looked like "ridiculous clothespin men on wooden horses" (135). The Sheridan project received funding from veterans as well as a congressional appropriation.

14. Gutzon Borglum to Helen Plane, August 17, 20, 1915, Caroline Helen Plane Papers, SMC; Gutzon Borglum, speech to Atlanta chapter, UDC, March 8, 1917, Borglum to Earl N. Findley, Sunday editor, *NYT*, December 14, 1915, *Scientific American*, August 1924, all in GB Papers; *AC*, September 26, 1915, May 22, 1916 (eight years to complete).

15. Gutzon Borglum to Leila Mechlin, January 18, 1906, GB Papers; Schaff and Schaff, *Six Wars at a Time*, 12–15, 115, 125, 147; Casey and Borglum, *Give the Man Room*, 46–49; *AC*, September 26, 1915. Lincoln Borglum became a successful sculptor in his own right. For Abraham Lincoln's image among Progressives, see Cook, *Civil War Memories*, 127–28.

16. Invitation to the dedication ceremony, May 20, 1916, GB Papers; Gutzon Borglum to Helen Plane, November 12, 1915, Caroline Helen Plane Papers, SMC; *AC*, September 26, 1915, May 21, 1916; Grace Elizabeth Hale, "Granite Stopped Time: Stone Mountain Memorial and the Representation of White Southern Identity," in Mills and Simpson, *Monuments to the Lost Cause*, 223–24; Lamar, *When All Is Said*, 153–54.

17. Helen Plane to Borglum, October 6, 1915 (telegram), December 4, 1917, Gutzon Borglum to Cordelia Powell Odenheimer, January 7, [1916], GB Papers; *Minutes of the Twenty-First Annual Convention of the Georgia Division United Daughters of the Confederacy Held in Thomasville, Georgia, November 16–20, 1915*, Gutzon Borglum to Helen Plane, October 24, 1915, Caroline Helen Plane Papers, SMC. The minutes also list small contributions from other chapters. Before World War I, the UDC funded monuments honoring Jefferson Davis in Richmond and Confederate soldiers at Shiloh battlefield as well as at Arlington National Cemetery. See Karen L. Cox, *Dixie's Daughters*, 52–56; LaCavera, *History of the Georgia Division*, 2:621.

18. Rawlings, *Second Coming*, 59–63; MacLean, *Behind the Mask of Chivalry*, 5–6. MacLean, whose book focuses on Athens, Georgia, analyzes the role of Edward Clarke and Mary Elizabeth Tyler in helping Simmons advertise and grow the KKK's membership.

19. Oney, *And the Dead Shall Rise*, 18–19, 88–89, 245–46, 400, 503, 506, 564, 574, 582, 648–49. Oney concludes that because of conflicting evidence, "there will never be a resolution to the Frank case" (649). For the cultural significance of the Frank case, see Melnick, *Black-Jewish Relations on Trial*, 3–29.

20. *AC*, November 28 (KKK meeting), December 7 (state charter), 1915, May 7, 1923 (KKK national membership); Rawlings, *Second Coming*, 62–63, 111–16, 177; Linda Gordon, *Second Coming of the KKK*, 2.

21. MacLean, *Behind the Mask of Chivalry*, 9; Kenneth T. Jackson, *Ku Klux Klan*, 29–44.

22. *AC*, August 20 (Governor Hardwick), September 5 (Labor Day parade), 1922, May 6, 7, 1923 (klonvocation); Jackson, *Ku Klux Klan*, 37. For additional articles about Klan parades and conventions, see *AC*, May 7, September 4, 1922, November 28, 1924. Linda Gordon, *Second Coming of the KKK*, 80–83, has noted that KKK parades were open to all white members of the public who wished to participate. Cross burnings were always held on high ground for maximum visibility.

23. Stokes, *D. W. Griffith's "The Birth,"* 74–75, 82, 207, 280; Piehler, *Remembering War the American Way*, 75.

24. Stokes, *D. W. Griffith's "The Birth,"* 108, 202–3, 216–17.

25. Rawlings, *Second Coming*, 51–53. Gallagher, *Causes Won, Lost, and Forgotten*, 45, notes that *The Birth of a Nation* "generated its largest profits in northern and western cities, where patrons likely were dazzled by Griffith's technical skill and masterful staging and little bothered by his racism."

26. *AC*, October 7, December 24, 1915; Rawlings, *Second Coming*, 51–53; Goodson, "This Mighty Influence," 41–42. Eagan was cofounder of the American Cast Iron Pipe Company.

27. *AC*, December 7, 9, 1915; *AJ*, December 7, 1915. For additional coverage of the film, see *AC*, December 11–15, 1915.

28. *AC*, December 13, 14 (veterans), 19, 20 (UDC), 25 (final performance), 1915; Goodson, "This Mighty Influence," 42.

29. Clarence G. Baxter to Gutzon Borglum, May 2, 1917, Borglum to Helen Plane, August 1, 1918, GB Papers; Lamar, *When All Is Said*, 152–53; David B. Freeman, *Carved in Stone*, 65. The minutes of the third annual meeting of the Stone Mountain Memorial Association organization, April 24, 1918, note "the conditions of war which have prevailed since the last annual meeting, and the urgent demands created by the American Red Cross activities . . . Liberty Loans . . . and other like demands" (Caroline Helen Plane Papers, SMC).

30. Helen Plane to Gutzon Borglum, February 1, 1919, Borglum to Plane, April 2, 1919, Hugh Dorsey to Sam Venable, January 24, 1919, GB Papers; David B. Freeman, *Carved in Stone*, 66–67. According to the minutes of the annual meeting of the SMCMA, April 24, 1918, the group had $475 cash on hand (SMCMA Records).

31. H. N. Randolph Personality File, AHC, including entry in *Who Was Who in America, 1897–1942* (Chicago: Marquis, n.d.); David B. Freeman, *Carved in Stone*, 66, 73. Randolph was active in the Chamber of Commerce (*City Builder*, December 1923, AHC). The Randolph-Lucas House (1924) was designed by P. Thornton Marye and modeled after Randolph's ancestral home, Dunlora, in Albemarle County, Virginia. Randolph, who died in 1938, is buried at Monticello, near his famous forebear. For a copy of Borglum's September 10, 1923, contract, see GB Papers. For a discussion of the Forward Atlanta campaign, see Newman, *Southern Hospitality*, 100–104.

32. Hollins Randolph to Gutzon Borglum, April 4, 1923, GB Papers; *AC*, Novem-

ber 4, 1923 (Founders Roll); Hollins Randolph to Hugh G. Gordon Jr., October 20, 1924, William G. McAdoo to Hollins Randolph, July 12, 1923, SMCMA Records. Although he did not endorse the Klan, McAdoo avoided criticizing the organization because of its support for his candidacy. See Pegram, *One Hundred Percent American*, 213–14.

33. Helen Plane to Gutzon Borglum, December 4, 1917, Borglum to Oswald Garrison Villard ("isms"), September 16, 1924, GB Papers; Nathan Bedford Forrest to Rogers Winter, May 8, 1925 (appointment to board), SMCMA Records; Schaff and Schaff, *Six Wars at a Time*, 103–9, 197–98, 201–3. Borglum endorsed women's suffrage and Prohibition in a 1921 commencement address at Wellesley College. See *Wellesley Alumnae Quarterly*, July 1921, copy in GB Papers. For another letter in which Forrest made a contribution, see Forrest to Winter, May 25, 1925, enclosing ten dollars from Wichita, Kansas, SMCMA Records. Schaff and Schaff note that when Adolf Hitler rose to power, Borglum quickly grasped the sinister implications of anti-Semitism and denounced Hitler at a time when few public figures did so (*Six Wars at a Time*, 104–9). For Borglum's meeting with Harding, see *AC*, December 20, 1922. Randolph was a McAdoo delegate to the 1924 Democratic National Convention.

34. *AC*, January 27, 1924; Mary Winter to John J. McSwain, January 12, 1925, SMCMA Records; Hollins Randolph to Gutzon Borglum, October 6, 1924, GB Papers.

35. Gutzon Borglum to Plato Durham, August 20, 1929, GB Papers; "A Token of American Re-entry and Fraternity, Dedicated Coins, Stone Mountain Memorial Half Dollar Issue," Miscellaneous Printed Material, SMC; N. B. Forrest to Roger[s] Winter, July 10, 1925, enclosing ten dollars for the coin campaign, SMCMA Records.

36. *AC*, August 12, 1923 (central group); *AJ*, February 25, 2017; "Greatness of Our Nation," *The Forum*, October 1923, Gutzon Borglum to Rogers Winter, [May] 26, 1923, GB Papers; Evie Terrono, "'Great Generals and Christian Soldiers': Commemorations of Robert E. Lee and Stonewall Jackson in the Civil Rights Era," in Savage, *Civil War in Art*, 153. See also *AC*, December 2, 1923, February 15, 1925. National publicity for the mountain included *NYT*, January 2, 1916; *Chicago Tribune*, November 22, 1922; *Scientific American*, August 1924.

37. Gutzon Borglum to Edward A. Rumely, January 24, 1924, GB Papers; *AC*, January 20, 1924; *AJ*, January 20, 1924; Lamar, *When All Is Said*, 161. On Rabbi Marx, see Oney, *And the Dead Shall Rise*, 575–77, 597. Lee manumitted his slaves before the Emancipation Proclamation went into effect. See Thomas, *Robert E. Lee*, 273–74.

38. *Thirtieth Annual Minutes, United Daughters of the Confederacy, Georgia Division, Quitman, Georgia, October 28–30, 1924*, copy in UDC Collection, AHC; *Address Delivered at the Annual Convention, United Daughters of the Confederacy, by Hollins N. Randolph, President, Stone Mountain Confederate Monumental Association, at Savannah, Georgia, Wednesday, November 19, 1924*, copy in E. Mer-

ton Coulter Collection, UGA; LaCavera, *History of the Georgia Division*, 1:108; *AC*, February 3, 1924; Hollins Randolph to Samuel Venable, June 11, 1924, Samuel Hoyt Venable Papers, SMC; David B. Freeman, *Carved in Stone*, 77–78.

39. Gutzon Borglum to Calvin Coolidge, January 31, 1925, Borglum diary entry, February 25, 1925, GB Papers; Winter diary, February 10, 12–14 ("pair of hyenas . . . plot to destroy"), 16, 19, 25, 1925, SMCMA Records; *AC*, February 22, 1925; David B. Freeman, *Carved in Stone*, 83–84. For receipts and correspondence relating to nonpayment of bills, see Gutzon Borglum Papers, SMC. Hale, "Granite Stopped Time," 225, suggests that Borglum and Randolph fought over politics and Klan factionalism.

40. Gutzon Borglum diary entry, February 25, 1925, GB Papers; Casey and Borglum, *Give the Man Room*, 212–13; Winter diary, February 25, 1925; *AC*, February 26, 1925; *AJ*, February 26, 1925 (headline); David B. Freeman, *Carved in Stone*, 85–86. Borglum's contract stated that the "models, drawings and designs" were his intellectual property and could not be copied or photographed without his consent. However, these items were "the property of the Association for the purpose of the completion of the work." On April 11, 1925, Borglum wrote that he had destroyed "the incomplete models to prevent their falling into the unfriendly hands of the Committee . . . to have the work executed by incompetent workmen" (Borglum to Calvin Coolidge, April 11, 1925, GB Papers). Dupre, *Monuments*, 110, describes Borglum and Randolph's relationship as a "clash of . . . titanic egos."

41. *Reasons Why It Was Necessary to Dismiss Gutzon Borglum*, Miscellaneous Printed Material, SMC; Winter diary, February 26, March 7, 1925; *AJ*, March 15, 1925. Winter had once served as a reporter for the *Journal*, and Arnold handled the newspaper's legal matters. Both men played roles in Frank's trial and its aftermath: Winter covered the trial and lynching for the paper, while Arnold served as a member of Frank's legal team.

42. Winter diary, February 26, 28, March 6, 1925 (extradition issue); UDC, undated petition advocating arbitration and an audit of Randolph's books, SMCMA Records; Ruby Jones Grace to UDC Executive Board and chapter presidents, April 3, 1925, SMCMA Records; program, Oglethorpe University, June 1, 1924, Mrs. William L. Colt, president, Women's University Club of New York, to Mary Borglum, June 17, 1925 (a women's club's sympathy for the sculptor), GB Papers; *AC*, April 12, 1925; *AJ*, April 26, 1925; *NYT*, March 1, 8, 1925. For additional coverage, see *NYT*, March 2, 3, 4, 6, 9, 10, 15, April 17, 1925.

43. *AC*, April 25, 1925; UDC resolution printed in LaCavera, *History of the Georgia Division*, 1:84–85. The *AJ*'s obituary, April 26, 1925, was titled "A Mother of the Confederacy."

44. *AC*, April 17, 1925. Borglum was living in Raleigh at the time of Lukeman's appointment. The State of North Carolina had commissioned him to create a memorial to its soldiers at Gettysburg National Military Park; it was completed in 1929.

45. Ibid., May 20, 21, 22, 1925; Winter diary, May 25, June 12, 1925.

46. Winter diary, April 22, June 12, 1925; Ruby Grace to Gutzon Borglum, February 25, 1925 (advocating arbitration), GB Papers; *AC*, February 26, 27, April 24, May

3, October 18, 1925. According to LaCavera, *History of the Georgia Division*, 1:109, Grace "steered the Division through the most trying times of its existence."

47. *Reasons Why the UDC Should With Hold Funds from the Stone Mountain Association*, October 5, 1925, Mrs. James S. Nichols Papers, SMC; Ruby Grace to Elizabeth Venable Mason, April 20, 1925, Gutzon Borglum Papers, SMC.

48. *AC*, October 29, 30 (quotations), 1925; *AJ*, October 29, 30, 1925; LaCavera, *History of the Georgia Division*, 2:643 (blackberries); Brundage, *Where These Memories Grow*, 14. For the UDC's definition of womanhood, see Karen L. Cox, *Dixie's Daughters*, 26–27.

49. Winter diary, April 22, June 12, 1925; Sumter L. Lowry to General Assembly of Georgia, July 10, 1927, ALMA to General Assembly of Georgia, August 8, 1927, Hollins Randolph to Rogers Winter, March 26, 1927, SMCMA Records; *AC*, October 31, 1926; Pamela H. Simpson, "The Great Lee Chapel Controversy and the 'Little Group of Willful Women' Who Saved the Shrine of the South," in Mills and Simpson, *Monuments to the Lost Cause*, 85–99.

50. *AC*, April 17, 1925.

51. Mildred Lewis Rutherford, *Truths of History* (n.d.), Mildred Lewis Rutherford, "Wrongs of History Righted" (speech delivered in Savannah, Georgia, November 13, 1914), copies in E. Merton Coulter Collection, UGA; Rutherford, *Measuring Rod*; Sarah Case, "Mildred Lewis Rutherford: The Redefinition of New South White Womanhood," in Chirhart and Wood, *Georgia Women*, 1:272–96.

52. Dolly Lamar referenced the UDC's schism in a letter to "Miss Millie" Rutherford, January 29, 1927, copy in GB Papers; *AC*, November 16, 18, 1927; Lamar, *When All Is Said*, 161–63; Case, "Mildred Lewis Rutherford," 286. For Rutherford's opposition to women's suffrage, see Rutherford to Hollins Randolph, December 10, 1926, SMCMA Records. McRae, "Caretakers of Southern Civilization," 801–2, calls Lamar and Rutherford "the most vocal anti-suffragists in Georgia politics." Some UDC members favored women's suffrage.

53. Augustus Lukeman, "An American Monument to Surpass the Pyramids," *Stone Mountain Memorial*, UDC edition [1926], *Stone Mountain Confederate Memorial News*, January 1927 (Randolph's remarks), H. F. Wilson to Rogers Winter, October 9, 1925 (approving Lukeman's design), SMCMA Records. For praise for Lukeman's model, which "will be finished and complete, made with mathematical precision," see Minutes, Board of Directors, SMCMA, June 23, 1925, Atlanta Ladies Memorial Association Records, AHC.

54. Casey and Borglum, *Give the Man Room*, 177. Winter called Mary Borglum "a fine little woman" (Winter diary, February 26, 1925). See also Gutzon Borglum to Helen Plane, September 11, 1916, GB Papers.

55. *AJ*, April 9, 1928; David B. Freeman, *Carved in Stone*, 110–16.

56. *AC*, April 10, 1928; *AJ*, April 9, 1928; David B. Freeman, *Carved in Stone*, 116–19.

57. Casey and Borglum, *Give the Man Room*, 179; *AC*, April 10, 1928.

58. Jesse O. Thomas to Hollins Randolph, June 5, 1925, Randolph to Thomas, June 11, 1925, SMCMA Records. A graduate of Tuskegee Institute and protege of

Booker T. Washington, Thomas held a number of important positions over a long public career as an advocate for African American educational, political, and social advancement. As the first black field secretary of a National Urban League southern office, he spoke out against racial discrimination and successfully lobbied for the hiring of black nurses in the Atlanta Public Schools. See Braxton, "Jesse O. Thomas."

59. Samuel Venable to Gutzon Borglum, August 20, 1926 (deed), Gutzon Borglum Papers, SMC; "SCV Urges Passage of Memorial Bill," *AJ*, July 11, 1927; *AC*, January 1, 1929 (UDC resolution); David B. Freeman, *Carved in Stone*, 116–19; *Opportunity* 3 (April 1925): 125, quoted in Gallagher, *Lee and His Generals*, 267. In his "Report to the Conference Committee," May 15, 1928, J. J. Haverty wrote of the "impossibility to raise any funds to complete . . . Lukeman's model" (Gutzon Borglum Papers, SMC. See also *AJ*, August 5, 1927. Randolph declared, "I have malice in my heart towards no person" (*AC*, April 12, 1928).

60. *Address of Judge Ernest C. Kontz, representing the Mayor of Atlanta at the Unveiling of the Statue of Alexander H. Stephens in the Hall of Fame, at the Capitol, Washington, D.C., December 8, 1927*, copy in E. Merton Coulter Collection, UGA; *AC*, November 13, 1927; *AJ*, November 13, 1927; Casey and Borglum, *Give the Man Room*, 18–19, 316. For one of many letters in which the sculptor expressed the desire to finish the carving as a matter of "common justice and good will," see Gutzon Borglum to Plato Durham, July 17, 1928, Gutzon Borglum Papers, SMC. Ten years later, Borglum expressed similar sentiments, adding that President Coolidge had asked that the feud with Randolph be kept out of the public eye. Borglum also claimed that the SMCMA owned him thirty-three thousand dollars (Borglum to Elizabeth Venable Mason and Sam Venable, April 5, 1938, GB Papers).

61. Lamar, *When All Is Said*, 119–20, 167–69; Clare, *Thunder and Stars*, 238–45. Although the episode faded from public memory, the controversy received considerable attention in the Daughters' centennial history. See LaCavera, *History of the Georgia Division*, 2:617–48.

62. Roth, *Matronage*, 54–55. In 1944, the Atlanta, Atlanta Fulton, and Rebecca Felton chapters of the UDC in Atlanta had 307 members, down from 1,702 in 1927. See United Daughters of the Confederacy Collection, AHC. According to LaCavera, *History of the Georgia Division*, 1:185–92, Atlanta eventually had seven UDC chapters: Admiral Raphael Semmes (founded 1960), Alfred Holt Colquitt (founded 1930), Atlanta (founded 1895), Crawford W. Long (founded 1929), Atlanta Fulton (founded 1921), Atlanta Georgia Centennial (1961), and Rebecca Latimer Felton (1927).

63. Linda Gordon, *Second Coming of the KKK*, 16–17, 191; Pegram, *One Hundred Percent American*, 20, 87, 219.

CHAPTER 5. ARTISTS, WRITERS, AND HISTORIANS OF THE 1920S–1930S

1. McDonough, "Remembering the Last Reunion"; MM to Henry Steele Commager, July 10, 1936, in MM, *Margaret Mitchell's "Gone with the Wind" Letters*, 37–40.

2. Huff, *My 80 Years in Atlanta*, 7–8, 15; *AJ*, July 21, 1935. By the time she published her stories, the city limits had been expanded to include the family's house. Sarah Huff's parents were Jeremiah Clayton "Jerry" Huff (1831–1907) and Elizabeth Huff (1821–1906); she and they are buried at Oakland Cemetery.

3. Huff, *My 80 Years in Atlanta*, 14, 17, 53, 90.

4. *AJ*, July 8, 1934, July 21, 1935. See also *AC*, August 12, 1930.

5. *AJ*, July 8, 15, 1934, July 21, 1935, July 12, 1936; Huff, *My 80 Years in Atlanta*, 22. Charlotte was no longer with the family by the time of the 1870 U.S. census.

6. *AJ*, May 13, 1954.

7. *AC*, May 7, 21, 1925, November 23, 25, 1931. Small embraced religion after attending an 1885 revival led by Rev. Sam Jones. See Minnix, *Laughter in the Amen Corner*, 92–94.

8. *AC*, November 30, 1925 (slave auction), January 5 (Confederacy's prospects), 6 (Lincoln's election), 1926. See also Samuel W. Small Scrapbook, AHC.

9. *AC*, January 7 (family details), 8 (Johnston), 9 (bombardment, Griffin), 11 (Calhoun), 1926.

10. Ibid., January 13, 1926.

11. Wilbur Kurtz to Wilbur Kurtz Jr. and Elma Kurtz, March 31, 1943, WGKS Papers.

12. Family history notes made by Wilbur Kurtz, May 28, 1954, and by his daughter, Annie Laurie Kurtz Lyon, March 28, 1967, WGKS Papers; Kurtz, "My Adventures with Atlanta History," 9; Kurtz, *Atlanta and the Old South*, 7; Sampson, "Pretty Damned Warm Times."

13. Kurtz, "My Adventures with Atlanta History," 9–11; Kurtz, *Atlanta and the Old South*, 7, 23–24. According to his grandson, family members often teased Kurtz about being "that Yankee who married Annie Laurie" (Wilbur G. Kurtz III, interview by author, August 25, 2018).

14. Franklin M. Garrett quoted in Kurtz, *Atlanta and the Old South*, 9; O'Connell, *Art and Life*, 29–51.

15. *AC*, August 20 (three stories), September 24, 1933.

16. Ibid., May 7, 1911. See also *AC*, April 4, 1911, April 14, 1912.

17. *Battle of Atlanta*, 15; Haden, *George V. Gress*, 7–11; *AC*, April 28, August 8, October 1, 2, 1921; "Salvation of Atlanta," 68–72.

18. Kurtz, "My Adventures with Atlanta History," 18–19; *AC*, January 15, November 4, 1934, May 29, 1937.

19. *AC*, June 22, 1930.

20. *AJ*, July 10, 1932. Kurtz also consulted Union brigadier general Jacob D. Cox's 1900 memoir, in which he wrote about women in a backyard pit "trying to sleep away the days of terror, while innocent-looking children, 4 or 5 years old, clustered around the air-hole, looking up with pale faces and great staring eyes." See Jacob D. Cox, *Military Reminiscences*, vol. 2., chap. 41.

21. Wilbur Kurtz Notebooks, April 8, 1933 (Saturday outings), WGKS Papers; Kurtz, "My Adventures with Atlanta History," 13–14; Lockerman, *Man Who Amazed Atlanta*, 71–75. Franklin Garrett Necrology Genealogical Resource, AHC. Kurtz

lived at 907 Penn Avenue, and Garrett lived at 811 Penn Avenue. The artillery shells collected by the DuBose men were donated to the Atlanta History Center and became the centerpiece of its Civil War exhibit, *Turning Point: The American Civil War*.

22. MM to Wilbur Kurtz, November 19, 1935, Kurtz to Margaret Baugh, February 8, 1960 (recalling his interactions with Mitchell), WGKS Papers; Kurtz, "My Adventures with Atlanta History," 14. For the Atlanta Historical Society and its membership of three hundred, see *AC*, September 3, 1939.

23. Gallagher, *Causes Won, Lost, and Forgotten*, 45; Newman, *Southern Hospitality*, 117.

24. Stephens Mitchell, "History of the Mitchell Ancestors," Stephens Mitchell, "Memoir of Margaret Mitchell" (including a copy of Maybelle's letter), Stephens Mitchell Family Papers, UGA; Kathleen Ann Clark, "Margaret Mitchell: What Living in the South Means," in Chirhart and Clark, *Georgia Women*, 191–94.

25. Stephens Mitchell, "Margaret Mitchell and Her People," 8–13, 20; MM interviewed by Medora Perkerson on WSB radio, July 4, 1936, reported in *AJ*, July 4, 1936; Fox-Genovese, "Scarlett O'Hara," 395; Pyron, *Southern Daughter*, 11–13; Groover, "Margaret Mitchell, the Lady," 56–57.

26. Stephens Mitchell, "Memoir of Margaret Mitchell," Stephens Mitchell Family Papers, UGA; Pyron, *Southern Daughter*, 35–36, 103.

27. Stephens Mitchell, "Memoir of Margaret Mitchell," Stephens Mitchell Family Papers, UGA; Pyron, *Southern Daughter*, 31–32, 55–56; Clark, "Margaret Mitchell," 200.

28. Stephens Mitchell, "Margaret Mitchell and Her People," 21, 24, (MM's debutante photograph in *AJ*, September 26, 1920); Pyron, *Southern Daughter*, 107, 130–41; Clark, "Margaret Mitchell," 198.

29. Medora Field Perkerson, "When Margaret Mitchell Was a Girl Reporter," in Harwell, *"Gone with the Wind,"* 39–45. MM's articles appeared in *AJ* on May 6, 1923 (Borglum), November 29 (Gordon), December 6 (Cobb), and December 13, 1925 (other three). The *Journal* printed a picture of the five generals on December 9, 1925. Mitchell's friends were surprised by her second marriage, believing that the vivacious Peggy would not be happy with a man Ralph McGill described as "solemn, slow-talking, serious John Marsh," but the marriage was a happy one. See "Little Woman, Big Book," in Harwell, *"Gone with the Wind,"* 73.

30. MM, "Margaret Mitchell," *Wilson Bulletin*, September 1936, in Harwell, *"Gone with the Wind,"* 37–38; MM to Julia Collier Harris, April 28, 1936, in MM, *Margaret Mitchell's "Gone with the Wind" Letters*, 2–6. See also Lois Dwight Cole, "The Story Begins at a Luncheon Bridge in Atlanta," in Harwell, *"Gone with the Wind,"* 55–61.

31. MM to Julia Collier Harris, April 28, 1936, MM to Donald Adams, July 9, 1936, MM to Fanny Butcher, July 11, 1936, in MM, *Margaret Mitchell's "Gone with the Wind" Letters*, 2–6, 30–31, 41; MM interviewed by Medora Perkerson, WSB radio, reported in *AJ*, July 4, 1936.

32. Edwards, *Road to Tara*, 138–39; Groover, "Margaret Mitchell, the Lady," 62.

For a lengthy discussion of the parallels between characters in the novel and Mitchell's family members, see Pyron, *Southern Daughter*, 238–59.

33. Edwards, *Road to Tara*, 155, 179–80, 188. Kurtz later recalled, "I found some confusion in references to the battle in East Atlanta, July 22d, and that affair in the Decatur public square where [Joseph] Wheeler's Cavalry attempted to capture [James] McPherson's wagon trains. They were separate engagements of the same date." See Kurtz to Margaret Baugh, February 8, 1960, WGKS Papers.

34. Pyron, *Southern Daughter*, 238–50; Cullen, *Civil War in Popular Culture*, 89; Crank, *New Approaches*, 2.

35. Cullen, *Civil War in Popular Culture*, 75.

36. *ADW*, December 12, 1936 (Hopkins Book and Furniture Store ad); July 25, 1937 (one of many references to the Gone with the Wind social club), February 26 ("greatest novel"), 1939. For the claim that African Americans liked the novel, see MM to Hershel Brickell, April 8, 1937, in MM, *Scarlett Letters*, 65. On December 26, 1936, the *ADW* noted that Rev. J. R. Henderson of Wheat Street Baptist Church would speak about *Gone with the Wind* but did not report on the event. Founded in 1928, the *ADW* became a daily newspaper in 1932. By 1945 it had a circulation of twenty-three thousand. The paper's owners, the Scott family, eventually started a number of papers as part of the Scott Newspaper Syndicate. See Aiello, *Grapevine of the Black South*, 1, 168.

37. MM to Thomas Dixon, August 15, 1936, in MM, *Margaret Mitchell's "Gone with the Wind" Letters*, 52–53; MM, *Gone with the Wind*, 447; Kenneth O'Brien, "Race, Romance, and the Southern Literary Tradition," in Pyron, *Recasting*, 157. For reverse anthropomorphism, see Cullen, *Civil War in Popular Culture*, 76–78.

38. *AJ*, June 28, 1936; Cullen, *Civil War in Popular Culture*, 67; Edwards, *Road to Tara*, 268.

39. *AJ*, June 28 (Tupper's review), July 4 (unsigned review), 1936; *AC*, June 28, 1936 (announcement of publication and Gwin's review); MM, *Gone with the Wind*, 957. Silber, *This War Ain't Over*, 125–37, discusses the Great Depression's revival of southern memories of Civil War adversity and analyzes white southerners' concerns regarding governmental overreach during the New Deal and the parallels they saw to Reconstruction.

40. *AJ*, June 29 (Davison's tea), July 4, 1936.

41. *AC*, July 9, 1936; Morton, "My Dear, I Don't Give," 55.

42. MM to Muriel King, October 15, 1937, in MM, *Scarlett Letters*, 96; *AC*, July 18 (movie rights), November 25, 1936; Edwards, *Road to Tara*, 250–51.

43. MM to Katharine Brown, February 14, March 8, 1937, in MM, *Scarlett Letters*, 48–50, 51–55. Brown worked for Selznick as East Coast story editor.

44. Kurtz, "My Adventures with Atlanta History," 15–18; Thomas Cripps, "Winds of Change: *Gone with the Wind* and Racism as a National Issue," in Pyron, *Recasting*, 141.

45. *AC*, February 26 (rail station, Jesse Clark), March 19 (five hundred employees), April 2 (barbecue), May 7 (additional buildings), 1939. See also articles by Kurtz, *AC*, April 23, May 14, June 11, December 2, 1939.

46. MM to Susan Myrick, January 19, February 10, 1939, MM to Wilbur Kurtz, May 8, 1939, MM to Virginius Dabney, July 23, 1942, in MM, *Scarlett Letters*, 171–74, 194–98, 224–26, 382–83; Bernstein, "Selznick's March," 10. Myrick compared Twelve Oaks to New York's Grand Central Station and noted that both director Victor Fleming and actor Clark Gable laughed at its appearance. See Susan Myrick diary, March 12, 1939, Susan Myrick Papers, UGA. The Myrick Papers at UGA also contain many memos from Myrick to Selznick employees about her dialect coaching of white and black actors.

47. Gallagher, *Causes Won, Lost, and Forgotten*, 46–50; Cullen, *Civil War in Popular Culture*, 82.

48. MM to David Selznick, May 11, 1938, in MM, *Scarlett Letters*, 119–20; Cripps, "Winds of Change," 144; Kenneth O'Brien, "Race, Romance and the Southern Literary Tradition," in Pyron, *Recasting*, 161; Cullen, *Civil War in Popular Culture*, 83–84. Myrick recalled MM's views about language in the film in "Margaret Mitchell, a Portrait," Susan Myrick Papers, UGA. On February 11, 1939, a leading African American newspaper, the *Chicago Defender*, urged readers to write directly to Will Hays, chair of the Motion Picture Producers and Distributors of America and namesake of the Hays Code, which provided guidelines for what could and could not be included in films, to demand that "the word 'nigger' be stricken" from the film."

49. Cripps, "Winds of Change," 143; Gerald Wood, "From *The Clansman* and *Birth of a Nation* to *Gone with the Wind*: The Loss of American Innocence," in Pyron, *Recasting*, 125; Cullen, *Civil War in Popular Culture*, 84; *ADW*, August 1, 1937, January 19 (casting Mammy), February 12, April 18 (casting Eddie Anderson as Uncle Peter), 1939. The *Chicago Defender* denounced the film on January 6, 1940, and October 10, 1942. It printed articles noting the casting of black actors on December 31, 1938 (Oscar Polk as Pork), February 11, 1939 (Butterfly McQueen as Prissy), and May 13, 1939 (Hattie McDaniel as Mammy). The article on McDaniel noted that the actress hoped to "glorify Race womanhood. Not the modern, streamlined type of Race woman, who attends teas and concerts . . . but the type of woman of the period that gave us Harriet Tubman [and] Sojourner Truth."

50. *AC*, November 27, 1939; Bernstein, "Selznick's March," 7–11, 18–19.

51. *AJ*, December 10 (two million copies), December 13, 14 (Rutherford), 1939; *AC*, December 12, 15, 1939; *NYT*, December 15, 1939 ("tumbledown shacks").

52. *AC*, December 14, 1939; *AJ*, December 14, 1939.

53. *AC*, December 14, 1939; *AJ*, December 14, 1939; *NYT*, December 15, 1939; Wilbur G. Kurtz Jr., "*Gone with the Wind* Premiere," 15–18.

54. *AC*, November 24, 1939; Wilbur G. Kurtz Jr., "*Gone with the Wind* Premiere"; MM to Mrs. Green Dodd Warren, November 1, 1939, MM to Mrs. W. Colquitt Carter, December 16, 1939, in MM, *Scarlett Letters*, 280–81, 323–24; Pyron, *Southern Daughter*, 375–78; Edwards, *Road to Tara*, 285.

55. *AC*, December 7 (contest), 9 (McGill), 15 (Palmer), 1939; *AJ*, December 15, 1939 (fifty in hoopskirts); *Atlanta Georgian*, November 20, 1939 (tickets), copy in Junior League of Atlanta Records, AHC.

56. *ADW*, December 14, 15, 16, 1939; *AJ*, December 15, 1939; King, *Papers of Martin Luther King*, 1:81.

57. *AC*, December 15, 1939; *AJ*, December 15, 1939.

58. *AC*, December 16, 1939; *AJ*, December 16, 1939; "Salvation of Atlanta," 74.

59. *ADW*, December 14 (black ushers), 16 (Big Bethel choir), 1939; *AC*, December 16, 1939; *AJ*, December 16, 1939; MM quoted in Bernstein, "Selznick's March," 24; Edwards, *Road to Tara*, 287–89.

60. *AC*, December 17, 1939 (two articles).

61. *AC*, December 17 (two articles), 21 ("Nuts"), 1939; *AJ*, December 24, 1939; *NYT*, December 10 (filming), 15 (premiere), 20 (quotations), 24, 1939; Bernstein, "Selznick's March," 28. *Gone with the Wind*'s initial run in Atlanta lasted until February 24, 1940, with 230,000 tickets sold. See MM, *Scarlett Letters*, 333n.

62. *ADW*, February 12 (dialect), December 15, 16 (three stories), 17 (dialect), 1939. On January 6, 1940, the *Chicago Defender*'s William L. Patterson condemned *Gone with the Wind* for glorifying slavery and serving as a sequel to *The Birth of a Nation* at a time when half of the U.S. black population was unemployed.

63. *AJ*, December 18, 1939.

64. MM to Lois Cole, December 10, MM to David Selznick, December 11, 1940, in MM, *Scarlett Letters*, 357–60; *AC*, December 8, 9, 12, 1940; Edwards, *Road to Tara*, 297–98.

## CHAPTER 6. THE CIVIL WAR CENTENNIAL

1. Transcript, Confederate States Civil War Centennial Commission meeting, July 21, 1960, DFC; Jon Wiener, "Civil War, Cold War, Civil Rights: The Civil War Centennial in Context, 1960–1965," in Fahs and Waugh, *Memory of the Civil War*, 208–25; Blight, *American Oracle*, 2–3. The Confederate States Civil War Centennial Commission consisted of southern state centennial commissions and was distinct from the U.S. CWCC.

2. *AC*, August 15, 1945; Newman, *Southern Hospitality*, 118–19, 140–42.

3. Newman, *Southern Hospitality*, 185–86.

4. *AC*, August 12, 17 (multiple stories), 1949; *ADW*, August 13, 18, 1949 (Scott); *AJ*, August 13, 17, 1949 (Scott). Kruse, *White Flight*, 185, characterizes Scott as the "the public voice of the old guard" of black leaders.

5. *AC*, August 18, 19, 1949; *ADW*, August 18, 19, 1949.

6. Cook, *Civil War Memories*, 156.

7. Ibid., 158–59.

8. Fortson, *Georgia Flags*; Coski, *Confederate Battle Flag*, 252–53.

9. Coski, *Confederate Battle Flag*, 252–55; Cobb, *Away Down South*, 291–92. On the image of the Confederate flag in Georgia, South Carolina, and Alabama, see James Foreman Jr., "Driving Dixie Down: Removing the Confederate Flag from Southern State Capitols," in Martinez, Richardson, and McNinch-Su, *Confederate Symbols*, 195–223.

10. *ADW*, February 14, 1956; Coski, *Confederate Battle Flag*, 255.

11. For its history, see the Atlanta Civil War Roundtable's website, atlantacwrt.org. Civil War Round Table of Atlanta Records, AHC, includes a "Directory of Civil War Round Tables" compiled by the Indianapolis Civil War Round Table, September 20, 1960. For more on roundtables, see Cook, *Civil War Memories*, 159.

12. Constitution, May 25, 1959, meeting about Longstreet, W. G. Ryckman to Mr. Stockard, February 10, 1960 (Perry); Wiley's motion to limit membership, January 24, 1961, Civil War Round Table of Atlanta Records, AHC. Today, the ACWRT requires only one current member to serve as sponsor.

13. Karl Betts, news release, September 13, 1958, GCWCC Collection; Cook, *Civil War Memories*, 164–65. For a discussion of the Cold War and Civil War memory, see Gannon, *Americans Remember Their Civil War*, 61–64; Wiener, "Civil War, Cold War," 215–17.

14. *AC*, April 11 (creation of Georgia CWCC and its committees), April 20, July 22 (Geer quote), August 30, October 11, 17, 30 (Wiley quote), 1959; Georgia CWCC goals printed in *Gone with the Wind* Centennial Benefit Costume Ball program, March 9, 1961, GCWCC Collection. Despite his campaign slogan, which promised "no, not one" black child in a white school, Vandiver became a moderate governor who presided over the peaceful integration of Georgia schools. See his obituary, *NYT*, February 23, 2005; Bodnar, *Remaking America*, 208.

15. Karl Betts planned Eisenhower's and the clergy's role well in advance. See his press release, January 27, 1960, GCWCC Collection. Cook, *Troubled Commemoration*, 49, 52, 58, 63 (quotation), 69, 76.

16. Carlon Carter to Stanley Rowland Smith, March 2, 1962, GCWCC Collection. See also Clyde A. Boynton to Smith, April 23, 1963, GCWCC Collection.

17. Cook, *Troubled Commemoration*, 81–82.

18. Minutes of the Georgia Civil War Centennial Ball Committee, May 2, June 10, July 8, December 29, 1960, program, Centennial Benefit Costume Ball, March 9, 1961, GCWCC Collection; Margaret Mitchell Memorial Room dedication program, WGKS Papers. Proceeds of the ball benefited three local charities. See *AC*, March 5, 1961.

19. Peter Zack Geer, press release, n.d., GCWCC Collection; *AC*, March 10, 11, 12, 23, 1961. According to Kreyling, *Late Encounter*, 33–34, "Hollywood magic" did not characterize the re-premiere.

20. Kruse, *White Flight*, 114–15, 184–93; Teel, *Ralph Emerson McGill*, 350–54; Hale, "Of the Meaning of Progress," 22–23; Thomas F. Jackson, *From Civil Rights*, 114–16. As Kruse points out, presidential candidate John F. Kennedy focused media attention on the situation by calling Martin Luther King Jr.'s wife, Coretta Scott King, a move that also helped him win black votes in the November election.

21. *Rich's Commemorates the Civil War Centennial 1861–1961* (brochure), DFC; *AC*, January 8, 10, 1961.

22. R. Loring Blackstone to Rowland Smith, December 28, 1960, DFC; *AC*, January 27, 1961; *AJ*, January 12, 1961. Most of the memorabilia for the exhibit was loaned by Beverly DuBose Jr.

23. Karl Betts to Everett J. Landers, March 8, 1961, BIW Papers; Cook, *Troubled Commemoration*, 88–94.

24. John F. Kennedy to Ulysses S. Grant III, March 14, 1961, Bell Wiley to Grant, March 22 [1961], *New York Herald Tribune*, March 22, 24, 1961, *NYT*, March 22, 1961, BIW Papers; *ADW*, March 26, 1961. Aiello, *Grapevine of the Black South*, 35, characterizes the *ADW* as "engaged in a practical radicalism that sought winnable racial battles." For extensive analysis of the Charleston meeting, see Cook, *Troubled Commemoration*, 95–105; Wiener, "Civil War, Cold War," 209–12..

25. Ashley Halsey Jr., speech, April 11, 1961, Donald Flamm, statement, April 12, 1961, BIW Papers; Cook, *Troubled Commemoration*, 112–19.

26. Press release, September 14, 1961, in minutes of the U.S. CWCC meeting, December 3, 1961, Fred Schwengel to Bell Wiley, September 30, 1961, White House press release, September 5, 1961 (with handwritten notation from Kennedy aide Harris Wofford, "Davenport is the highest-ranking Negro in the Defense Department"), BIW Papers; Karl Betts to Peter Zack Geer, October 6, 1961, GCWCC Collection; Ralph Righton to Betts, May 2, 1961 (indicating that Georgia senator Richard Russell hoped to restore the U.S. CWCC's budget but the outcome was uncertain), Civil War Round Table of Atlanta Records, AHC; *ADW*, December 6, 1961. Betts died in 1962 and Grant in 1968. For Davenport's background, see *Ebony* 18 (April 1963): 86.

27. *AC*, April 8, 13, 1961 (McGill). In his editorial, McGill erroneously claimed that there were black Confederate regiments as well as black Union regiments. See Teel, *Ralph Emerson McGill*, 353–54.

28. *ADW*, February 17, 1956 (Negro History Week).

29. *Campus Mirror*, January 15, 1933; *ADW*, December 5, 1934 (White), January 2, 1938 (Borders), January 2, 1944 (parade).

30. *ADW*, December 30, 1952 (rallies), January 2, 1955 (Marshall); speeches of Walden (1960) and Mays (n.d.) reported in *Pittsburgh Courier* press service, Trezzvant W. Anderson Collection, AUC.

31. *ADW*, December 30, 1962, January 2, 1963. Union Baptist was located at the corner of Simpson and Hightower Roads. On Hollowell's background, see *NYT*, January 2, 2005. The centenary of the Emancipation Proclamation also inspired McGill to praise Lincoln's action against slavery: "The Confederacy was doomed because it put itself on the wrong side of this moral question" (*AC*, January 5, 1963). African Americans in other states staged similar celebrations. John Bodnar, *Remaking America*, 210–11, discusses an event in Springfield, Illinois, sponsored by the Negro Emancipation Centennial Authority of Chicago.

32. *ADW*, January 13, 15, 19, 1963.

33. Cook, *Troubled Commemoration*, 146, 149, 152–53.

34. Ibid., 172–77; *ADW*, September 21, 1962; *NYT*, September 18, 1962.

35. *ADW*, September 23, 26, 1962; Cook, *Troubled Commemoration*, 170–77. Representing the national African American media, *Jet* magazine issued a September 27, 1962, press release, copy in Johnson Publishing Company clipping file, AUC, about the "lilywhite aspects" of the event. In addition to the U.S. CWCC, cohosts of

the event were the U.S. Civil Rights Commission and the centennial agencies of several northern states.

36. Garrow, *Bearing the Cross*, 32–90. For a recap of the civil rights movement to date, see *NYT*, August 29, 1963.

37. King, *Papers of Martin Luther King*, 1:109–11; *ADW*, April 16, 1944.

38. "Address of the Reverend Dr. Martin Luther King, Jr., New York Civil War Centennial Commission—Park Sheraton Hotel, New York City—Wednesday, September 12, 1962," Morehouse College Martin Luther King, Jr. Collection, AUC; *NYT*, September 13, 15, 18, 1962 (quotations); Cook, *Troubled Commemoration*, 187–88.

39. King, *Papers of Martin Luther King*, 7:308–10, 349; *ADW*, October 19, 1961; Garrow, *Bearing the Cross*, 161, 169–70, 199; Blight, *American Oracle*, 17. See also *ADW*, October 17, 1962. Jon Wiener "Civil War, Cold War," 218–19, points out that Kennedy's press secretary, Pierre Salinger, gave the president a draft of a "second Emancipation Proclamation" in December 1962, but Kennedy declined to issue it.

40. *ADW*, April 20, August 29 (two stories), 30, 1963; *AC*, August 30, 1963; Garrow, *Bearing the Cross*, 173–230, 246, 269; Rieder, *Gospel of Freedom*, 43–49, 137, 157–58.

41. *AC*, August 29, September 30, 1963, January 28, 1965; *ADW*, August 29, 1963; *NYT*, August 29, 1963; Garrow, *Bearing the Cross*, 283–86. King subsequently used Civil War themes less often, though he did so again in 1965 during the Alabama voting rights campaign, ending a speech at the State Capitol by quoting the "Battle Hymn of the Republic." See Cook, *Civil War Memories*, 177.

42. Beverly DuBose Jr., *Report of the Georgia Civil War Centennial Commission Commemorating the War between the States 1959-1965* (n.d., n.p.), DFC.

43. Peter Zack Geer, press release, September 30, 1961, February 28, 1962, ACWRT program, April 13, 1962, GCWCC newsletter, March 1962, GCWCC Collection; copy of Kurtz's remarks, April 13, 1962, in WGKS Papers. Kurtz told his daughter that the raid "was the greatest of the Civil War events memorialized in the state of Georgia." See Annie Laurie Kurtz Lyon notes on family history, January 3, 1967, WGKS Papers.

44. Senators Richard Russell and Herman Talmadge wrote to Smith regarding a commemorative stamp on July 27, 1961. See Stanley Rowland Smith to Karl Betts, January 5, 1962, GCWCC Collection. Betts endorsed the plan in a January 15, 1962, letter to Smith and wrote again on April 16, 1962, to congratulate Georgia on keeping "the centennial where it belongs," away from politics (GCWCC Collection).

45. *AJ*, March 1, 1962; Kurtz, *Atlanta and the Old South*, 7. See also *AC*, September 10, 15, 16, 22, 1962.

46. Governor Carl Sanders, executive order appointing Beverly DuBose Jr. as Georgia CWCC chair, August 2, 1963, DuBose to Sanders, December 30, 1963, DFC; DuBose to Paul Heffernan, March 20, 1964 (two thousand dollars), DuBose to James I. Robertson Jr., March 30, 1964 (no budget), DuBose to Lila Stenz, April 7, 1964, GCWCC Collection; *AC*, August 30, November 18, 1964.

47. *AC*, February 3, 1964.

48. Program of the Seventh National Assembly Sponsored by the U.S. Civil War Centennial Commission, Atlanta, June 10–12, 1964, DFC; *AC*, June 11, 1964; *AJ*, June 11, 1964.

49. Program of the Seventh National Assembly Sponsored by the U.S. Civil War Centennial Commission, Atlanta, June 10–12, 1964, DFC; *AC*, June 11, 13, 1964. During July 1964, a meeting of the Confederate States Centennial Committee took place. See *Report of the Georgia CWCC*, DFC. See also *AC*, June 4, 12, 1964. Wiley is best remembered for his seminal works about common soldiers, *The Life of Johnny Reb* and *The Life of Billy Yank*.

50. *AC*, April 18, July 22, 1959.

51. *AC*, February 15, 1958; *AJ*, February 21, 1945 (Hartsfield); Freeman, *Carved in Stone*, 135, 142–46. *Stone Mountain Memorial Association* had also been the original name of Plane's organization.

52. *AC*, June 21, 1946, July 5, and 9, 1962. In 1990, the Georgia Supreme Court validated the state's 1951 antimask law. See *NYT*, December 6, 1990. For an overview of the issue, see J. Vincent Lowery, "A Monument to Many Souths: Tourists Experience Southern Distinctiveness at Stone Mountain," in Karen L. Cox, *Destination Dixie*, 223–43.

53. *AC*, July 8, 9 (two stories), 10 (two stories), 15, 1962; unsigned letter to the editor, *AC*, July 14, 1962.

54. Albert D. Putnam to Beverly DuBose Jr., June 16, 1964, Phil Campbell to DuBose, July 7, 1964, DFC; *AC*, June 15, 1964. See also *AC*, June 7, 13, July 12, 1964 (Sanders). *AC*, June 23, 1963, called Davis a "sensitive, devoted talent." *AJ*, June 12, 1963, pointed out that the novel, a Literary Guild selection for July 1963, made Davis the first local author to win a book club endorsement since Margaret Mitchell.

55. Beverly DuBose Jr., "Battle Plan Stone Mountain, July 25, 1964," n.d., GCWCC Collection.

56. Beverly DuBose Jr. to Paul M. Heffernan, March 20, 1964, DuBose to Lila Stenz, April 7, 1864, DuBose to Ivan Allen Jr., June 17, 1965, copy of Chickamauga program, GCWCC Collection; *AC*, July 26, August 29, 1964; *AJ*, July 26, 1964.

57. Beverly DuBose Jr., *Report of the Georgia Civil War Centennial Commission*, DFC; *AC*, June 26, 1964; *AJ*, October 1, 1964. See also *AC*, September 27 (Hartsfield), October 2 (photograph of set), 5 (Fitch), 1964.

58. Peter Zack Geer, press releases, n.d., "General Outline of Proposed Projects," August 16, 1963, James I. Robertson to Edward Downer, August 14, 1963, GCWCC Collection; *AC*, May 12 (public library), September 11 (speakers), 1964; Bodnar, *Remaking America*, 215. The judges for the essay contest were college professors.

59. See, for example, "War Diary," *AC*, February 16, 1964; "Atlanta Century," *AJ*, June 12, 1964; "War for the Union," *ADW*, April 5, June 14, 1964; *AJ*, June 16, 1961 (Grant). Additional media discussed in Beverly DuBose Jr., *Report of the Georgia Civil War Centennial Commission*, DFC.

60. *7 Georgia Centennial Tours, 1961–1965* (n.p., n.d.), copy in DFC; *Aids for Ad-*

*vertisers*, July 1961, John Riggall, to Wilbur Kurtz Jr., June 27, 1961, Peachtree Creek pamphlet sponsored by Trust Company, Coca-Cola ad, n.d., WGKS Papers; *AC*, May 10, 1964.

61. Beverly DuBose Jr., *Report of the Georgia Civil War Centennial Commission*, May 5, 1864, DFC.

62. *ADW*, February 13, 1963. This article suggested that the Association for the Study of Negro Life and History (later renamed Association for the Study of African American Life and History), founded in 1915 by Carter Woodson and based in Washington, D.C., might work with the CWCC. The article also noted that "materials related to the Negro are available in Civil War official records but are completely omitted in popular history books used in our schools."

### CHAPTER 7. SHADES OF GRAY

1. *AJC*, September 1, 2016. For a discussion of the "Atlanta Way," see *AJC*, July 7, 2019. See also Henry, "Resurrected Mims Park." In the 1950s, land from the first Mims Park was used for a public school. In the summer of 2019, the park became contentious again after the death of longtime local city council member Ivory Lee Young Jr., who had supported the decision to name the park for Cook. Led by Antonio Brown, several members of the Atlanta City Council tried to revisit the issue, but the city council voted nine to six not to reopen the matter (*AJC*, July 7, 2019).

2. David B. Freeman, *Carved in Stone*, 141–49. McQueen quit after she sued but lost a court case in which she claimed that her name was being used without permission. See Bourne, *Butterfly McQueen Remembered*, 80.

3. *AJC*, October 4, 9, 1964; LaCavera, *History of the Georgia Division*, 1:582–88. In 1948, when all of the Confederate veterans had died, the Confederate Soldier's Home became the Home for Confederate Widows. In 1963, the handful of remaining widows were moved elsewhere and the facility was closed. See LaCavera, *History of the Georgia Division*, 2:523–27; David B. Freeman, *Carved in Stone*, 150. Confederate Hall was later renamed Memorial Hall, although Stone Mountain now has another building named Confederate Hall.

4. *AJC*, May 31, June 1, 1964; David B. Freeman, *Carved in Stone*, 151–52.

5. *AC*, March 8, 9, 1963; Hancock, *Sculptor's Fortunes*, 130, 176–80, 219–20, 261, 266; David B. Freeman, *Carved in Stone*, 157–64.

6. *AC*, March 3, 1963; Hancock, *Sculptor's Fortunes*, 220.

7. Hancock designed sculptures called *Valor* and *Sacrifice* that were completed and unveiled in 1977. See Hancock, *Sculptor's Fortunes*, 222–23; David B. Freeman, *Carved in Stone*, 180–81; Hudson and Mirza, *Atlanta's Stone Mountain*, 97.

8. Herman Talmadge to Richard Nixon, November 12, 1969, press release, December 1, 1969, BIW Papers.

9. *New York Times*, May 10, 1970.

10. *Savannah Morning News*, May 8, 1970, *Richmond Times-Dispatch*, May 8, 1970, *Tampa Tribune*, May 8, 1970, *Los Angeles Times*, May 8, 1970, *Binghamton*

*Press*, May 9, 1970, copies in BIW Papers; Mrs. C. W. Reid to Wiley, May 12, 1970, in BIW Papers; *AC*, May 7, 8, 1970.

11. Stone Mountain Memorial Carving Dedication program, May 9, 1970, copy in BIW Papers; *AC*, May 8, 9, 1970 (quotation).

12. On May 10, 1970, the *AC* reported on Billy Graham's "unexplained absence" and "Sen. Richard Russell's need to attend the dedication in his honor of a federal laboratory in Athens." See also *AC*, May 9, 10, 11, 1970. *AJ*, May 10, 1970, reported that "Agnew's appearance . . . put the national seal of approval" on the project. See also *ADW*, May 14, 1970. Rosemary Cox, daughter of Stone Mountain's horticulturalist, Harold Cox, recalled that the event "went off without a hitch," to the relief of Stone Mountain employees (interview by author, September 17, 2018).

13. *AC*, May 9, 10, 1970.

14. Ibid., May 9, 15, 16, 23, 1970; Mills and Simpson, *Monuments to the Lost Cause*, xv. Agnew resigned the vice presidency in 1973 after pleading guilty to tax evasion.

15. *AC*, July 22, 1979 (history), February 2, 1980 (clay), December 21, 1980 (structural problems), March 25, 1982 (rat poison).

16. Ibid., September 22, 1974, May 11, 1975.

17. *AJ*, July 25, September 28, 1975; *AC*, October 17, 1973 (Jackson's election), July 23, 1975 (Cyclorama). Records relating to the citizens group Cyclorama Restoration, including newsletters pertaining to fundraising efforts, in Cyclorama Restoration, Inc. Records, AHC. In 1975, *AC* readers voted overwhelmingly in favor of restoring the Cyclorama, with 4,797 respondents to a poll supporting the idea and only 25 opposing it (*AC*, August 5, 1979). For Jackson's background and distinguished family, see Pomerantz, *Where Peachtree Meets Sweet Auburn*, 128, 197–98, 238–43, 362, 420–21. Between 1960 and 1970, Atlanta's black population rose from 38.3 percent to 51.3 percent. Jackson won 95 percent of the African American vote and 17.5 percent of the white vote. See Bayor, *Race and the Shaping*, 7, 48–52.

18. *AC*, June 9, 1976 (downtown), March 20, 25, 26, April 5, 1977. See also *AC*, April 25, June 11, July 4, August 29, September 10, 1976.

19. Ibid., November 30 (seven million dollars), December 1 (minority employment), 1977, July 3, 10, 1978, February 27, July 22 (funding formula), August 28 (lightning strike and closure), 1979. For the effort to move the Cyclorama to Stone Mountain, see *AC*, September 20, 1978, January 21, February 6 (Jackson's response). The Jackson administration developed a plan requiring 25 percent minority contractors for city projects. See Minority Business Utilization Plan, 1980, copy in Maynard Jackson Mayoral Administrative Records, AUC; Bayor, *Race and the Shaping*, 49.

20. Cyclorama Historical Conservation update, May 15, 19, 1980, Maynard Jackson Mayoral Administrative Records, AUC; Cyclorama Architects/Engineers, "Renovation/Restoration Design" (press release), n.d., EWF Consulting Engineers, "Innovative Space Frame for Atlanta's Cyclorama Roof" (press release), December 1981 ("100% minority-owned"), Battle of Atlanta, Cyclorama Restoration Records, AHC;

*AC*, December 23, 1977, February 19 (Berger), July 30 (*Texas*), 1978, December 15 (holes, auditorium, film), 1981, May 23 (poison removal), 1982.

21. *AC*, May 30, June 2, 10, 1982 (Grizzard).

22. Young, Newman, and Young, *Andrew Young*, 20–21 (quotation), 155 (biography).

23. Allen Freeman, "Battle for Atlanta," 82.

24. *AC*, July 9, 1984 (Sibley). See letters to the editor, *AC*, June 3, July 24, 30, September 3, December 24, 1987, January 11, 1988.

25. Margaret Mitchell Collection, Special Collections Department, Atlanta-Fulton Public Library System, Central Library. The Mitchell fountain was refurbished in 2012. See "Mayor Kasim Reed and Atlanta VIPs Celebrate Margaret Mitchell Square Restoration," Central Atlanta Progress press release, July 5, 2012, www.atlantadowntown.com; *AC*, December 12, 1984.

26. *AC*, December 18, 1987 (Trammel Crow's efforts to demolish the Mitchell House); *NYT*, January 29, 1988 (Young's decision); Atlanta Urban Design Commission, "Atlanta's Lasting Landmarks" (1987), "Suggested Remarks for Mayor Young at the AUDC Awards Ceremony," May 12, 1982, in Andrew J. Young Papers, Auburn Avenue Research Library; Dickey, *Tough Little Patch of History*, 110–16. For Young's ties to the business community, see Bayor, *Race and the Shaping*, 52.

27. Edmunds, "There's Something about Mary," 114. Taylor had seen the film version of *Gone with the Wind* for the first time at age sixteen.

28. Allen Freeman, "Battle for Atlanta," 78–82; Dickey, *Tough Little Patch of History*, 118–19.

29. *AJ*, September 16, 1991; Dickey, *Tough Little Patch of History*, 120–21.

30. *AC*, August 11, 1994. On September 18, 1994, the *AC* covered the fire and quoted Penny Lawing, executive assistant of Margaret Mitchell Inc., as saying, "Our goal has always been to have it up and running by the Olympics."

31. *AJC*, February 8, 1995, May 13, 1996. Contractors had installed a sprinkler system but had not yet connected it. Neither arson case has been solved.

32. *Washington Post*, July 27, 1996 (Fortain); *Atlanta Business Chronicle*, June 5–11, 1997. The *Washington Post* also reported that the French admired Mitchell because she gave money to rebuild the city of Vimoutiers after World War II. Mitchell's fiancé, Clifford Henry, had been killed in France in 1918 while serving in World War I. Dickey, *Tough Little Patch of History*, 150, notes that Mayor Bill Campbell committed the city to ten thousand dollars toward renovation after the second fire.

33. Dickey, *Tough Little Patch of History*, 129–38; Allen Freeman, "Battle for Atlanta," 78–82. For fundraisers, including invitations, see Margaret Mitchell House institutional records, AHC.

34. Dickey, *Tough Little Patch of History*, 161–65.

35. Dickey, *Tough Little Patch of History*, 150–53, 165. In 2013, Cleage became playwright in residence at the Alliance Theatre.

36. Ibid., 166–70.

37. *NYT*, January 25, 1987; "'Racial Cleansing' That Drove 1,100 Black Residents out of Forsyth County, Georgia"; Coski, *Confederate Battle Flag*, 255–56.

38. *Clark Atlanta University Panther*, October 9, 1991; *AC*, January 13, 1993; *AJ*, January 13, 1993; Coski, *Confederate Battle Flag*, 256–58. Miller defeated Andrew Young and Roy Barnes to win the Democratic primary and defeated Republican Johnny Isakson for the governorship.

39. Tom Murphy quoted in Martinez, "Georgia Confederate Flag Dispute," 208; Coski, *Confederate Battle Flag*, 258–60. According to the *AC*, January 13, 1993, "In perhaps the finest moment of a long political career, Mr. Miller ripped aside the illusions that have clouded debate over the state flag." *AJ* columnist Dick Williams wrote on January 14, 1993, "We honor our past, not disown it, when we return to the pre-1956 state flag that bears the official standard of the Confederacy, not the misused battle flag." The *AC* reported on January 21, 2001, that "more and more Georgians have been flying the pre-1956 flag, as if the official version didn't exist."

40. *AJ*, July 20, 1996.

41. "WXIA Atlanta Coverage of Opening Ceremony of the 1996 Summer Olympics," Parts 1–8," YouTube.com; Newman, *Southern Hospitality*, 276–79; Young, Newman, and Young, *Andrew Young*, 248–50. In conjunction with the Games, the Southern Crossroads Festival at Centennial Olympic Park drew two million guests who watched performances on three stages. See Margaret M. Gold and George Revill, "The Cultural Olympiads: Reviving the Panegyris," in Gold and Gold, *Olympic Cities*, 76–77.

42. *AC*, January 23, 31, 2001 (multiple articles), including an analysis of the vote in the legislature with 90 percent support among Democrats and 75 percent opposition from Republicans; Martinez, "Confederate Flag Dispute," 217–22; Coski, *Confederate Battle Flag*, 260–61.

43. Martinez, "Confederate Flag Dispute," 225–26; Coski, *Confederate Battle Flag*," 261–63. *AC*, March 3, 2004, reported the referendum results and noted that the Perdue flag was "modeled after the first national flag of the Confederacy," an irony lost on many Georgians. For the movement of rural white Georgia voters into the Republican Party over this and other issues, see Hayes and McKee, "Booting Barnes," 709, 724.

44. For the text of the marker, see the Georgia Historical Society website, https://georgiahistory.com/ghmi_marker_updated/the-burning-and-destruction-of-atlanta/. See Ray Henry, "Civil War Marker in Atlanta Stirs Controversy," *Charleston Post and Courier*, April 11, 2011, https://www.postandcourier.com/civil-war-marker-in-atlanta-stirs-controversy/article_59cacdca-6413-5938-97b8-d35c0c438a6e.html; *AJC*, April 12, 20, 2011.

45. *AJC*, July 26, 2014, April 12, June 19, 2017 (Juneteenth). Books published during the sesquicentennial include Link, *Atlanta*; Venet, *Changing Wind*; Rubin, *Through the Heart of Dixie*; Stephen Davis, *What the Yankees Did to Us*.

46. *AJC*, July 15, 2015, February 10, 2017; "Salvation of Atlanta," 75.

47. *AJC*, January 10, 2016 (NAACP), April 25 (New Orleans), August 17 (Baltimore), 2017. See also *Time*, April 2, 2018 (New Orleans). For a discussion of national debates over Confederate statues, see Clinton, *Confederate Statues and Memorialization*.

48. *Washington Post*, July 2, 2018; *Time*, July 3, 2017; Marie Tyler-McGraw, "Southern Comfort Levels: Race, Heritage Tourism, and the Civil War in Richmond," in Horton and Horton, *Slavery and Public History*, 157–67. The commission also noted that although Davis and his family are buried in Richmond's Hollywood Cemetery, he "was not from Richmond or Virginia." Both Jackson and Lee were natives of the Old Dominion, although Jackson was born in Clarksburg, which is now in West Virginia.

49. Horwitz, *Confederates in the Attic*, 288.

50. Al Such, "10 Monuments That Pay Tribute to Black Atlanta History," WABE radio, February 1, 2018, atlantaplanit.wabe.org/2018/02/01/11-monuments-that-pay-tribute-to-atlanta-black-history; John Riddle Jr. obituary, *Los Angeles Times*, March 9, 2002; *AJC*, August 28, 2017; Crimmins and Farrisee, *Democracy Restored*, 150–52; *High Life*, fall 2018, 13.

51. *AJC*, October 11, 2013, June 11, 2017; Atlanta History Center, "Confederate Monument Interpretation Guide," https://www.atlantahistorycenter.com/research/confederate-monuments, accessed February 8, 2020. African American columnist Gracie Bonds Staples endorsed Hale's efforts in a column in the *AJC*, March 6, 2016.

52. Ibid., January 12, 2017, April 5, 2018. See also Michael Thurmond, "Don't Let Stone Mountain's History Divide Us," *AJC*, May 6, 2018; Jim Galloway, "Michael Thurmond Gambles on a Better History for Stone Mountain," *AJC* Political Insider blog, March 24, 2018, https://www.ajc.com/blog/politics/michael-thurmond-gambles-better-history-for-stone-mountain/MPrb1xjDhvebgoSRzRx6oK/. Thurmond left the board, and Deal appointed African American Gregory Levett Sr. as his replacement in December 2018.

53. *AJC*, November 29, 2015, January 10 ("not useful"), March 27, 2017, January 6 (Ralston), 2018.

54. *AJC* Political Insider blog, August 15, 2017 (Abrams), https://www.ajc.com/news/politics-blog/; *AJC*, September 1, 2016 (Young), August 31, 2017 (Congressman David Scott), April 15, 2018 (Congressman Hank Johnson). For Lewis's position, see *AJC* Political Insider blog, July 25, 2015. All states have two statues in the National Statuary Hall; Georgia's other statue is medical pioneer Crawford Long. Stephens's statue was sculpted by Gutzon Borglum.

55. *AJC*, August 21, 31, September 9, 12, October 2, 22, 25, December 6, 17, 2017, January 4, April 27, July 15, 2018.

56. Ibid., August 15, October 14, November 6, 17, 2017; "Crossfire Hits Home in Buckhead," *Reporter Newspapers*, September 1, 2017. Reed had the support of Atlanta's city council in convening the committee. For these and a complete list of Confederate monuments in Fulton and DeKalb Counties, see Hagler, *Georgia's Confederate Monuments in Honor*.

57. *AJC*, July 26, August 24 (Atlanta), September 13 (Decatur), 2019. Signage at Oakland Cemetery's obelisk identifies the Atlanta Ladies Memorial Association's role in memorializing the dead and African Americans' commitment to fight for civil rights. The Lion of Atlanta is identified as "a visual representation of the Lost Cause."

58. "What Does Freedom Look Like," NAACP Atlanta Jubilee Day 2018, January 1, 2018, Cascade United Methodist Church, program and author notes.

59. Alfred Colquitt Chapter, UDC, "Confederate Memorial Day, Historic Oakland Cemetery, 28 April 2018," program and author notes. According to the program, the ALMA dissolved in 1989, and the Alfred Holt Colquitt Chapter carried on the Confederate Memorial Day tradition. According to Ava Cheryl Manley, in 2018, Georgia had sixty-two UDC chapters and five chapters of Children of the Confederacy.

60. *AJC*, September 1, 2016.

# BIBLIOGRAPHY

MANUSCRIPT COLLECTIONS

*ATLANTA HISTORY CENTER, KENAN RESEARCH CENTER*

Atlanta Gas Light Company Records
Atlanta Ladies Memorial Association Records
Atlanta Pioneer Women's Society Collection
Myrta Lockett Avary Papers
Carrie Berry Papers
Calhoun Family Papers
Civil War Round Table of Atlanta Records
Confederate Soldier's Home of Georgia Register of Inmates
Cyclorama Restoration, Inc. Records
DuBose Family Collection
Sarah Huff Family Correspondence and Receipt
Junior League of Atlanta Records
Wilbur G. Kurtz Sr. Papers
Helen Dortch Longstreet Papers
Millie J. McCreary Diary
Margaret Mitchell Collection
Margaret Mitchell House Archives
Stephens Mitchell Papers
C. Helen Plane Collection
Hollins Randolph Personality File
Richards Family Papers

Sidney Root Papers
Samuel W. Small Scrapbook
Sons of Confederate Veterans Collection
United Confederate Veterans Collection
United Daughters of the Confederacy Collection
Winship-Flournoy Family Papers

*ATLANTA PUBLIC LIBRARY*

Margaret Mitchell

*ATLANTA UNIVERSITY CENTER, ROBERT W. WOODRUFF LIBRARY*

Trezzvant W. Anderson Collection
John H. Calhoun Jr. Papers
Maynard Jackson Mayoral Administrative Records
Johnson Publishing Company Clipping Files Collection
Martin Luther King Jr. Collection

*AUBURN AVENUE RESEARCH LIBRARY, ATLANTA*

Edward Randolph Carter and Andrew Jackson Lewis Collection
Andrew J. Young Papers

*EMORY UNIVERSITY, STUART A. ROSE MANUSCRIPT,
ARCHIVES, AND RARE BOOK LIBRARY, ATLANTA*

Henry Woodfin Grady Papers
Stone Mountain Collection
    Gutzon Borglum Papers (series 2)
    Miscellaneous Printed Material (series 6)
    Mrs. James S. Nichols Papers (series 5)
    Caroline Helen Plane Papers (series 4)
    Stone Mountain Confederate Monumental Association Records (series 1)
    Samuel Hoyt Venable Papers (series 3)
Bell Irvin Wiley Papers

*GEORGIA STATE ARCHIVES, MORROW*

Georgia Civil War Centennial Commission
Vanishing Georgia

*GEORGIA STATE UNIVERSITY, ATLANTA*

*Atlanta Journal-Constitution* Photographs
Lane Brothers Photographs

*LIBRARY OF CONGRESS, WASHINGTON, D.C.*

Gutzon Borglum Papers
Miscellaneous Manuscript Collection

*UNIVERSITY OF GEORGIA, HARGRETT RARE BOOK
AND MANUSCRIPT LIBRARY, ATHENS*

E. Merton Coulter Collection
John Brown Gordon Family Papers
Stephens Mitchell Family Papers
Susan Myrick Papers
United Confederate Veterans/United Daughters of the Confederacy Collection

*UNIVERSITY OF MASSACHUSETTS, AMHERST LIBRARIES,
SPECIAL COLLECTIONS AND UNIVERSITY ARCHIVES*

W. E. B. Du Bois Collection

### BOOKS AND ARTICLES

Aiello, Thomas. *The Battle for the Souls of Black Folk: W. E. B. Du Bois, Booker T. Washington, and the Debate That Shaped the Course of Civil Rights*. Santa Barbara, Calif.: Praeger, 2016.

———. *The Grapevine of the Black South: The Scott Newspaper Syndicate in the Generation before the Civil Rights Movement*. Athens: University of Georgia Press, 2018.

*Atlanta Chapter United Daughters of the Confederacy, 1897–1922*. N.p.: 1922.

Avary, Myrta Lockett. *Dixie after the War*. New York: Appleton, 1906.

———. *A Virginia Girl in the Civil War, 1861–1865*. New York: Appleton, 1903.

Avary, Myrta Lockett, and Isabella Martin, eds. *Diary from Dixie*. New York: Appleton, 1905.

Barber, J. Max. "The Atlanta Tragedy." *The Voice* 3 (October 1906): 473–79.

*Battle of Atlanta: Story of the Cyclorama of the Johnston-Sherman Campaign*. Atlanta: n.p., 1919.

Bayor, Ronald H. *Race and the Shaping of Twentieth-Century Atlanta*. Chapel Hill: University of North Carolina Press, 1996.

Bellows, Barbara L. *God and General Longstreet: The Lost Cause and the Southern Mind*. Baton Rouge: Louisiana State University Press, 1982.

Bernstein, Matthew. "Selznick's March: The Atlanta Premiere of *Gone with the Wind*." *Atlanta History* 63 (Summer 1999): 7–33.

Blair, Ruth. "Atlanta's Monuments." *Atlanta Historical Bulletin* 5 (October 1940): 273–77.

Blair, William A. *Cities of the Dead: Contesting the Memory of the Civil War in the South, 1865–1914*. Chapel Hill: University of North Carolina Press, 2004.

Blight, David W. *American Oracle: The Civil War in the Civil Rights Era*. Cambridge: Belknap Press of Harvard University Press, 2011.

———. *Race and Reunion: The Civil War in American Memory*. Cambridge: Belknap Press of Harvard University Press, 2001.

Bodnar, John. *Remaking America: Public Memory, Commemoration, and Patriotism in the Twentieth Century*. Princeton: Princeton University Press, 1992.

Bourne, Stephen. *Butterfly McQueen Remembered*. Lanham, Md.: Scarecrow, 2008.

Braxton, Rosemary. "Jesse O. Thomas." *New Georgia Encyclopedia*. https://www .georgiaencyclopedia.org/articles/history-archaeology/jesse-o-thomas-1885 -1972. Last edited January 24, 2014.

Brown, Thomas J. *Civil War Canon: Sites of Confederate Memory in South Carolina*. Chapel Hill: University of North Carolina Press, 2015.

———, ed. *Remixing the Civil War: Meditations on the Sesquicentennial*. Baltimore: Johns Hopkins University Press, 2011.

Brundage, W. Fitzhugh. *Lynching in the New South: Georgia and Virginia, 1880– 1930*. Urbana: University of Illinois Press, 1993.

———. *The Southern Past: A Clash of Race and Memory*. Cambridge: Harvard University Press, 2005.

———, ed. *Where These Memories Grow: History, Memory, and Southern Identity*. Chapel Hill: University of North Carolina Press, 2000.

Bryan, Ferald J. *Henry Grady or Tom Watson: The Rhetorical Struggle for the New South, 1880–1890*. Macon, Ga.: Mercer University Press, 1994.

Buck, Paul H. *The Road to Reunion, 1865–1900*. Boston: Little, Brown, 1937.

Cardon, Nathan. *A Dream of the Future: Race, Empire, and Modernity at the Atlanta and Nashville World's Fairs*. New York: Oxford University Press, 2018.

Carter, E. R. *The Black Side: A Partial History of the Business, Religion, and Education of the Negro in Atlanta*. Atlanta: n.p., 1894.

Casey, Robert J., and Mary Borglum. *Give the Man Room: The Story of Gutzon Borglum*. New York: Bobbs-Merrill, 1952.

Censer, Jane Turner. *The Reconstruction of White Southern Womanhood, 1865– 1895*. Baton Rouge: Louisiana State University Press, 2003.

Chirhart, Ann Short, and Kathleen Ann Clark, eds. *Georgia Women: Their Lives and Times*. Vol. 2. Athens: University of Georgia Press, 2014.

Chirhart, Ann Short, and Betty Wood, eds. *Georgia Women: Their Lives and Times*. Vol. 1. Athens: University of Georgia Press, 2009.

Clare, Virginia. *Thunder and Stars: The Life of Mildred Rutherford*. Atlanta: Oglethorpe University Press, 1941.

Clark, Kathleen Ann. *Defining Moments: African American Commemoration and Political Culture in the South, 1863–1913*. Chapel Hill: University of North Carolina Press, 2005.

Clinton, Catherine, ed. *Confederate Statues and Memorialization*. Athens: University of Georgia Press, 2019.

Cobb, James C. *Away Down South: A History of Southern Identity*. New York: Oxford University Press, 2005.

Connelly, Thomas L., and Barbara L. Bellows. *God and General Longstreet: The Lost Cause and the Southern Mind*. Baton Rouge: Louisiana State University Press, 1982.

Cook, Robert J. *Civil War Memories: Contesting the Past in the United States since 1865*. Baltimore: Johns Hopkins University Press, 2017.

———. "The Quarrel Forgotten: Toward a Clearer Understanding of Sectional Reconciliation." *Journal of the Civil War Era* 6 (September 2016): 413–36.

———. *Troubled Commemoration: The American Civil War Centennial, 1961–1965.* Baton Rouge: Louisiana State University Press, 2007.

Cooper, Walter G. *The Cotton States and International Exposition and South Illustrated.* Atlanta: Illustrator Company, 1896.

Coski, John M. *The Confederate Battle Flag: America's Most Embattled Emblem.* Cambridge: Belknap Press of Harvard University Press, 2005.

Cox, Jacob D. *Military Reminiscences of the Civil War.* 2 vols. New York: Scribner's, 1900.

Cox, Karen L., ed. *Destination Dixie: Tourism and Southern History.* Gainesville: University Press of Florida, 2012.

———. *Dixie's Daughters: The United Daughters of the Confederacy and the Preservation of Confederate Culture.* Gainesville: University Press of Florida, 2003.

Crank, James A., ed. *New Approaches to "Gone with the Wind."* Baton Rouge: Louisiana State University Press, 2015.

Crimmins, Timothy J., and Anne H. Farrisee. *Democracy Restored: A History of the Georgia State Capitol.* Athens: University of Georgia Press, 2007.

Cullen, Jim. *The Civil War in Popular Culture: A Reusable Past.* Washington, D.C.: Smithsonian Institution Press, 1995.

Daily, Jane, Glenda Elizabeth Gilmore, and Bryant Simon, eds. *Jumpin' Jim Crow: Southern Politics from Civil War to Civil Rights.* Princeton: Princeton University Press, 2000.

Davis, Harold E. *Henry Grady's New South: Atlanta, a Brave and Beautiful City.* Tuscaloosa: University of Alabama Press, 1990.

Davis, Jefferson. *The Rise and Fall of the Confederate Government.* 2 vols. 1881. New York: Da Capo, 1990.

Davis, Maggie. *The Far Side of Home.* New York: Macmillan, 1963.

Davis, Ren, and Helen Davis. *Atlanta's Oakland Cemetery: An Illustrated History.* Athens: University of Georgia Press, 2012.

Davis, Stephen. *What the Yankees Did to Us: Sherman's Bombardment and Wrecking of Atlanta.* Macon, Ga.: Mercer University Press, 2012.

Dickey, Jennifer W. *A Tough Little Patch of History: "Gone with the Wind" and the Politics of Memory.* Fayetteville: University of Arkansas Press, 2014.

Dixon, Thomas. *The Clansman.* New York: Doubleday, 1905.

Dorsey, Allison. *To Build Our Lives Together: Community Formation in Atlanta.* Athens: University of Georgia Press, 2004.

Drago, Edmund L. *Black Politicians and Reconstruction in Georgia: A Splendid Failure.* Baton Rouge: Louisiana State University Press, 1982.

Du Bois, W. E. B. *The Autobiography of W. E. B. Du Bois: A Soliloquy on Viewing My Life from the Last Decade of Its First Century.* 1968. New York: International Publishers, 1991.

———. *Black Reconstruction in America.* New York: Russel and Russel, 1935.

———. *The Souls of Black Folk.* 1903. New York: Modern Library, 2003.

Dupre, Judith. *Monuments: America's History in Art and Memory.* New York: Random House, 2007.

Dyer, Thomas G. *Secret Yankees: The Unionist Circle in Confederate Atlanta.* Baltimore: Johns Hopkins University Press, 1999.

Eckert, Ralph L. "The General and the Editor: John B. Gordon, Henry W. Grady, and the Georgia Gubernatorial Race of 1886." *Atlanta History* 32 (Spring 1988): 5–16.

———. *John Brown Gordon: Soldier, Southerner, American.* Baton Rouge: Louisiana State University Press, 1989.

Edmunds, Emma. "There's Something about Mary." *Atlanta Magazine* 58 (October 1998): 58–61, 113–17.

Edwards, Anne. *Road to Tara: The Life of Margaret Mitchell.* New York: Ticknor and Fields, 1983.

Emert, Barbara Jean, ed. *The Georgia Division, Children of the Confederacy History, 1912–1987.* N.p.: Georgia Division, Children of the Confederacy, 1988.

Fahs, Alice, and Joan Waugh, eds. *The Memory of the Civil War in American Culture.* Chapel Hill: University of North Carolina Press, 2004.

Fairman, Henry Clay. *Chronicles of the Old Guard of the Gate City Guard, Atlanta Georgia, 1858–1915.* 2 vols. Atlanta: Byrd, 1915.

Faust, Drew Gilpin. *This Republic of Suffering: Death and the American Civil War.* New York: Vintage, 2008.

Felton, Rebecca Latimer. *My Memoirs of Georgia Politics.* Atlanta: Index Printing, 1911.

Fortson, Ben W. *Georgia Flags.* Atlanta: n.p., 1963.

Foster, Gaines M. *Ghosts of the Confederacy: Defeat, the Lost Cause, and the Emergence of the New South, 1865–1913.* New York: Oxford University Press, 1987.

Fox-Genovese, Elizabeth. "Scarlett O'Hara: The Southern Lady as New Woman." *American Quarterly* 33 (Autumn 1981): 391–411.

Freeman, Allen. "Battle for Atlanta." *Preservation* 50 (March–April 1998): 76–82.

Freeman, David B. *Carved in Stone: The History of Stone Mountain.* Macon, Ga.: Mercer University Press, 1997.

Gallagher, Gary W. *Causes Won, Lost, and Forgotten: How Hollywood and Popular Art Shape What We Know about the Civil War.* Chapel Hill: University of North Carolina Press, 2008.

———. *The Confederate War: How Popular Will, Nationalism, and Military Strategy Could Not Stave Off Defeat.* Cambridge: Harvard University Pres, 1997.

———. *Jubal A. Early, the Lost Cause, and Civil War History: A Persistent Legacy.* Milwaukee, Wis.: Marquette University Press, 1995.

———. *Lee and His Generals in War and Memory.* Baton Rouge: Louisiana State University Press, 1998.

Gallagher, Gary W., and Alan T. Nolan, eds. *The Myth of the Lost Cause and Civil War History.* Bloomington: Indiana University Press, 2000.

Gannon, Barbara A. *Americans Remember Their Civil War.* Santa Barbara, Calif.: ABC-CLIO, 2017.

Gardner, Sarah E. *Blood and Irony: Southern White Women's Narratives of the Civil War, 1861–1937*. Chapel Hill: University of North Carolina Press, 2004.

Garrett, Franklin M. *Atlanta and Environs: A Chronicle of Its People and Events*. 2 vols. Athens: University of Georgia Press, 1954.

Garrow, David J. *Bearing the Cross: Martin Luther King, Jr., and the Southern Christian Leadership Conference*. New York: Morrow, 1986.

Gaston, Paul M. *The New South Creed: A Study in Southern Mythmaking*. New York: Knopf, 1970.

Gay, Mary A. H. *Life in Dixie during the War*. 1897. Atlanta: Darby, 1979.

Godshalk, David Fort. *Veiled Visions: The 1906 Race Riot and the Reshaping of American Race Relations*. Chapel Hill: University of North Carolina Press, 2005.

Gold, John R., and Margaret M. Gold, eds. *Olympic Cities: City Agendas, Planning, and the World's Games, 1896–2012*. New York: Routledge, 2007.

Goodson, Steve. "'This Mighty Influence for Good or for Evil': The Movies in Atlanta, 1895–1920." *Atlanta History* 39 (Fall–Winter 1995): 28–47.

Gordon, John B. *Reminiscences of the Civil War*. New York: Scribner's, 1903.

Gordon, Linda. *The Second Coming of the KKK: The Ku Klux Klan of the 1920s and the American Political Tradition*. New York: Liveright, 2017.

Groover, Robert L. "Margaret Mitchell, the Lady from Atlanta." *Georgia Historical Quarterly* 52 (March 1968): 53–69.

Guelzo, Allen C. *Reconstruction: a Concise History*. New York: Oxford University Press, 2018.

Hacker, J. David. "A Census-Based Count of the Civil War Dead." *Civil War History* 57 (December 2011): 307–48.

Haden, Charles J. *George V. Gress: Donor of the Cyclorama of the Battle of Atlanta and the Atlanta Zoo*. Atlanta: n.p., 1940.

Hagler, Gould B., Jr. *Georgia's Confederate Monuments in Honor of a Fallen Nation*. Macon, Ga.: Mercer University Press, 2014.

Hain, Pamela Chase. *Murder in the State Capitol: The Biography of Lieutenant Colonel Robert Augustus Alston*. Macon, Ga.: Mercer University Press, 2013.

Hale, Grace Elizabeth. "'Of the Meaning of Progress': A Century of Southern Race Relations." *Atlanta History* 44 (Winter 2001): 20–41.

Hancock, Walker. *A Sculptor's Fortunes*. Gloucester, Mass.: Cape Ann Historical Association, 1997.

Harris, Joel Chandler. *Life of Henry W. Grady Including His Writings and Speeches*. New York: Cassell, 1890.

Harris, M. Keith. *Across the Bloody Chasm: The Culture of Commemoration among Civil War Veterans*. Baton Rouge: Louisiana State University Press, 2014.

Harvey, Bruce. *World's Fairs in a Southern Accent: Atlanta, Nashville, and Charleston, 1895–1902*. Knoxville: University of Tennessee Press, 2014.

Harvey, Bruce, and Lynn Watson-Powers. "'The Eyes of the World Are upon Us': A Look at the Cotton States and International Exposition of 1895." *Atlanta History* 39 (Fall–Winter 1995): 5–12.

Harwell, Richard, comp. and ed. *"Gone with the Wind" as Book and Film*. Columbia: University of South Carolina Press, 1983.

Hayes, Danny, and Seth C. McKee. "Booting Barnes: Explaining the Historic Upset in the 2002 Georgia Gubernatorial Election." *Politics and Policy* 32 (December 2004): 708–38.

Henry, Scott. "Resurrected Mims Park Will Offer a Lesson in Atlanta Race Relations." *Atlanta Magazine* online, January 27, 2017. https://www.atlanta magazine.com/news-culture-articles/resurrected-mims-park-will-offer -lesson-atlanta-race-relations/.

Higginbotham, Evelyn Brooks. *Righteous Discontent: The Women's Movement in the Black Baptist Church, 1880–1920*. Cambridge: Harvard University Press, 1993.

Horton, James Oliver, and Lois E. Horton, eds. *Slavery and Public History: The Tough Stuff of American Memory*. New York: New Press, 2006.

Horwitz, Tony. *Confederates in the Attic: Dispatches from the Unfinished Civil War*. New York: Random House, 1998.

Hudson, Paul Stephen, and Lora Pond Mirza. *Atlanta's Stone Mountain: A Multicultural History*. Charleston, S.C.: History Press, 2011.

Huff, Sarah. *My 80 Years in Atlanta*. Atlanta: n.p., 1937.

Inscoe, John, ed. *Georgia in Black and White: Explorations in Race Relations of a Southern State*. Athens: University of Georgia Press, 1994.

Jackson, Kenneth T. *The Ku Klux Klan in the City, 1915–1930*. Chicago: Dee, 1992.

Jackson, Thomas F. *From Civil Rights to Human Rights: Martin Luther King, Jr., and the Struggle for Economic Justice*. Philadelphia: University of Pennsylvania Press, 2007.

Jacob, Kathryn Allamong. *Testament to Union: Civil War Monuments in Washington, D.C.* Baltimore: Johns Hopkins University Press, 1998.

Janney, Caroline E. *Burying the Dead but Not the Past: Ladies' Memorial Associations and the Lost Cause*. Chapel Hill: University of North Carolina Press, 2008.

———. "'I Yield to No Man an Iota of My Convictions': Chickamauga and Chattanooga National Military Park and the Limits of Reconciliation." *Journal of the Civil War Era* 2 (September 2012): 394–420.

———. *Remembering the Civil War: Reunion and the Limits of Reconciliation*. Chapel Hill: University of North Carolina Press, 2013.

Jones, Carroll. *The 25th North Carolina Troops in the Civil War: History and Roster of a Mountain-Bred Regiment*. Jefferson, N.C.: McFarland, 2009.

Kammen, Michael. *Mystic Chords of Memory: The Transformation of Tradition in American Culture*. New York: Vintage, 1993.

King, Martin Luther, Jr. *The Papers of Martin Luther King Jr*. Ed. Clayborne Carson. 7 vols. Berkeley: University of California Press, 1992–2014.

Kreyling, Michael. *A Late Encounter with the Civil War*. Athens: University of Georgia Press, 2013.

Kruse, Kevin M. *White Flight: Atlanta and the Making of Modern Conservatism*. Princeton: Princeton University Press, 2005.

Kurtz, Wilbur G. *Atlanta and the Old South: Paintings and Drawings*. Atlanta: American Lithographs, 1969.

———. "My Adventures with Atlanta History as Told to Charlotte Hale Smith." *Atlanta Historical Bulletin* 12 (March 1967): 9–21.

Kurtz, Wilbur G., Jr. *"Gone with the Wind* Premiere: Excerpts from the Diary of Wilbur G. Kurtz, Jr." *Atlanta Historical Bulletin* 12 (September 1967): 15–22.

Kytle, Ethan J., and Blain Roberts. *Denmark Vesey's Garden: Slavery and Memory in the Cradle of the Confederacy*. New York: New Press, 2018.

LaCavera, Tommie Phillips, comp. and ed. *A History of the Georgia Division of the United Daughters of the Confederacy, 1895–1995*. 2 vols. Atlanta: United Daughters of the Confederacy, 1995.

Lamar, Dolly Blount. *When All Is Said and Done*. Athens: University of Georgia Press, 1952.

Lewis, David Levering. *W. E. B. Du Bois: Biography of a Race, 1868–1919*. New York: Holt, 1993.

Link, William A. *Atlanta, Cradle of the New South: Race and Remembering in the Civil War's Aftermath*. Chapel Hill: University of North Carolina Press, 2013.

Litwack, Leon F. *Trouble in Mind: Black Southerners in the Age of Jim Crow*. New York: Knopf, 1998.

Lockerman, Doris. *The Man Who Amazed Atlanta: The Journey of Franklin Miller Garrett*. Atlanta: Longstreet, 1996.

Longstreet, Helen D. *Lee and Longstreet at High Tide: Gettysburg in the Light of the Official Records*. Gainesville, Ga.: the Author, 1905.

Lumpkin, Katharine Du Pre. *The Making of a Southerner*. New York: Knopf, 1947.

MacLean, Nancy. *Behind the Mask of Chivalry: The Making of the Second Ku Klux Klan*. New York: Oxford University Press, 1994.

Marten, James. *Sing Not War: The Lives of Union and Confederate Veterans in Gilded Age America*. Chapel Hill: University of North Carolina Press, 2011.

Martinez, J. Michael. "The Georgia Confederate Flag Dispute." *Georgia Historical Quarterly* 92 (Summer 2008): 200–228.

Martinez, J. Michael, William D. Richardson, and Ron McNinch-Su, eds. *Confederate Symbols in the Contemporary South*. Gainesville: University Press of Florida, 2000.

Matthews, John M. "Negro Republicans in the Reconstruction of Georgia." *Georgia Historical Quarterly* 60 (Summer 1976): 145–64.

McCarty, Laura. "Civil War Centennial." *New Georgia Eycyclopedia*. https://www.georgiaencyclopedia.org/articles/history-archaeology/civil-war-centennial. Last edited September 9, 2014.

McDonough, John. "Remembering the Last Reunion of Civil War Veterans." NPR, July 3, 2009. https://www.npr.org/templates/story/story.php?storyId=106259780.

McElya, Micki. *Clinging to Mammy: The Faithful Slave in Twentieth Century America*. Cambridge: Harvard University Press, 2007.

——. *The Politics of Mourning: Death and Honor in Arlington National Cemetery*. Cambridge: Harvard University Press, 2016.

McPherson, James M. *Embattled Rebel: Jefferson Davis as Commander in Chief.* New York: Penguin, 2014.

McRae, Elizabeth Gillespie. "Caretakers of Southern Civilization: Georgia Women and the Anti-Suffrage Campaign, 1914–1920." *Georgia Historical Quarterly* 82 (Winter 1998): 801–28.

Melnick, Jeffrey. *Black-Jewish Relations on Trial: Leo Frank and Jim Conley in the New South*. Oxford: University Press of Mississippi, 2000.

Miller, Brian Craig. *Empty Sleeves: Amputation in the Civil War South*. Athens: University of Georgia Press, 2015.

Mills, Cynthia, and Pamela H. Simpson, eds. *Monuments to the Lost Cause: Women, Art, and Landscapes of Southern Memory*. Knoxville: University of Tennessee Press, 2003.

Minnix, Kathleen. *Laughter in the Amen Corner: The Life of Evangelist Sam Jones*. Athens: University of Georgia Press, 1993.

Mitchell, Margaret. *Gone with the Wind*. 1936. New York: Scribner, 1964.

——. *Margaret Mitchell's "Gone with the Wind" Letters, 1936–1949*. Ed. Richard Harwell. New York: Macmillan, 1976.

——. *The Scarlett Letters: The Making of the Film "Gone with the Wind."* Ed. John Wiley Jr. New York: Taylor, 2014.

Mitchell, Stephens. "Margaret Mitchell and Her People in the Atlanta Area." *Atlanta Historical Bulletin* 9 (May 1950): 5–27.

Mixon, Gregory. *The Atlanta Riot: Race, Class, and Violence in a New South City*. Gainesville: University Press of Florida, 2005.

Morton, Marian J. "'My Dear, I Don't Give a Damn': Scarlett O'Hara and the Great Depression." *Frontiers: A Journal of Women Studies* 5 (Autumn 1980): 52–56.

Neff, John R. *Honoring the Civil War Dead: Commemoration and the Problem of Reconciliation*. Lawrence: University Press of Kansas, 2005.

Newman, Harvey K. *Southern Hospitality: Tourism and the Growth of Atlanta*. Tuscaloosa: University of Alabama Press, 1999.

Nixon, Raymond B. *Henry W. Grady: Spokesman of the New South*. New York: Knopf, 1943.

O'Connell, David. *The Art and Life of Atlanta Artist Wilbur G. Kurtz: Inspired by Southern History*. Charleston, S.C.: History Press, 2013.

Oney, Steve. *And the Dead Shall Rise: The Murder of Mary Phagan and the Lynching of Leo Frank*. New York: Random House, 2004.

Pegram, Thomas R. *One Hundred Percent American: The Rebirth and Decline of the Ku Klux Klan in the 1920s*. Chicago: Dee, 2011.

Perdue, Theda. *Race and the Atlanta Cotton States Exposition of 1895*. Athens: University of Georgia Press, 2010.

*Photo-Gravures of the Cotton States Exposition: Atlanta, 1895*. New York: Wittemann, 1895.

Piehler, G. Kurt. *Remembering War the American Way*. Washington, D.C.: Smithsonian Institution Press, 1995.

Pierce, Haywood J., Jr. *Benjamin H. Hill: Secession and Reconstruction*. Chicago: University of Chicago Press, 1928.

Pioneer Citizens' Society of Atlanta. *Pioneer Citizens' Story of Atlanta 1833–1902*. Atlanta: Byrd, 1902.

Pomerantz, Gary M. *Where Peachtree Meets Sweet Auburn: A Saga of Race and Family*. New York: Penguin, 1996.

Prince, K. Stephen. "A Rebel Yell for Yankee Doodle: Selling the New South at the 1881 Atlanta International Cotton Exposition." *Georgia Historical Quarterly* 92 (Fall 2008): 340–71.

——. *Stories of the South: Race and the Reconstruction of Southern Identity, 1865–1915*. Chapel Hill: University of North Carolina Press, 2014.

Pyron, Darden Asbury, ed. *Recasting: "Gone with the Wind" in American Culture*. Miami: University Presses of Florida, 1983.

——. *Southern Daughter: The Life of Margaret Mitchell*. New York: Oxford University Press, 1991.

Rabinowitz, Howard N. *Race Relations in the Urban South, 1865–1890*. Athens: University of Georgia Press, 1996.

"The 'Racial Cleansing' That Drove 1,100 Black Residents Out of Forsyth County, Georgia." NPR, December 8, 2017. https://www.npr.org/2017/12/08/569156832/the-racial-cleansing-that-drove-1-100-black-residents-out-of-forsyth-county-ga.

Randall, Alice. *The Wind Done Gone*. Boston: Houghton Mifflin, 2001.

Rawlings, William. *The Second Coming of the Invisible Empire: The Ku Klux Klan in the 1920s*. Macon, Ga.: Mercer University Press, 2016.

Reed, Wallace. *History of Atlanta, Georgia*. Syracuse, N.Y.: Mason, 1889.

Richards, Samuel P. *Sam Richards's Civil War Diary: A Chronicle of the Atlanta Home Front*. Ed. Wendy Hamand Venet. Athens: University of Georgia Press, 2009.

Rieder, Jonathan. *Gospel of Freedom: Martin Luther King, Jr.'s Letter from a Birmingham Jail and the Struggle That Changed a Nation*. New York: Bloomsbury, 2013.

Rodgers, Robert L., comp. *History of [the] Confederate Veterans' Association of Fulton County, Georgia*. Atlanta: Sesson, 1890.

Rosenburg, R. B. *Living Monuments: Confederate Soldiers' Homes in the New South*. Chapel Hill: University of North Carolina Press, 1993.

Roth, Darlene Rebecca. *Matronage: Patterns in Women's Organizations, Atlanta, Georgia, 1890–1940*. Brooklyn, N.Y.: Carlson, 1994.

Rubin, Anne Sarah. *Through the Heart of Dixie: Sherman's March and American Memory*. Chapel Hill: University of North Carolina Press, 2014.

Russell, James Michael. *Atlanta, 1847–1890: City Building in the Old South and New*. Baton Rouge: Louisiana State University Press, 1988.

Rutherford, Mildred Lewis. *A Measuring Rod to Test Text Books and Reference Books in Schools, Colleges, and Libraries.* Athens, Georgia: n.p., 1920.

Rydell, Robert W. *All the World's a Fair: Visions of Empire at American International Expositions, 1876–1916.* Chicago: University of Chicago Press, 1984.

"The Salvation of Atlanta." *Smithsonian* 49 (December 2018): 68–72.

Sampson, Robert D. "'Pretty Damned Warm Times': The 1864 Charleston Riot and 'the Inalienable Right of Revolution.'" *Illinois Historical Journal* 89 (Summer 1996): 99–116.

Savage, Kirk, ed. *The Civil War in Art and Memory.* New Haven: Yale University Press, 2016.

———. *Standing Soldiers, Kneeling Slaves: Race, War, and Monument in Nineteenth-Century America.* Princeton: Princeton University Press, 1997.

Schaff, Howard, and Audrey Karl Schaff. *Six Wars at a Time: The Life and Times of Gutzon Borglum, Sculptor of Mount Rushmore.* Sioux Falls, S.D.: Center for Western Studies, 1995.

Silber, Nina. *The Romance of Reunion: Northerners and the South, 1865–1900.* Chapel Hill: University of North Carolina Press, 1993.

———. *This War Ain't Over: Fighting the Civil War in New Deal America.* Chapel Hill: University of North Carolina Press, 2018.

Slide, Anthony. *American Racist: The Life and Films of Thomas Dixon.* Lexington: University Press of Kentucky, 2004.

Stephens, Alexander H. *Recollections of Alexander H. Stephens: His Diary Kept When a Prisoner at Fort Warren, Boston Harbour, 1865.* Ed. Myrta Lockett Avary. New York: Doubleday, 1910.

Still, William. *The Underground Railroad.* 1872. New York: Arno, 1968.

Stokes, Melvyn. *D. W. Griffith's "The Birth of a Nation": A History of the Most Controversial Motion Picture of All Time.* New York: Oxford University Press, 2007.

Swain, Martha H., Elizabeth Anne Payne, and Marjorie Julian Spruill, eds. *Mississippi Women: Their Histories, Their Lives.* Athens: University of Georgia Press, 2003.

Tankersley, Allen P. *John B. Gordon: A Study in Gallantry.* Atlanta: Whitehall, 1955.

Teel, Leonard Ray. *Ralph Emerson McGill: Voice of the Southern Conscience.* Knoxville: University of Tennessee Press, 2001.

Thomas, Emory. *Robert E. Lee: A Biography.* New York: Norton, 1995.

Trowbridge, John Townsend. "The Wilderness." *Atlantic Monthly,* January 1866, 39–46.

United Daughters of the Confederacy. *Minutes of the Fourteenth Annual Convention, Georgia Division, United Daughters of the Confederacy, Held at Savannah, Georgia October 27, 28, 29, 1908.* Rome, Ga.: Clement, 1908.

Varon, Elizabeth R. *Appomattox: Victory, Defeat, and Freedom at the End of the Civil War.* New York: Oxford University Press, 2014.

Venet, Wendy Hamand. *A Changing Wind: Commerce and Conflict in Civil War Atlanta.* New Haven: Yale University Press, 2014.

Washington, Booker T. *Booker T. Washington Papers*. Ed. Louis R. Harlan. 14 vols. Urbana: University of Illinois Press, 1972–89.

Wert, Jeffry D. *General James Longstreet: The Confederacy's Most Controversial Soldier*. New York: Touchstone, 1993.

Wiley, Bell Irvin. *The Life of Billy Yank: The Common Soldier of the Union*. Indianapolis: Bobbs-Merrill, 1952.

——. *The Life of Johnny Reb: The Common Soldier of the Confederacy*. Indianapolis: Bobbs-Merrill, 1943.

Wilson, Charles Reagan. *Baptized in Blood: The Religion of the Lost Cause, 1865–1920*. Athens: University of Georgia Press, 1980.

Woodward, C. Vann. *Origins of the New South, 1877-1913*. Baton Rouge: Louisiana State University Press, 1951.

Wynne, Lewis N. "The Bourbon Triumvirate: A Reconsideration." *Atlanta Historical Journal* 24 (Summer 1980): 39–55.

Young, Andrew, Harvey Newman, and Andrea Young. *Andrew Young and the Making of Modern Atlanta*. Macon, Ga.: Mercer University Press, 2016.

# INDEX

CPSIA information can be obtained
at www.ICGtesting.com
Printed in the USA
LVHW041742080920
665361LV00003B/404